Bloom's Modern Critical Views

Modern Critical Views

MARK TWAIN

Edited and with an introduction by
Harold Bloom
Sterling Professor of the Humanities
Yale University

CHELSEA HOUSE PUBLISHERS
Philadelphia

Jacket illustration by Robert Trask

Mark Twain is seen against the background of
his Life on the Mississippi, *while Huck Finn*
amiably idles, surveying Tom Sawyer painting the
fence. —H.B.

Printed and bound in the United States of America

10

Library of Congress Cataloging-in-Publication Data
Mark Twain.
    (Modern critical views)
    Bibliography: p.
    Includes index.
    1. Twain, Mark, 1835–1910—Criticism and
interpretation—Addresses, essays, lectures.
I. Bloom, Harold.   II. Series.
PS1338.M27   1986   818'.409   86–2577
ISBN 0–87754–698–3

Contents

Editor's Note

This book gathers together a representative selection of the best criticism devoted to the writings of Mark Twain that has been published during the last forty years. I am grateful to Eden Quainton for his erudition and insight in helping me to choose the essays that constitute this volume.

The introduction centers upon Twain's undoubted masterpiece, *Huckleberry Finn*, emphasizing the secular intensities of Twain's loving study of his own nostalgia for the freedom of storytelling. Bernard De Voto's overview of Twain's career commences the chronological sequence, and usefully integrates life, work, and socio-historical context. It is followed here by the classic study of *Pudd'nhead Wilson* by F. R. Leavis, with its characteristic emphasis upon the book's "moral astringency." J. Hillis Miller, in his own earlier critical phase as a "critic of consciousness," contrasts first-person expressions of a consciousness in the narrators of *David Copperfield* and *Huckleberry Finn*.

A more formalist, New Critical reading of Twain is represented here by the distinguished poet and novelist Robert Penn Warren, whose essay analyzes *Huckleberry Finn* and *A Connecticut Yankee* as structures that tell Twain's own self-divided story of personal and creative anguish. Related closely to Warren's essay, but even more biographically oriented, is Judith Fetterley's meditation upon what she calls Twain's "anxiety of entertainment," his sense of himself as public performer, the artist as showman.

Twain's anxious vision, as turned upon boyhood, is the subject of Cynthia Griffin Wolff's dark study of *Tom Sawyer*, which she reads as a nightmare vision of the self's defeat. That image of defeat certainly gets into the shaping of Twain's *The Mysterious Stranger*, analyzed by Bruce Michelson as a remarkable instance of the power of great fiction to affirm life even as it denies all of the illusions that constitute life. Such a paradox is akin to what Alfred Kazin explores as Twain's power to make us accept how "life becomes farce without ceasing to be horror."

A more genial Twain is presented by James M. Cox as he revisits *Life on the Mississippi*, and ironically urges deconstructive critics to address themselves to what is most problematic in our greatest comic writer. Roy Harvey Pearce also confronts Twain where he is most baffling, in the image of Huck Finn as the self that tells lies in order to be free to get at the truth. The challenge to contemporary criticism is taken up by Douglas Robinson and by Cleo McNelly Kearns. Considering *A Connecticut Yankee* as an American apocalypse, Robinson maps Twain's revisionary relationship to the long tradition that extends from the Bible's Book of Revelation to nineteenth-century Romanticism. McNelly Kearns sets *Huckleberry Finn* against the current literary "science" of semiotics, and sees the book as a triumph that transcends the limits of semiotics, while carrying us to the antithetical borders of silence and of prophecy. Her strenuous reading fitly ends this book, reminding us again that *Huckleberry Finn* is one of the central American books, indispensable for our understanding of ourselves.

Introduction

I

> After supper she got out her book and learned me about Moses
> and the Bulrushers, and I was in a sweat to find out all about
> him; but by-and-by she let it out that Moses had been dead a
> considerable long time; so then I didn't care no more about him;
> because I don't take stock in dead people.

Huck Finn's American vision has this in common with Captain Ahab's
or Walt Whitman's, that Huck too would strike the sun if it insulted him.
The three best American books—*Huckleberry Finn*, *Moby-Dick*, *Leaves of
Grass*—have in common also that they are each the most American of books.
Twain's masterpiece is essentially comic, Melville's is tragic, Whitman's is
beyond characterization or categorization, except that despite its humor and
its Emersonian hopes for America, we remember it best for its dark shadows.
Huckleberry Finn, shrewd and grim as it is sometimes compelled to be, remains
unique in our national literature for its affirmative force. Fecund in its prog-
eny—as diverse as Kipling's *Kim*, Eliot's *The Dry Salvages*, Hemingway's *The
Sun Also Rises*, and Mailer's *Why Are We in Vietnam?*—the book is likely to
go on engendering our strongest writers, with only *Leaves of Grass* as a rival
in that role.

What is the secret of an appeal that affected Eliot and Faulkner, Hemingway and Joyce, with almost equal intensity? Is it because the book tells
the truth? That was the judgment of Lionel Trilling, and I am not moved
to dismiss such a judgment lightly. The book tells a story which most Amer-

icans need to believe is a true representation of the way things were, are, and yet might be. Huck lives in a complex reality that nevertheless does not negate his freedom. Yet that freedom is also a solitude, and is purchased by a series of lies, noble in their intention, but lies nevertheless. Without a family, yet with a murderous father always apt to turn up again, Huck perpetually experiences a primal loneliness that he both welcomes and dreads:

> Miss Watson she kept pecking at me, and it got tiresome and lonesome. By-and-by they fetched the niggers in and had prayers, and then everybody was off to bed. I went up to my room with a piece of candle and put it on the table. Then I set down in a chair by the window and tried to think of something cheerful, but it warn't no use. I felt so lonesome I most wished I was dead. The stars was shining, and the leaves rustled in the woods ever so mournful; and I heard an owl, away off, who-whooing about somebody that was dead, and a whippowill and a dog crying about somebody that was going to die; and the wind was trying to whisper something to me and I couldn't make out what it was, and so it made the cold shivers run over me. Then away out in the woods I heard that kind of a sound that a ghost makes when it wants to tell about something that's on its mind and can't make itself understood, and so can't rest easy in its grave and has to go about that way every night grieving. I got so down-hearted and scared, I did wish I had some company. Pretty soon a spider went crawling up my shoulder, and I flipped it off and it lit in the candle; and before I could budge it was all shriveled up. I didn't need anybody to tell me that that was an awful bad sign and would fetch me some bad luck, so I was scared and most shook the clothes off of me. I got up and turned around in my tracks three times and crossed my breast every time; and then I tied up a little lock of my hair with a thread to keep witches away. But I hadn't no confidence. You do that when you've lost a horse-shoe that you've found, instead of nailing it up over the door, but I hadn't ever heard anybody say it was any way to keep off bad luck when you'd killed a spider.

Huck, like any American, does not feel free unless he is alone, and yet solitude makes him fear that he is no part of the creation, however the world happened or came about. His extraordinary pathos results from his ambivalence towards a freedom he necessarily cannot evade for very long at a time.

II

V. S. Pritchett found in *Adventures of Huckleberry Finn* evidence of an American limitation, when compared to the more civilized modes of European literature:

> It is not a book which grows spiritually, if we compare it to *Quixote*, *Dead Souls* or even *Pickwick*; and it is lacking in that civilised quality which you are bound to lose when you throw over civilisation—the quality of pity. One is left with the cruelty of American humor.

Pritchett perhaps forgot that throwing over civilization and its discontents is not so easily accomplished. Huck's discomfort with culture is acute, but he is hardly "a natural anarchist and bum" to whom ideas and ideals are "repugnant," as Pritchett thought. Nor is he "the servant of the river-god," which was Lionel Trilling's trope, a mythologization that derived Huck's supposedly "very intense moral life" from his "perpetual adoration of the Mississippi's power and charm." That is to compound Huck with T. S. Eliot, for whom "the Boy is also the spirit of the River." Huck indeed is now part of the American mythology, but hardly because he is the spirit of the river, which is not a god for Twain, whatever it was to be for Trilling and for Eliot. Twain tells us that the Mississippi is well worth reading about, is remarkable, and manifests many eccentricities. Huck too is well worth reading about, is quite remarkable, and is a wonderfully eccentric boy. Critics are fond of finding a moral in him, or at least want to see him as a kind of Sancho Panza to Tom Sawyer's Don Quixote. Tom Sawyer, alas, is something of a bore and not very quixotic, and Huck has little in common with the shrewd and pragmatic Sancho. There is however a touch of the quixotic in Huck, who is a great storyteller, a boy who lies merely to keep in practice.

Huck's fictions are lies *against* time, against an impossible father, against society and history, but not against reason and nature. They are not lies *for* anything; Huck does not seek benefits from them. Like the strong poets, Huck always has the desire to be different, the desire to be elsewhere. Change and travel are necessary for Huck; without them he cannot be independent. But we would do him wrong if we judged him as seeking freedom above everything else. Except for Joyce's Poldy Bloom, Huck Finn must be the most good-natured and tolerant representation of a human being in the fiction of the English language. The freedom he must have, because he is that freedom, is a freedom that he wants for everyone else. It is the freedom of the storyteller, Twain's own freedom.

That freedom, by common consent, has something to do with postponing death, with deferring the fear of dying. Divination, the sidestepping of dangers to the magic, occult, ontological self, is a fundamental component of the urge to tell stories. Huck of course is never going to be an adult, and so never will have to die. Yet that sounds wrong, because Huck rejects a maturation that is merely the death drive. The superego haunts Huck, yet cannot dominate him, because Huck will not surrender his gift for lying. "You don't know about me," Huck begins by saying, and he ends with the insistence that he will be out there ahead of the rest of us:

> But I reckon I got to light out for the Territory ahead of the rest,
> because Aunt Sally she's going to adopt me and sivilize me and
> I can't stand it. I been there before.

Huck's discomfort with civilization stems from his wholehearted rejection of guilt, sin, and solipsism, all of them Eliotic attributes, or should one say virtues? We can call Huck's attributes his virtues, because Huck, like his creator, is essentially an enlightened rationalist, though retaining considerable zest for the romance of superstitions. Unlike Eliot, Huck is not a Christian, and his prayer is not, "And let my cry come unto Thee," but something more naturalistic and buoyant:

> Sometimes we'd have that whole river all to ourselves for the
> longest time. Yonder was the banks and the islands, across the
> water; and maybe a spark—which was a candle in a cabin win-
> dow—and sometimes on the water you could see a spark or two—
> on a raft or a scow, you know; and maybe you could hear a fiddle
> or a song coming over from one of them crafts. It's lovely to live
> on a raft. We had the sky, up there, all speckled with stars, and
> we used to lay on our backs and look up at them, and discuss
> about whether they was made, or only just happened—Jim he
> allowed they was made, but I allowed they happened; I judged
> it would have took too long to *make* so many. Jim said the moon
> could a *laid* them; well, that looked kind of reasonable, so I didn't
> say nothing against it, because I've seen a frog lay most as many,
> so of course it could be done. We used to watch the stars that
> fell, too, and see them streak down. Jim allowed they'd got spoiled
> and was hove out of the nest.

This delightful compromise upon a myth of creation is "kind of reasonable," and wholly characteristic of Huck's cheerful skepticism. Even more characteristic is the joy of being that opens chapter 19 with what must be the most beautiful prose paragraph yet written by any American:

Two or three days and nights went by; I reckon I might say they swum by, they slid along so quiet and smooth and lovely. Here is the way we put in the time. It was a monstrous big river down there—sometimes a mile and a half wide; we run nights, and laid up and hid day-times; soon as night was most gone, we stopped navigating and tied up—nearly always in the dead water under a tow-head; and then cut young cottonwoods and willows and hid the raft with them. Then we set out the lines. Next we slid into the river and had a swim, so as to freshen up and cool off; then we set down on the sandy bottom where the water was about knee deep, and watched the daylight come. Not a sound, any-wheres—perfectly still—just like the whole world was asleep, only sometimes the bull-frogs a-cluttering, maybe. The first thing to see, looking away over the water, was a kind of dull line—that was the woods on t'other side—you couldn't make nothing else out; then a pale place in the sky; then more paleness, spreading around; then the river softened up, away off, and warn't black any more, but gray; you could see little dark spots drifting along, ever so far away—trading scows, and such things; and long black streaks—rafts; sometimes you could hear a sweep screaking; or jumbled up voices, it was so still, and sounds come so far; and by-and-by you could see a streak on the water which you know by the look of the streak that there's a snag there in a swift current which breaks on it and makes that streak look that way; and you see the mist curl up off of the water, and the east reddens up, and the river, and you make out a log cabin in the edge of the woods, away on the bank on t'other side of the river, being a wood-yard, likely, and piled by them cheats so you can throw a dog through it anywheres; then the nice breeze springs up, and comes fanning you from over there, so cool and fresh, and sweet to smell, on account of the woods and the flowers; but sometimes not that way, because they've left dead fish laying around, gars, and such, and they do get pretty rank; and next you've got the full day, and everything smiling in the sun, and the song-birds just going it!

This is a cosmos that was not made, but "only just happened." It is no part of romance or legend, not myth, but a representation of a natural reality seen in its best aspect, where the days and nights swim and slide by. We hesitate to call this a fiction, since it lacks any residual Platonism. Even Freud had his last touch of Platonism, the transcendentalism that he called the "reality principle." Twain and Huck tell us a story about reality, but without reference to any principle.

III

Eminent critics have disagreed vigorously over the way in which Twain chose to end his masterpiece. That something is seriously wrong with the conclusion is palpable, but what is wrong may only be that in this book no conclusion is possible anyway. T. S. Eliot and Lionel Trilling both argued the formal adequacy of the long episode at the Phelps place, in which Tom Sawyer arrives again to organize the "rescue" of Jim, the runaway slave who in some clear sense has become Huck's true family. But the critical decision here certainly goes to Leo Marx, who sees the novel's end as its self-defeat:

> Should Clemens have made Huck a tragic hero? Both Mr. Eliot and Mr. Trilling argue that that would have been a mistake, and they are very probably correct. But between the ending as we have it and tragedy in the fullest sense, there was vast room for invention. Clemens might have contrived an action which left Jim's fate as much in doubt as Huck's. Such an ending would have allowed us to assume that the principals were defeated but alive, and the quest unsuccessful but not abandoned. This, after all, would have been consonant with the symbols, the characters, and the theme as Clemens had created them—and with history.

Marx is aware that he asks for too much, but that is the lasting power of the book that Twain wrote until he reached the Phelps place episode. We are so transported by *Huckleberry Finn* that we cannot surrender our hopes, and of these the largest is a refusal to abandon the desire for a permanent image of freedom. Twain could not extend that image into a finality, but the image endures nevertheless, as a permanent token of something evermore about to be.

BERNARD DE VOTO

Mark Twain and the Great Valley

The first truly American literature grew out of the tidewater culture of the early republic. It was the culture of a people who, whatever their diversity, were more homogeneous in feeling and belief than Americans as a people have ever been since them. We have come to think of the literature whose greatest names are Emerson and Poe, Thoreau and Melville, Hawthorne and Whitman, as our classic period, and in a very real sense the republic that shaped their mind was classical. It felt a strong affinity for the Roman Republic, it believed that Roman virtues and ideas had been expressed in the Constitution, it gave us a great architectural style because it identified its own emotions in the classic style. When Horatio Greenough let a toga fall from Washington's naked shoulders he was not out of tune with contemporary taste: Washington seemed a kind of consul, so did Jefferson, and in the portraits of them which our stamps and coins preserve they have a Roman look. This classical republican culture was at its most vigorous when our classic writers were growing up. But there is an element of anachronism in all literature, and while these men were themselves in full vigor American culture entered a new phase.

The culture of the early republic crossed the Alleghenies in two streams, one Southern, the other mainly New England; but they were more like each other than either was like the one which their mingling presently helped to produce. For beyond the mountains people found different landscapes, different river courses, different relationships of sky and wind and water, dif-

From *The Portable Mark Twain*. ©1946, renewed 1974 by The Viking Press, Inc. Originally entitled "Introduction."

ferent conceptions of space and distance, different soils and climates—
different conditions of life. Beyond still farther mountains lay Oregon and
California—and they were implicit in the expanding nation as soon as the
treaty that gave us Louisiana was signed—but first the United States had to
incorporate the vast expanse between the eastern and the western heights of
land. That area is the American heartland. Its greatest son was to call it the
Egypt of the West because nature had organized it round a central river and
it touched no ocean, but it came into the American consciousness as the
Great Valley. When the tidewater culture came to the Great Valley it necessarily broke down: new conditions demanded adaptations, innovations,
new combinations and amplifications. The new way of life that began to
develop there had a different organization of feeling, a different metabolism
of thought. It was no more native, no more "American," than that of the
first republic, but it was different and it began to react on it.

The heartland was midcontinental and its energies were oriented toward
the river at its center—and were therefore turned away from Europe, which
had been a frontier of the early republic. And life in the heartland, with its
mingling of stocks, its constant shifting of population, and its tremendous
distances, led people in always increasing numbers to think continentally.
Both facts were fundamental in the thought and feeling of the new culture.

The American littoral came only slowly, with greater slowness than the
fact demanded, to realize that the nation's center of gravity was shifting
westward. It tragically failed to understand one consequence of that shift,
thirty years of contention between the Northeast and the South to dominate
the Great Valley or at least achieve a preferential linkage with it. The failure
to understand was in great part a failure to think continentally—as was made
clear at last when the Civil War demonstrated that no peaceful way of resolving the contention had been found. Even now too many Americans fail
to understand that the war, the resolution by force, only made explicit the
organization of our national life that is implicit in the geography which the
Great Valley binds together. Abraham Lincoln understood our continental
unity; he argued it persistently down to the outbreak of the war and from
then on. And Lincoln was a distillation of the heartland culture.

Lincoln's feeling for the continentalism of the American nation was so
intense that it almost transcended the transcendent facts. It was a deposit in
the very cells of his bones from the soil of the Great Valley. He was, Herndon
rightly says, one of the limestone men, the tall, gaunt, powerful, sallow,
saturnine men who appear in quantity enough to constitute a type when the
wilderness on both sides of the Ohio comes under the plow. His radical
democracy was wrought from the experience of the Great Valley. In his

ideas and beliefs as in the shadowed depths of his personality there is apparent
a new articulation of American life. His very lineaments show it. When you
turn from the Jefferson nickel to the Lincoln penny as when you turn from
Jefferson's first inaugural address to any of Lincoln's state papers, in the flash
of a total and immediate response you understand that you have turned from
one era to a later one. You have turned from the tidewater republic to the
continental empire.

Lincoln expressed a culture and brought a type to climax. Similarly,
when that culture found major literary expression it did so from a rich and
various, if humble, literary tradition. As always, the literary expression was
the later one; the economic, social, and political impact was felt much earlier.
The lag, however, was not so great as Walt Whitman thought. Whitman
was sixty when in 1879 he traveled across the Great Valley to its western
limit, where the Front Range walls it off. He traversed it with a steadily
growing conviction that here in the flesh were the people whose society he
had envisioned in so many rhapsodies, Americans who had been fused,
annealed, compacted (those are his words) into a new identity. He felt that
literature had not yet spoken to these prairie people, "this continental inland
West," that it had not yet spoken for them, that it had not made images for
their spirit.

The poet supposed that he was speaking of things still to come but he
was already wrong by a full ten years. The thing had happened. And the
first notification that it had happened can be dated with an exactness not
often possible in the history of literature. That notification came in 1869
with the appearance of a book of humorous travel sketches by Samuel Langhorne Clemens, who, faithful to the established tradition, signed it with a
pen name, Mark Twain.

Innocents Abroad was greeted with an enthusiasm that made Mark Twain
a celebrity overnight, and with too much misunderstanding of a kind that
was to persist throughout his career. It was a funny book and a cardinal part
of its fun was its disdain of European culture. This disdain, the mere fact
of making humor of such disdain, and its frequent exaggeration into burlesque
all produced an effect of shock—in most ways a delightful shock but in some
ways an uneasy one. Yet the point was not the provinciality of such humor,
though it was frequently provincial, and not its uncouthness, though it was
sometimes uncouth, but the kind of consciousness it implied. Again it is
absurd to speak of this as the first American literature that was independent
of European influences, for our literature had obediently divorced itself from
Europe as soon as Emerson ordered it to. The humorous core of *Innocents
Abroad* was not independence of Europe, but indifference to it. Thoreau and

Emerson and Poe were detached from Europe but completely aware of being heirs to it, but here was a literature which had grown up in disregard of Europe—which had looked inward toward the Mississippi and not outward beyond the Atlantic. Failure to appreciate the implications of this difference was one reason, no doubt the weightiest one, why for two full generations literary critics thought of Mark Twain as no more than a clown. But the same identity, the same organization of personality, that made Lincoln the artificer of our continental unity was what made Mark Twain a great writer.

There are striking affinities between Lincoln and Mark Twain. Both spent their boyhoods in a society that was still essentially frontier; both were rivermen. Both absorbed the midcontinental heritage: fiercely equalitarian democracy, hatred of injustice and oppression, the man-to-man individualism of an expanding society. Both were deeply acquainted with melancholy and despair; both were fatalists. On the other hand, both were instinct with the humor of the common life and from their earliest years made fables of it. As humorists, both felt the basic gravity of humor; with both it was an adaptation of the mind, a reflex of the struggle to be sane; both knew, and Mark Twain said, that there is no humor in heaven. It was of such resemblances that William Dean Howells was thinking when he called Mark Twain "the Lincoln of our literature."

II

Samuel Clemens was born at Florida, Monroe County, Missouri, on November 30, 1835, a few months after his parents reached the village from Tennessee. His father was a Virginian, his mother a Kentuckian, and as a family they had made three moves before this one. Florida was a handful of log cabins only two hundred miles east of the Indian Country and in the earliest stage of frontier economy. Though he could have only a generalized memory of it, Sam's earliest years were thus spent in the "Sweet Betsy from Pike" society which has contributed a color and a flavor of its own to American legendry. More: the town was located at the forks of that Salt Creek which figures in the folk proverbs. He could retain little conscious memory of the chinked-log, open-fireplace hamlet with its woods-runners and movers; mostly it would mean the immediacy of nature, the infinity of the forest, the ease of escape into solitude and an all-encompassing freedom. He was still short of four when the Clemenses made their last move, this time eastward. They seem to have been movers by force of circumstance, not instinct; it was always the pressure of poverty and the hope of betterment that impelled them on. But they bequeathed restlessness to their son.

The final move brought them to Hannibal, an older settlement than Florida and perhaps four times as large but still short of five hundred inhabitants. Hannibal is the most important single fact in the life of Samuel Clemens the person and Mark Twain the writer. It too was lapped round by forest; it maintained the romantic mystery, the subliminal dread, and the intimacy with nature that he had been born to; but it had passed the pioneering stage. It must be seen as a later stage that characterized all our frontiers east of the great plains, after the actual frontier of settlement had pushed westward, after the farms had been brought in and functional communities had been established, but while the frontier crafts and values and ways of thinking lingered on, a little mannered perhaps, a little nostalgic, but still vital. The frontier thugs had passed to other fields or degenerated to village loafers and bullies. There were a few Indians near by and sizable numbers not too far away but they were a spectacle, not a threat. A few hunters and trappers ranged the woods but they were relics, brush folk, not of the great race. There were as many frame houses as log cabins; if the schoolhouse had a puncheon floor, the squire's wife had a silk dress from St. Louis. Caste lines were almost nonexistent. Hannibal was a farmers' market village. More than half of its inhabitants were Southerners, but Southerners modified by the Great Valley. Its slaves were servants, not gang laborers.

But also Hannibal was on the Mississippi. Here enters the thread of cosmopolitanism that is so paradoxically interwoven with the extreme provincialism of this society. Steamboats bore the travelers and commerce of half a continent past the town wharf. Great rafts of logs and lumber—it was the latter kind that Huck and Jim traveled on—came down from Wisconsin. A population of freighters, movers, and mere drifters in shanty boats, keelboats, broadhorns, mackinaws, and scows added pageantry. Other types and other costumery came down from the lakes and northern rivers: voyageurs, trappers, winterers, Indians of the wilderness tribes always seen in ceremonial garments on their way to make treaties or collect annuities. All these belonged to the rapidly widening movement of the expanding nation. Moreover, Hannibal was within the aura of St. Louis, eighty miles away, and St. Louis was the port through which the energies of a truly imperial expansion were moving toward Santa Fe, Oregon, and California. Perhaps dimly but quite permanently any river town so near St. Louis would give even the most local mind an awareness of the continental divide, the Columbia, the Pacific, the Southwest. A town that may have never heard of Zebulon Pike or John Ledyard or Jonathan Carver nevertheless felt the national will that had turned them westward. The year of Mark's birth, 1835, may properly be taken as the year when the final phase of our continental expansion began. And the fruitfulness of Hannibal for Mark's imagination may reasonably be said to have stopped with his tenth year, just before that final phase raised up the irrepressible conflict.

For two things remain to be said of the society that shaped Sam Clemens's mind and feelings: that its post-pioneer, frontier stage stops short of the industrial revolution, and that the sectional conflict which produced the Civil War has not yet shown itself. The life which is always most desirable in Mark's thinking is the pre-industrial society of a little river town; it is a specific identification of Hannibal. Whereas the evils of life are the eternal cruelties, hypocrisies, and stupidities of mankind which have nothing to do with time or place but result from Our Heavenly Father's haste in experimenting when He grew dissatisfied with the monkey.

As the St. Petersburg of *Tom Sawyer*, Hannibal is one of the superb idyls of American literature, perhaps the supreme one. A town of sun, forest shade, drowsy peace, limpid emotions, simple humanity—and eternity going by on the majestic river. Even here, however, a mood of melancholy is seldom far away: a melancholy of the river itself, of our westering people who had always known solitude, and of a child's feeling, which was to grow through the years, that he was a stranger and a mysterious one under the stars. And below the melancholy there is a deeper stratum, a terror or disgust that may break through in a graveyard at midnight or at the sound of unidentified voices whispering above the water. This is in part fantasy, but in part also it is the weary knowledge of evil that paints Hannibal in far different colors in *Pudd'nhead Wilson* or *Huckleberry Finn*.

Almost as soon as he begins to write, Mark Twain is a citizen of the world, but he is always a citizen of Hannibal too. He frequently misunderstood himself, but he knew that quite clearly. In a postscript to [a] fragment of a letter "to an unidentified person," . . . he says:

> And yet I can't go away from the boyhood period & write novels because *capital* [that is, personal experience] is not sufficient by itself & I lack the other essential: interest in handling the men & experiences of later times.

While still a boy, he was apprenticed to a printer and so got the education that served more nineteenth-century American writers than any other. (It was a surprisingly extensive education. By twenty he knew the English classics thoroughly, was an inveterate reader of history, and had begun to cultivate his linguistic bent.) The trade eventually led him to newspaper reporting but first it took him on a series of *Wanderjahre* toward which heredity may have impelled him. At eighteen he went to St. Louis and on to New York. Philadelphia followed, Muscatine, St. Louis again, Keokuk (where he began to write humorous newspaper sketches), and Cincinnati, always setting type on a newspaper or in a job shop. He was twenty-two years old (and, if his memory can be trusted, ripe with a characteristic fantasy of South American adventure) when the American spectacle caught him up. In 1857 he began his apprenticeship to a Mississippi pilot. . . .

"Old Times on the Mississippi," a study in pure ecstasy, . . . is . . . stamped from his memory, which was always nostalgic, and from the romancing half of his twinned talent. It records a supreme experience about whose delight there can be no doubt whatever, and it testifies to Mark's admiration of all skills and his mastery of one of the most difficult. But piloting gave him more than ever got into "Old Times" or its enlargement, *Life on the Mississippi*. "Flush Times" would have done as well as "Old Times" to describe the climactic years of the prewar Mississippi Valley, with the rush and fever of the expanding nation. Those years vastly widened Mark's knowledge of America and fed his insatiable enjoyment of men, his absorbed observation of man's depravity, and his delight in spectacle.

The Civil War put an end to piloting. Mark has described his experience and that of many others in that war, in all wars, in a sketch which is one of the best things he ever wrote. "The Private History of a Campaign That Failed" could not be spared from the mosaic of our national catastrophe; it is one of the contexts in which Mark Twain has perfectly refracted a national experience through a personal one. When his military career petered out in absurdity, he joined the great national movement which even civil war could not halt. His older brother, the gentle zany Orion, was made Secretary of the Territory of Nevada and, paying the Secretary's passage west, Mark went along. In Nevada he found another national retort, another mixed and violent society, another speculative flush times. He became a drunkard of speculation, a prospector, a hunter of phantasmal mines, a silver miner, a laborer in a stamp mill, and at last a newspaperman. He went to work for that fabulous paper *The Territorial Enterprise* of Virginia City as an "editor," that is to say a reporter. And it was here that he took his immortal *nom de plume*, a phrase from the pilot's mystery. "Mark Twain" was signed to a species of humor in which Sam Clemens had been immersed ever since his apprenticeship, the newspaper humor of the Great Valley, which was in turn a development of the pungent oral humor he had heard from childhood on. Far from establishing a literary tradition, Mark Twain brought one to culmination.

After less than two years on the *Enterprise* he went to California, in

1864. He had met Artemus Ward in Nevada; now he joined the transient, bright Bohemia of the Golden Gate: Bret Harte, Prentice Mulford, Charles Warren Stoddard, Charles H. Webb, Ada Clare, Ina Coolbrith, still slighter and more forgotten names. He got a new kind of companionship and his first experience of literary sophistication. After a short time as a reporter he began to write humor for the Coast's literary papers, the *Californian* and the *Golden Era*. Promptly his work developed a strain of political and ethical satire which it never lost: the humorist was seldom separable from the satirist from this year on. That is to say, the individual humor of Mark Twain with its overtones of extravaganza and its undercurrent of misanthropy was, however crude and elliptical, fully formed by the end of 1864. He had not yet revealed the novelist's power to endow character with life, but it—together with a memorable talent for the vernacular—was made clear to anyone with eyes on December 16, 1865, when the New York *Saturday Press* published "Jim Smiley and His Jumping Frog."

The immortal story derived from still another Western experience, one which had made Mark, however lackadaisically, a pocket miner. He had sent it east at Artemus Ward's suggestion, but only an accident got it into type. It was a momentary smash hit, and so Mark was not altogether an unknown when he went to New York in 1867. Before he went there, however, he had reached the farthest limit of the expansionist dream, having gone to the Sandwich Islands as a newspaper correspondent. That voyage in turn had initiated his career as a lecturer. He had a marked histrionic talent; for years he barnstormed or made occasional appearances as a public "reader" and storyteller; all his life was making the after-dinner appearances of that vanished age, which pleased his vanity and gratified the longings of an actor *manqué*. But he went to New York as a correspondent: he had arranged to travel to Europe and the Holy Land with a conducted tour. In 1867 he published his first book, a collection of sketches called *The Celebrated Jumping Frog of Calaveras County* after the best of them, but the year is more notable for the travel letters he wrote for the *Alta California* and the New York *Tribune*. He made a book of them after his return, meanwhile writing free-lance humor and Washington correspondence. The book, *Innocents Abroad*, was published in 1869.

All this has been detailed to show how deep and various an experience of American life Mark Twain had had when he began to write. The rest of his biography is also strikingly typical of nineteenth-century America, but the seed-time has now been accounted for. It is not too much to say that he had seen more of the United States, met more kinds and castes and conditions of Americans, observed the American in more occupations and moods and tempers—in a word had intimately shared a greater variety of the characteristic experiences of his countrymen—than any other major American writer. . . .

III

Mark Twain was a man of moods, of the extreme of moods. He had a buoyancy which, twinned as it was with gentleness and intuition and wit, gave him a personal magnetism which his friends did not hesitate to call enchantment. Yet it alternated with an anger that readily became fury and was rooted in a revulsion between disgust and despair. The alternation suggests a basic split; it is clearly marked in his personality and equally evident in his books. The splendor his friends felt, his kindness to the unfortunate and the lowly and the oppressed, his generosity, his sensitiveness unite in a singular luminosity of spirit. Yet he was capable of savage vindictiveness, he exaggerated small or imaginary grievances out of all reason, and on little or no provocation he repeatedly believed himself misrepresented or betrayed. One doubts if any other American writer was ever so publicly beloved or privately adored; one is certain that no other was involved in so many lawsuits. "I am full of malice, saturated with malignity," he wrote eight months before his death. His malice and malignity of that moment were for the damned human race, but he could feel them in his private life whenever he thought he had been wronged. When *A Connecticut Yankee* was finished he wrote Howells that if he could write it over again "there wouldn't be so many things left out. They burn in me and they keep multiplying and multiplying, but now they can't even be said. And besides they would require a library—and a pen warmed up in hell." With a pen warmed up in hell he did fill a library and an extraordinary bulk of letters too. If it was sometimes avenging personal, usually imaginary wrongs, that private activity was only a reflex of the public function. For what burned in him was hatred of cruelty and injustice, a deep sense of human evil, and a recurrent accusation of himself. Like Swift he found himself despising man while loving Tom, Dick, and Harry so warmly that he had no proper defense against the anguish of human relationships. The trouble was that in terms of either earth or heaven he was never sure what to make of Samuel L. Clemens and so is recorded on both sides.

He is usually to be found on both sides of any question he argues. His intelligence was intuitive, not analytical. He reasoned fluently, with an avidity that touched most of the surface flow of his time, but superficially and with habitual contradictions. He had little capacity for sustained thought and to get to the heart of a question had to abandon analysis and rely on feeling. The philosophy which he spent years refining and supposed he had perfected is a sophomoric determinism. Even so, it is less a philosophy than a symbol or a rationalization; the perceptions it stood for are expressed at the level of genius in his fiction—not as idea but in terms of human life. Most of the nineteenth century's optimisms were his also. He fiercely championed the democratic axioms; they are the ether of his fiction and the fulcrum of his satire. He thought too that the nineteenth century, especially as Progress, and more especially as Progress in the United States, was the happiest estate of man; he believed that it was bringing on a future of greater freedom and greater happiness. This was basic and spontaneous in his mind, but at the same time he felt something profoundly wrong. There seemed to be some limitation to freedom, some frustration of happiness. He never really came to grips with the conflict. Only in the last fifteen years of his life did he ascribe any part of what might be wrong to any but superficial injustices in American life or any but slight dislocations in our system. By the time he became aware of serious threats to freedom they did not seem to matter much: he was so absorbed in the natural depravity of man that the collapse or frustration of democracy, which he was by then taking for granted, seemed only an unimportant detail. Ideally, his last years would have been spent in more rigorous analysis—if not of the objective data, then of his intuitive awareness of them. They were not and so his judgments remained confused—and his principal importance in our literature belongs to his middle years, the period when his mind and feelings are in healthy equilibrium. It is an importance of his perceptions, not his thinking, and it exists primarily in his fiction, most purely in *Huckleberry Finn*. The best of Mark Twain's fiction is, historically, the first mature realization in our literature of a conflict between the assumptions of democracy and the limitations on democracy. Between the ideal of freedom and the nature of man.

Not less important is the fact that there is a reconciliation, even an affirmation. Detachment could be no greater but it is still somehow compassionate; condemnation could be no more complete, but it is somehow magnanimous. The damned human race is displayed with derision and abhorrence, yet this is on the ground that it has fallen short of its own decencies. Moreover at least *Huckleberry Finn* has a hero, the only heroic character (apart from Joan of Arc, a debauch of gyneolatry) he ever drew, and it is the essence of what Mark Twain had to say that the hero is a Negro slave. It has also a vindication not only of freedom, but of loyalty and decency, kindness and courage; and it is the essence of Mark Twain that this vindication is made by means of a boy who is a spokesman of the folk mind and whom experience has taught wariness and skepticism. Like all great novels *Huckleberry Finn* moves on many levels of significance, but it describes a flight and a struggle for freedom, and the question it turns on is a moral question.

Mark found zest and gusto—nouns that do not describe very much American literature of the first rank—in whatsoever was alive. He liked few novels except those of his intimate friends. What he praised in the ones he did like was reality of behavior, speech, or motive; his notebooks are sulphurous with comments on merely literary, that is false, characters. His taste was for biography, autobiography, history—life direct, men revealing themselves. No doubt the race was damned but it was fascinating. And that was proper for if his fiction is the best of his work, his most salient talent as a novelist is the life-giving power. It is a careless and prodigal fecundity, but nevertheless remarkably concentrated. Old Man Finn, for instance, is greatly imagined and he seems to fill the first half of the book, yet he appears in only a few pages. Mrs. Judith Loftus lives completely in a single chapter. A mere passerby, a casual of the river or a thug heard talking in a frowzy town, may reveal a whole personality in a few paragraphs. Nor is this fecundity confined to Mark's fiction, for the framework of all his books is anecdotal and all the people in them are dramatized. The whole population of his principal books, nine-tenths of the population of all his books, has the same vividness. Boys, villagers, the rivermen, the Negroes, Colonel Sellers, the two great vagabonds—there is nothing quite like the Mark Twain gallery elsewhere in American literature.

But there is a striking limitation: nowhere in that gallery are there women of marriageable age. No white women, that is, for the slave Roxana in *Pudd'nhead Wilson* lives as vividly as Old Man Finn himself. It must be significant that the only credible woman of an age that might sanction desire is withdrawn from desire behind the barrier of race. None of Mark Twain's nubile girls, young women, or young matrons are believable; they are all bisque, saccharine, or tears. He will do girl children in the romantic convention of boys' books and he is magnificent with the sisterhood of worn frontier wives whom Aunt Polly climaxes, but something like a taboo drains reality from any woman who might trouble the heart or the flesh. There is no love story in Mark Twain, there is no love at all beyond an occasional admission, for purposes of plot only, that someone is married or is going to be. Women seldom have husbands and men seldom have wives unless they are beyond middle age. Mark's endless absorption in human motives did not, for literary purposes at least, extend to sexual motives. Sex seems to be forbidden unless it can be treated mawkishly, and this writer of great prose who habitually flouted the genteel proprieties of language was more prudish than the most tremulous of his friends in regard to language that might suggest either desire or its gratification. So there is a sizable gap in the world he created. That gap has never been accounted for. Certainly there was nothing bloodless about Mark Twain; and his marriage, one of the happiest of literary marriages, was clearly passionate. Yet he did not marry till he was thirty-five (1870), and there may have been something permissive—to a man whose characters have usually lost a father if not both parents—in the fact that he married an invalid.

Few Americans have written as much as Mark Twain. His published works are not much greater in bulk than his unpublished manuscripts, the books he finished fewer than the ones he broke off and abandoned. He wrote on impulse and enthusiasm and while they lasted he wrote easily, but he wrote as needs must, for he had little faculty of self-criticism and but small ability to sustain or elaborate an idea. He was best at the short haul. Not only his fiction but the personalized narrative that is the vehicle of *Innocents Abroad, A Tramp Abroad, Life on the Mississippi*, and much else is episodic. When what he was writing was in circuit with his deepest perceptions he was superb. The breaking of the circuit always threw him into extemporization, which meant that fiction fell away into extravaganza and satire into burlesque. At such times he did not know that he was flatting; the serious artist could become a vaudeville monologuist in a single page without being aware that the tone had changed. That such a well-imagined novel as *Pudd'n-head Wilson* was written round the grotesque joke called "Those Extraordinary Twins" would be incredible if the same tone-deafness were not plentifully evident elsewhere. He thought the mawkish *Joan of Arc* and the second-rate *The Prince and the Pauper* his best work. He interrupted his masterpiece before it was half-finished, liking it so little that he threatened to burn it, and ignored it for six years during which, though he wrote constantly, he wrote nothing of importance. Then he finished it almost as casually as he had begun it. There is no greater book in American literature, but critics agree that the last quarter of it is impaired by the extravaganza that begins when Huck gets to Uncle Silas's farm. It is typical of Mark Twain that he felt no difference in kind or key between this admittedly superb extravaganza and the searching of American society and human experience that precedes it. In fact, the delivery of Jim from the dungeon was one of Mark's favorite platform readings.

Furthermore, he lacked the attribute of the artist—whatever it may be— that enables him to think a novel through till its content has found its own inherent form. Of his novels only *Joan of Arc, The Prince and the Pauper*, and *Tom Sawyer* have structures that have developed from within; significantly, all are simple and only one is first-rate. Mark lived with his material for a long time, sometimes for many years, but not consciously, not with critical or searching dissatisfaction. A book must come of its own momentum from the unconscious impulse, be it as a whole, as a fragment, or as something that hardly got started before it broke off. This is to say that he had no conscious esthetic. He stood at the opposite pole from Henry James, with the other great contemporary of both, Howells, in between but nearer to James. Yet he had as large a share as either of them in creating the modern American novel.

The explanation for his lack of self-criticism and for his innocence of esthetics is not to be found in the supposed naiveté of the society that bore him. In the first place, that society was far from naive; in the second place, not only did the fine artist Howells come from it, but Mark himself raised its native tale-telling to a fine art, which surely establishes a discipline. He had, besides, two other disciplines: that of the daily job, which he observed as faithfully as any writer who ever lived, and the taskmastership of a great style. Nor can Mark's own explanation, which he pleads so earnestly in the letter to Andrew Lang, be supported: that he wrote for the belly and members only. *Huckleberry Finn* is no more written for the belly and members only than *War and Peace* is or *Recherche du Temps Perdu*. But it is written at the behest of an instinctive drive, and explanation need go no farther if it could, for this time at least Mark's whole personality was behind it. In short, he wrote trivially or splendidly or magnificently as what appears to have been little more than chance might determine: he was not a fully self-conscious artist. But when he wrote greatly he was writing from an inner harmony of desire and will. Or call it a harmony of his deepest self and his inheritance from the Great Valley.

Only that harmony, seen in relation to time and history, can explain him. For no man ever became a great writer more inadvertently than Mark Twain. He first became famous as a superior Artemus Ward, and that corresponded to his idea of himself. A long time passed before he had any desire to be more. He exploited a joke-maker's talent as systematically as a production manager could have done it for him, delighted by the discovery that he could raise his status, prestige, and income beyond Tom Sawyer's dreams. Nevertheless there is the paradox that almost from the beginning the attack of the funny man had been supported by that of a serious artist. Already in "The Jumping Frog" mastery of fictional character is clearly presaged, and the prophecy is fulfilled as early as *The Gilded Age* (1873). By *The Gilded Age* also a satirist is dealing maturely with a wide expanse of American life. From this composite the funny man cannot be separated out for a long time, and

during that time there are only sporadic indications that Mark saw either the
novelist or the satirist as more than instrumentalities of the humorist. The
paradox resists criticism. One can only repeat that Mark Twain's greatness
developed because the time and the continent had shaped him at their core.

This representative centrality goes on undiminished after the establishment of his fame. Following his marriage he was briefly a newspaper owner
in Buffalo but abandoned that career to move to a provincial New England
city, Hartford, and set up as a professional writer. His periodic restlessness
continued; he never spent the full year in Hartford, he made at least twelve
trips abroad, and he once expatriated himself for nine years. The Hartford
period, 1874–91, covered his greatest happiness and the beginning of his
catastrophe. His was an unusually happy family life, and he was the center
of an always widening circle. Howells and the Rev. Joseph Twichell were
his closest friends; Cable, Aldrich, most of the leading writers of his generation were of the circle, and it widened to include the rich, the famous,
the powerful, and the great. Mark ruled it by divine right: there have always
been conflicting opinions about his books, but only one has ever been possible
about his dominion over men's affections. He seemed alien to mortality. A
fantasy of his childhood is frequently set down in notes and fragments of
manuscript: the child had identified himself with a romantic stranger in
Hannibal, a mysterious, perhaps supernatural visitor from Elsewhere. As
the one-gallus village boy came to be a world figure, that fantasy seemed on
the way to being confirmed. There was further confirmation as the author
of *The Gilded Age* entered with a blithe and innocent heart on another career
as a speculator, and the stamp-mill operator and tramp printer, who sincerely
believed all his life that he was a member of the laboring class, undertook
with the same innocence to be an industrial promoter.

Always convinced that his publishers were defrauding him, Mark had
established his own firm to publish his books. The expansion it underwent
in order to handle the bestseller of the generation, *Personal Memoirs of U. S.
Grant*, could not be sustained. The firm sank into insolvency and finally went
bankrupt. It could probably have been saved except that the most fantastic
of Mark's promotions failed at the same time and left him bankrupt. For
years he had been pouring his earnings and his wife's fortune into a mechanical typesetter which would indeed have made him a multimillionaire
if it had succeeded. Its failure and that of the publishing firm were only the
beginning of a series of disasters on the same scale as his fantastic rise. He
paid off his indebtedness by a heroic lecture tour that took him round the
world but his health broke. The oldest of his three daughters, the one who
seemed most like him in temperament and talent, died during his absence.

An agonizing personality change in his youngest daughter was finally diagnosed as epilepsy. Mrs. Clemens declined into permanent invalidism and in 1904 died.

This prolonged catastrophe brought Mark's misanthropy out of equilibrium; it dominated the rest of his life. The disasters were, of course, personal and yet it is hardly straining the facts to find him here also representative of the nineteenth-century America that had already found so much expression in him. As the century neared its end there was a good deal of pessimism and disenchantment in the United States. A wave of doubt and questioning swept many minds. The people who began an imperialistic adventure in the Pacific with the same naive enthusiasm that had taken Mark Twain into the industrial life were widely, at the very time they stepped out on the world stage, beginning to be troubled about themselves. The nineteenth century, looking back on its course, found cause to be dismayed. Was the democratic dream being served as well as the nation had assumed? Had the United States gone wrong somewhere during the avalanche of expansion? Were there, then, limits to what democracy could do, or flaws or contradictions in its theses, or impassable barriers in its path? Was the good time ending, were the vigorous years running out under a gathering shadow?

However deep or shallow this *fin de siècle* weariness may have been in the United States at large, Mark Twain's last fifteen years must be seen as related to it, if only distantly. During this period he wrote as much as in any similar length of time in his life, perhaps more, but most of it is fragmentary, unfinished. Almost all of it deals with the nature of man, man's fate, and man's conceptions of honor and morality. There are fables, dialogues, diatribes—sometimes cold, sometimes passionate, derisive, withering, savage. Mark sees the American republic perishing, like republics before it, through the ineradicable cowardice, corruption, and mere baseness of mankind. He elaborates theories, which he embodies in imaginary histories of the world (and sometimes of extra-mundane societies) to support his prophecy, and yet he cannot be much troubled by the going-down of this western land, for year by year he is writing a general apocalypse. The Old Testament fables had always served him for humorous derision of man's gullibility, but now he uses them as missiles in a ferocious attack on human stupidity and cruelty. Man is compact of malignity, cowardice, weakness, and absurdity, a diseased organism, a parasite on nature, a foolish but murderous animal much lower than the swine.

Yet *What Is Man?* (published anonymously in 1906 but written before the turn of the century), the fullest of many developments of these themes, cannot be seen solely as a document in anthropophobia. It is also in complex

ways a justification, even a self-justification. Its fixed universe, with an endless chain of cause and effect from the beginning of time, permits Mark to
compose many variations on the theme of human pettiness, but also it serves
to free man of blame—and thus satisfies a need deeply buried in Mark's
personal remorse. To this period also belongs *Mark Twain's Autobiography*,
which serves him as an escape into the security of the boyhood idyl he had
made immortal in *Tom Sawyer*. The need to escape is significant, but the
release is even more so, for it breaks the obsession signified by *What Is Man?*
But a much truer release and a fulfillment as well came, as always, when
Mark turned from reasoning to the instinctual portions of his mind. The
highest reach of his last period is *The Mysterious Stranger*. It is an almost
perfect book—perfect in expression of his final drive, in imaginative projection of himself, in tone and tune, in final judgment on the nature of man
and the experience of Mark Twain. It is on a humbler level than his great
books. More than any of them it is Mark Twain somewhat in disregard of
America. It is not, finally, a major work; but in its small way it is a masterpiece. Those who know and love Mark Twain will always find it as
revealing as *Huckleberry Finn*.

IV

Mark Twain died in 1910 with, as he had foretold, the return of the
mysterious visitor from beyond the solar system under whose sign he had
been born, Halley's comet. His last years had been as full of honors as his
middle years had been of fame. Even so, in 1910 it was hardly possible to
define his importance in American literature as clearly as we can after another
generation.

No doubt his first importance in that literature is the democratizing
effect of his work. It is a concretely liberating effect, and therefore different
in kind from Whitman's vision of democracy, which can hardly be said to
have been understood by or to have found a response among any considerable
number of Americans. Mark Twain was the first great American writer who
was also a popular writer, and that in itself is important. Much more important is the implicit and explicit democracy of his books. They are the
first American literature of the highest rank which portrays the ordinary
bulk of Americans, expresses them, accepts their values, and delineates their
hopes, fears, decencies, and indecencies as from within. The area proper to
serious literature in the United States was enormously widened by them, in
fact widened to the boundaries it still observes today. There have been no
acknowledged priorities of caste in American writing since Mark Twain.

Moreover, in his native equalitarian point of view, in his assertion of the basic democratic axioms, in his onslaught on privilege, injustice, vested power, political pretense, and economic exploitation (much of it admittedly superficial or confused, though much else is the most vigorous satire we have), in his transmutation of the town-meeting or country-store sharpness of judgment into a fine art—he is mid-nineteenth-century American democracy finding its first major voice in literature, ultimately its strongest voice. In him the literature of democracy becomes more robust than it had been before, such part of that literature, at least, as may be said to contain multitudes and speak to them. And this, to return to our starting point, embodies the transforming experience of the American people as they occupied the Great Valley and pushed beyond it, on the way forging the continental mind.

The nature of his writing is hardly less important. Mark Twain wrote one of the great styles of American literature, he helped develop the modern American style, he was the first writer who ever used the American vernacular at the level of art. There has been some failure to understand this achievement. Shortly before this [essay] was written, the most pontifical American critic guessed that Mark must have turned to the vernacular of *Huckleberry Finn* because he lacked education, was unacquainted with literary traditions, and therefore wrote thin or awkward prose. That absurdity disregards Mark's life and his books as well. The reader may determine . . . whether the style of *The Mysterious Stranger* lacks strength or subtlety, lacks any quality whatever for the effects required of it, or if that represents too late a period, may turn to "Old Times on the Mississippi," which was written before *Huckleberry Finn*, or "The Private History of a Campaign That Failed," which was written while *Huck* was still half finished. Mark Twain wrote English of a remarkable simplicity and clarity, and of singular sensitiveness, flexibility, and beauty as well. Its simplicity might deceive a patronizing reader for the sentence structure is not involved, usually consisting of short elements in natural sequence, and in order to understand without analysis how much art has gone into it one must have an ear for the tones and accents of speech as well as some feeling for the vigor of words. It is so lucid that it seems effortless—but just what is style?

Now, it is important that Mark made the American vernacular the medium of a great novel. Even before that he had used local, class, and racial dialects with immeasurably greater skill than anyone before him in our literature. "The Jumping Frog" raised such dialects above the merely humorous use which was the only one they had previously had and gave them a function in the writing of fiction. And the first two chapters of *The Gilded Age* bring to American literature genuine Negro speech and a rural dialect that are both genuine and an instrument of art—literally for the first time. In the rendition of Negro speech he may have had one equal, though there are those who will not grant that Harris is an equal; but it is doubtful if anyone has used the dialects of the middle South, or for that matter any other American dialect, as well as he. This on the basis of *The Gilded Age* and its immediate successors: the achievement of *Huckleberry Finn* is greater still. Huck's style, which is the spoken language of the untutored American of his place and time, differentiates the most subtle meanings and emphases and proves capable of the most difficult psychological effects. In a single step it made a literary medium of the American language; the liberating effect on American writing could hardly be overstated. Since *Huckleberry Finn* the well of American undefiled has flowed confidently.

Nevertheless, Mark's principal service to the American language was not Huck's vernacular: it lay within the recognized limits of literary prose. Within those limits he was a radical innovator, a prime mover who changed the medium by incorporating in it the syntax, the idioms, and especially the vocabulary of the common life. The vigor of his prose comes directly from the speech of the Great Valley and the Far West. A superlative may be ventured: that Mark Twain had a greater effect than any other writer on the evolution of American prose.

His place in that evolution cannot be analyzed or even illustrated here. He is in the direct succession and he powerfully accelerates the movement. The evolution is of course older than our independence, even older than our nationality—which it helped to produce. Only an American could have said, "We must all hang together, or assuredly we shall all hang separately" in the traditional context. Only an American could have written, "It is not necessary that a man should earn his living by the sweat of his brow unless he sweats easier than I do." Only an American could have written, "the calm confidence of a Christian with four aces." The sequence is Franklin, Thoreau, Mark Twain; and the point here made lightly can be made with as profound a search into the fusion of thought, expression, and nationality as anyone may care to undertake. But before Mark Twain no American, no one writing in English, could have launched a novel into the movement of fiction with such a passage as:

> At the end of an hour we saw a far-away town sleeping in a valley
> by a winding river, and beyond it on a hill, a vast gray fortress
> with towers and turrets, the first I had ever seen out of a picture.

"Bridgeport?" said I, pointing.
"Camelot," said he.

Such questions as these, however, interest the historian of literature more than the general reader. The general reader who, it may be worth reminding you, continues to read Mark Twain, here and in Europe, more often by far than any other of our great dead. It is not difficult to say why.

The Americanism just mentioned is part of it. Any unidentified quotation from Mark Twain will be recognized at sight as American. It is, furthermore, a national Americanism; his great books are set along the Mississippi, but no one can think of them as local or regional. But there is also a kind of centripetal Americanism, so that he seems frequently to speak for the nation. The character of national spokesman is in his work as early as *Innocents Abroad;* by *Huckleberry Finn* it is self-evident. Fifteen years before he died it was generally acknowledged—so that if the nation's mood changed or its honor came in peril, the newspapers could hardly be put to bed till Mark Twain had spoken.

But there is something more basic. What the millions who have gone on reading Mark Twain since 1869 have chiefly wanted and received from him is precisely those images which, three years after *Tom Sawyer* and four years after "Old Times on the Mississippi" had been published, Walt Whitman was still hoping someone would forge from the new national life.

So long as anyone may be interested in our past there will be readers for the books in which Mark embodied his plentiful share of it. These are chiefly *Life on the Mississippi, Roughing It,* and the *Autobiography.* But he is so persistently an autobiographer that the same lens repeatedly refracts something deeply American and casual contexts suddenly rise to the level of his better books. It may be a lynching in Marion County, a reminiscence of General Grant, a pocket-miner's tomcat, Harriet Beecher Stowe in her dotage fetching a warwhoop behind someone's ear—but it is more likely to be a page or two of dialogue which make a society transparent and register a true perception forever. This more than the verbal humor is likely to preserve some of the lesser books, perhaps even *Following the Equator,* though the always painful burlesque that is now intolerable predominates in others. The humor that was the essential Mark Twain remains; it is interstitial, it is the breathing of his mind. Whether it be exuberance, an individual way of letting light in, the passion of a man hardly able to contain his wrath, or the deadlier laughter in suspension that means a tortured mind's adaptation to reality, it is the fundamental attribute of Mark Twain. The critic who for a moment forgets that Mark was a humorist is betrayed.

In the end, however, Mark's fiction is the best part of him. *The Prince and the Pauper* and *Joan of Arc* have already lost their luster, though the first still charms children as it once charmed Victorian adults. A middle group which lost their audience for a while have begun to regain it, books with great qualities in them but marred by the improvisation or the failure of artistic intelligence that have been described above. *Pudd'nhead Wilson*, the most courageous of Mark's books, has a fine verve, a theme he never dared to face outside it, the magnificent Roxana, and a certain historical importance as one of the few serious treatments in American fiction of any aspect of slavery. It is a matter of some regret that Mark began writing fiction with *The Gilded Age*, for he was still inexpert at narrative and in fact hardly in earnest as a novelist, and the exceedingly serious book suffers in consequence. It is also too bad that he wrote it with a collaborator, for Mark would have contributed enough mistakes by himself, whereas Charles Dudley Warner quadruples them, adding the melodrama of the wronged girl for good measure. Nevertheless *The Gilded Age* named an era for all American thinking since it and remains one of the very few contemporary attacks on that venal period. Finally, it has Colonel Sellers in it and so is immortal.

Shorter pieces range from the fathomlessly mawkish "Horse's Tale" and "Dog's Tale" (a similar and worse one of the same kind remains unpublished) to "The Man That Corrupted Hadleyburg" and "Captain Stormfield's Visit to Heaven," which are part of the Mark Twain canon and contain essential portions of his quarrel with mankind. The best of his shorter pieces, however, is "Tom Sawyer Abroad." Presumably because the setting (a navigable balloon) makes it look like burlesque, most critics have ignored it. It is a deliberate exploration of the provincial mind and its prejudices, ignorances, assumptions, wisdoms, cunning. It memorably differentiates three stages of that mind, by way of the familiar Tom, Huck, and Nigger Jim. It is among the very best of Mark's work, frequently on a level with *Huckleberry Finn* itself, and must eventually be recognized as what it is.

A Connecticut Yankee in King Arthur's Court is the most tragically marred of Mark's books. It might have been a masterpiece, it repeatedly flashes to greatness, some of its satire is Mark Twain at his most serene or most savage; but nothing is sustained, tinny extravaganza or burlesque sooner or later spoils every clearly sounded note, and in short the book is at war with itself. Within a single set of covers Mark repeated every error of judgment that can be found in the Collected Works. Probably it will always be read for its fine moments but no one will ever name it among his great books.

Those are *The Adventures of Tom Sawyer* and *Adventures of Huckleberry*

Finn. Here the images Walt Whitman desired of and for the new society are actually forged. They are the America of their time speaking with many voices—and the sharp difference between them corresponds not only to the dichotomy in Mark's mind but to one that is basic in our thinking about ourselves. Between them the idyllic *Tom* and the corrosive *Huck* express most of the American consciousness. Forgetting that he himself had made several plays of it, Mark once refused to let an applicant dramatize *Tom Sawyer* because you cannot make a hymn into a play. It is a hymn: to boyhood, to the fantasies of boyhood, to the richness and security of the child's world, to a phase of American society now vanished altogether, to the loveliness of woods and prairies that were the Great Valley, to the river, to many other things in which millions of readers have recognized themselves and their inheritance. It is wrought out of beauty and nostalgia. Yet Mark is nowhere truer to us, to himself, or to childhood than in the dread which holds this idyl inclosed. The book so superbly brings the reader within its enchantment that some reflection is required before he can realize of what ghastly stuff it is made—murder and starvation, grave-robbery and revenge, terror and panic, some of the darkest emotions of men, some of the most terrible fears of children, and the ghosts and demons and death portents of the slaves. The book could have been written nowhere but in America and by no American but Mark Twain, but it has passed out of our keeping. It is the fantasy of boyhood in world literature.

Huckleberry Finn also has become a universal possession. It is a much deeper book than *Tom Sawyer*—deeper as of Mark Twain, of America, and of humanity. When after some stumbling it finds its purpose, it becomes an exploration of an entire society, the middle South along the river. In accomplishing this purpose it maintains at the level of genius Mark's judgment in full on the human race. It is well to remember that no one had spoken so witheringly to Americans about themselves before Huck raised his voice. But the book is not only the judgment on the damned human race which the much later *What Is Man?* only tried to be, it is also incomparably rich with the swarming life that so absorbed Mark Twain—and contains a forthright assertion of the inalienable dignity of man. It is the most complete expression of Mark Twain.

Like *Tom* and in much greater measure it has a mythic quality. This is in part the river itself, the Mississippi which had dominion over Mark's imagination and here becomes a truly great symbol. It is in part the symbol of the downriver journey—made the more momentous by a boy's bewilderment and a slave's flight for freedom. But in greater part it is the developing pageantry which becomes ecstatic when two vagabonds join Jim and Huck, and the Duke of Bilgewater and the "pore disappeared Dauphin, Looy the Seventeen," take their place in a small company of literature's immortals.

Thus realism, fantasy, satire, mythology, and the tragic knowledge of man, all of them a good many layers deep, united in Mark Twain's masterpiece. It is the book he was meant to write. A book of itself alone, unlike any other, unique, essentially Mark Twain, essentially America, it also has transcended our national literature. Every new generation of readers discovers that it belongs to mankind.

F. R. LEAVIS

Mark Twain's Neglected Classic

Pudd'nhead Wilson is not faultless—no book of Mark Twain's is that—but it is all the same the masterly work of a great writer. Yet it is very little known. One cannot easily find anyone, English or American, who has read it (at least that is my experience), and it would seem never at any time to have had the beginnings of the recognition that is its due. Its reputation— if it may be said to have a reputation—would not encourage a strenuous search for a copy of the book, unless in an admirer of *Huckleberry Finn* who was curious to look over one of the author's ephemeral productions, one that also dealt in its way with life in Hannibal, Missouri, the village of Mark Twain's childhood.

The explanation, I think, is partly that *Pudd'nhead Wilson* is so very unlike *Huckleberry Finn*. But it is also, I think, that the nature of the greatness of *Huckleberry Finn* itself tends not to be fully recognized. There are, then, two reasons for hoping that *Pudd'nhead Wilson* may come to be appreciated as it deserves: it is a classic in its own right (if an unrecognized classic may be said to *be* one); and, further, for all the unlikeness, it bears a very close relation to *Huckleberry Finn*; a relation of such a kind that to appreciate the lesser work is to have a surer perception of the greatness of the greater.

Huckleberry Finn, by general agreement Mark Twain's greatest work, is supremely the American classic, and it is one of the great books of the world. The significance of such a work doesn't admit of exhaustive recognition in a simple formula, or in several. Mark Twain himself was no simple being,

From *Commentary* (February 1956). © 1956 by F. R. Leavis. Originally entitled "Mark Twain's Neglected Classic: The Moral Astringency of *Pudd'nhead Wilson*."

and the complexity of his make-up was ordinarily manifested in strains, disharmonies, and tormenting failures of integration and self-knowledge. These, in his supreme masterpiece, can be seen to provide the creative drive. There is of course the aspect of return to boyhood, but the relation to complexity and strain represented by *Huckleberry Finn* is not one of escape from them—in spite of the qualities that have established the book as a classic for children (and in spite of Mark Twain's conviction, at times, that its appeal should be as such). It is true that the whole is given through Huck, the embodiment of that Western vernacular, or of the style created out of that, in which the book is written. But that style, perfectly as it renders the illiterate Huck, has been created by a highly sophisticated art to serve subtle purposes, and Huck himself is of course not merely the naive boyish consciousness he so successfully enacts; he is, by one of those triumphant sleights or equivocations which cannot be judiciously contrived, but are proof of inspired creative possession, the voice of deeply reflective maturity—of a life's experience brooded on by an earnest spirit and a fine intelligence. If Mark Twain lacked art in Arnold Bennett's sense (as Arnold Bennett pointed out), that only shows how little art in Arnold Bennett's sense matters, in comparison with art that is the answer of creative genius to the pressure of a profoundly felt and complex experience. If *Huckleberry Finn* has its examples of the unintelligence that may accompany the absence of sustained critical consciousness in an artist, even a great one, nevertheless the essential intelligence that prevails, and from the poetic depths informs the work, compels our recognition—the intelligence of the whole engaged psyche; the intelligence that represents the integrity of this, and brings to bear the wholeness.

For in his supreme creation the complex and troubled Mark Twain did achieve a wholeness; it is manifested in the nature of the creative triumph. The charged significance of *Huckleberry Finn* brings together a strength of naiveté and a strength of mature reflective wisdom. Let me quote, with immediate relevance, Mr. Bernard De Voto, most penetrating of the commentators on Mark Twain I am acquainted with: "fundamentally Huck is an expression—a magnificent expression, a unique expression—of the folk mind. The folk mind, that is, in mid-America in the period of the frontier and immediately following, the folk mind shaped for use by the tremendous realities of conquering a hostile wilderness and yet shadowed by the unseen world. He is one of the highest reaches of American fiction.

"But if Huck expresses the folk mind, he is also Mark Twain's surrogate, he is charged with transmitting what that dark, sensitive, and complex consciousness felt about America and the human race. . . . Mark Twain was not a systematic thinker. Customarily, like the creature of fable who was his

brother Orion, he held in succession all possible opinions about every ↑
he tried to analyze, held none of them long, and was able to drive nou.. ....,
deep beneath the surface. Especially as a metaphysician he was as feeble a
novice as ever ventured into that stormy sea. But in what he perceived, in
what he felt, in the nerve-ends of emotion, in the mysterious ferments of art
which transform experience, he was a great mind—there has been no greater
in American literature. Be it said once more and ever so wearily: insuffi-
ciencies and mental defects prevented him from ever completely imple-
menting the artist throughout the whole course of a book. That does not
matter—in *Huckleberry Finn* we get the finest expression of a great artist, the
fullest report on what life meant to him."

When Mr. De Voto speaks of the "folk mind" in *Huckleberry Finn* he is
making a plainly valid observation; an observation duly offset, as the quoted
passage shows, by the recognition of quite other aspects of the book. But
insistence on the "folk" element sometimes goes with an attempt to make
Huckleberry Finn American in a sense that would make it an immeasurably
lesser thing than the great work it is. Mr. Van Wyck Brooks, in *The Times
of Melville and Whitman*, writes: "He was the frontier storyteller, the great
folk writer of the American West, and raised to a pitch unparalleled before
him the art of oral storytelling and then succeeded in transferring its effects
to paper." Such an account (and there is a formidable representative intention
behind it) serves as a license for insisting on the force of the reply—the
obvious and unanswerable reply: Mark Twain was something very much
more than a folk-writer, and the art of *Huckleberry Finn* is no mere matter of
managing effects—suspense, surprise, climax, and so on. One cannot intel-
ligently discuss the art without discussing the complex and reverse of naive
outlook it conveys. Mr. Brooks, recognizing, as any reader must, an insistent
moral preoccupation in the theme, quotes Paine, Mark Twain's biographer:
"the author makes Huck's struggle a psychological one between conscience
and the law on one side, and sympathy on the other." But there is more to
the moral theme of *Huckleberry Finn* than that suggests. What the book conveys is the drama in a mind in which conscience finds that it is not single,
and that the "law" doesn't speak with one voice, and that what Paine calls
"sympathy" itself engages a moral imperative. In fact, *Huckleberry Finn* has
as a central theme the complexity of ethical valuation in a society with a
complex tradition—a description that applies (for instance) to any "Christian"
society.

The book is a profound study of civilized man. And about its attitude
towards civilization as represented by the society depicted in it there is
nothing simple or simplifying, either in a "frontier" spirit or in a spirit of

reductive pessimism. It is not to the point to adduce such private utterances of Mark Twain's as: "We have no real morals, but only artificial ones—morals created and preserved by the forced suppression of natural and healthy instinct." "Never trust the artist; trust the tale": Lawrence's dictum might have been addressed to Mark Twain's case. *Huckleberry Finn*, the tale, gives us a wholeness of attitude that transcends anything ordinarily attainable by the author. The liberation effected by the memories of youth and the Mississippi was, for the creative genius at his greatest, not into irresponsibility but the reverse. The imaginatively recovered vitality of youth ministered, in sum, no more to the spirit of "Pudd'nhead Wilson's Calendar" than to nostalgia or daydream, but to the attainment of a sure and profound moral maturity. That is, to call *Huckleberry Finn* a great work is not an exaggeration.

I insist in this way because of a tendency in America (and transatlantic fashions regarding American literature tend to be taken over uncritically in England) to suggest that the beginnings of the truly American in literary tradition come from the frontier and the West. According to this view Mark Twain is a more truly American writer than Hawthorne or Henry James. It is a view that, in offering to exalt him, actually denies his greatness, for it makes the attributed advantage in Americanness a matter of his being alienated from English and European tradition as Hawthorne and James are not. Such an alienation could only be an impoverishment: no serious attempt has been made to show that any sequel to disinheritance could replace the heritage lost. Mark Twain is indeed "frontier" and Western, but in being greatly American he bears as close and essential a relation to England and Europe as that which we recognize in Hawthorne or in James (in some ways he strikes an English reader as being less foreign, less positively un-English, than either of them). The Americanness of alienation may be represented by Dreiser, Scott Fitzgerald, and Hemingway: the author of *Huckleberry Finn*, when we think of those writers, seems to belong to another world. Nor as we read the book are we prompted to reflect that he is a fellow countryman of Walt Whitman.

It is not my business here to enforce these observations in a detailed analysis of *Huckleberry Finn*, but, with them in view, to suggest how that book is related to *Pudd'nhead Wilson*, which, different as it is (it makes no show of frontier naiveté, but belongs frankly to sophisticated literary tradition), is nevertheless unmistakably by the same hand, develops the same preoccupations, and expresses the same moral outlook. With the oral tradition of storytelling, the potent element of recovered boyhood that has so recommended *Huckleberry Finn* is absent too. But the Mississippi *is* there in *Pudd'nhead Wilson*, and its evoked presence occasions a significant expansion:

The hamlet's front was washed by the clear waters of the great river; its body stretched itself rearward up a gentle incline; its most rearward border fringed itself out and scattered its houses about the base-line of the hills; the hills rose high, inclosing the town in a half-moon curve clothed with forests from foot to summit.

Steamboats passed up and down every hour or so. Those belonging to the little Cairo line and the little Memphis line always stopped; the big Orleans liners stopped for hails only, or to land passengers or freight; and this was the case also with the great flotilla of 'transients.' These latter came out of a dozen rivers—the Illinois, the Missouri, the Upper Mississippi, the Ohio, the Monongahela, the Tennessee, the Red River, the White River, and so on; and were bound every whither and stocked with every imaginable comfort or necessity which the Mississippi's communities could want.

Here, quite plainly, speaks a proud imaginative delight in the memory of the great river; the great river as Mark Twain had known it in boyhood and in his piloting days; and in the memory, or vision, we feel the sense of freedom, beauty, and majesty that informs *Huckleberry Finn*; but there is something further: the passage unmistakably conveys the sense, sanguine and exalted, of an expanding and ripening civilization.

Mark Twain, we are told, was brought up in a frontier society. "Think," it has been written, "of the squalor of those villages, their moral and material squalor, their dim and bounded horizon, their petty taboos: repression at one extreme, eruption at the other, and shiftlessness for a golden mean." But what *Pudd'nhead Wilson* should make us recognize is that "frontier" is an insidious term. It suggests cultural deprivation and loss—a dropping of the heritage in the battle with pioneer hardship. And no doubt it could be argued that the account just quoted fairly describes Dawson's Landing; or that so we should have agreed if we had had to live there. But as a matter of fact this is not the tone, this is not how the stress falls, in *Pudd'nhead Wilson*. After the evocation of the river we read:

The town was sleepy and comfortable and contented. It was fifty ·
years old, and was growing slowly—very slowly in fact, but still
it was growing.

It may have been sleepy, but what Mark Twain conveys with great power is an effect quite other than one of rawness and squalor:

In 1830 it was a snug little collection of modest one- and two-storey frame dwellings whose white-washed exteriors were almost concealed from sight by climbing tangles of rose-vines, honey-suckles, and morning-glories. Each of these pretty homes had a garden in front, fenced with white palings and opulently stocked with hollyhocks, marigolds, touch-me-nots, prince's feathers and other old-fashioned flowers; while on the window-sills of the houses stood wooden boxes containing moss-rose plants and terra-cotta pots in which grew a breed of geraniums whose spread of intensely red blossoms accented the prevailing pink tint of the rose-clad house-front like an explosion of flame. When there was room on the ledge outside of the pots and boxes for a cat, the cat was there—in sunny weather—stretched at full length, asleep and blissful, with her furry belly to the sun and a paw curved over her nose. Then that house was complete, and its contentment and peace were made manifest to the world by this symbol, whose testimony is infallible. A home without a cat—and a well-fed, well-petted, and properly revered cat—may be a perfect home, perhaps, but how can it prove title?

All along the streets, on both sides, at the outer edge of the brick sidewalks, stood locust-trees with trunks protected by wooden boxing, and these furnished shade for summer and a sweet fragrance in spring when the clusters of buds came forth.

The comfort, well-being, and amenity evoked here have more than a material significance; they are the outward signs of an inward grace. Provincial as Dawson's Landing may be, it represents a society that has kept its full heritage of civilization. True, it *is* provincial, and Wilson's fate—the "Pudd'nhead" and the long failure to make way against that estimate—figures for us its attitude towards originality of mind. Moreover an English reader gets what are for him (the human world presented being so essentially un-foreign) startling glimpses of mob lawlessness as an accepted social institution. Yet the effect of the opening description of Dawson's Landing remains: this is a civilized community—one qualified to have exacted a very much more favorable report than any brought back by Martin Chuzzlewit.

And further, it is not unaware of its provinciality, and is far from having lost the desire to keep in touch with the remoter centers of its civilization and with its past. This comes out notably in its reception of the twins, the presentment of which illustrates the complex poise of Mark Twain's attitude. The comedy of the reception is not satiric. Dawson's Landing displays, not merely its crudenesses and limitations, but also a touching positive humility, a will to pay homage to something other than provinciality and philistinism and the standards of everyday life. The exhibition of democratic *moeurs* at Aunt Patsy's is finely and subtly done, and quite clear in its significance. These democrats, without being in the least inclined to go back on their democracy, respond imaginatively to their traditional memories and to the sense of ideal values belonging to a richer life that is now remote from them. It is an utterly different thing from snobbery, and, as Mark Twain presents it, something that the social crudity of the occasion sets off as the reverse of trivial or crude:

> None of these visitors was at ease, but, being honest people, they didn't pretend to be. None of them had ever seen a person bearing a title of nobility before, and none had been expecting to see one now, consequently the title came upon them as a kind of pile-driving surprise, and caught them unprepared. A few tried to rise to the emergency, and got out an awkward 'My lord,' or 'Your lordship,' or something of that sort, but the great majority were overwhelmed by the unaccustomed word and its dim and awful associations with gilded courts and stately ceremony and anointed kingship, so they only fumbled through the handshake and passed on, speechless.

Then, significantly, this homage to a glimpsed ideal superiority is followed by the homage to art:

> Here a prodigious slam-banging broke out below, and everybody rushed down to see. It was the twins knocking out a classic four-handed piece on the piano in great style. Rowena was satisfied—satisfied down to the bottom of her heart.
>
> The young strangers were kept long at the piano. The villagers were astonished and enchanted with the magnificence of their performance, and could not bear to have them stop. All the music that they had ever heard before seemed spiritless prentice-work and barren of grace or charm when compared with these intoxicating floods of melodious sound. They realized that for once in their lives they were hearing masters.

The poise is beautifully maintained; those first two sentences serve only to enforce the serious and profound significance of the last, the closing one of the chapter.

In its whole attitude towards distinction that appeals to standards other than the "democratic," Dawson's Landing represents a subtler civilization than accounts of "the pioneer community" might suggest. Consider, for instance, the special license accorded Judge Driscoll in an environment that doesn't encourage moral independence or free play of mind. "Judge Driscoll," says Mark Twain, "could be a freethinker and still hold his place in society because he was the person of most consequence in the community, and therefore could go on his own way and follow out his own notions." But York Leicester Driscoll isn't represented as having achieved his leading place by preeminence in the qualities that one would have expected to tell most among pioneering democrats. We are told of him:

> He was very proud of his old Virginian ancestry, and in his hospitalities and his rather formal and stately manners he kept up the tradition. He was fine and just and generous. To be a gentleman—a gentleman without stain or blemish—was his only religion, and to it he was always faithful. He was respected, esteemed, and beloved by all the community.

It is quite unequivocal: he is "respected, esteemed and beloved" (a set of terms that defines something quite different from the attitudes towards the smart and therefore successful man) because he is a "gentleman," representing as such an ideal that doesn't belong to the realm of material "success" and is above the attainment of the ordinary member of the community. And we come here to that complexity of ethical background which I have spoken of as providing a central preoccupation of Mark Twain's, in *Pudd'nhead Wilson* as in *Huckleberry Finn*. I am not thinking merely of the persistence of an aristocratic tradition in a democratic society. That society has also its Christian allegiance, and, while the Judge is "just and generous," the total concept of "gentleman" is decidedly not Christian. When we come to Pembroke Howard, for whom to be a gentleman is *not* his only religion, the situation, with its irony, is focused in the one actor:

> He was a fine, brave, majestic creature, a gentleman according to the nicest requirements of the Virginian rule, a devoted Presbyterian, an authority on the 'code,' and a man always courteously ready to stand up before you in the field if any act or word of his had seemed doubtful or suspicious to you, and explain it with any weapons you might prefer from bradawls to artillery. He was very popular with the people, and was the Judge's dearest friend.

For the gentleman, "honor stood first": the laws of honor "required certain things of him which his religion might forbid him: then his religion must yield—the laws could not be relaxed to accommodate religion or anything else." And the Christian and democratic community, with a complete and exalted conviction, gave its approval.

> The people took more pride in the duel than in all the other events put together, perhaps. It was a glory to the town to have such a thing happen there. In their eyes, the principals had reached the summit of human honor.

There is nothing remarkable about the ability to observe such facts. What is remarkable is the subtlety of the appraising attitude that Mark Twain, in terms of impersonal art, defines towards them—as towards the whole inclusive situation presented in the book. Astringent as is the irony of *Pudd'n-head Wilson*, the attitude here has nothing of the satiric in it (the distinctively satiric plays no great part in the work as a whole). Mark Twain unmistakably admires Judge Driscoll and Pembroke Howard. And it is important to note that, if they are "fine," the "fineness" is not a mere matter of their being "just and generous." The total attitude where they are concerned is not altogether easy to describe, not because it is equivocal, but because it is not a simple one, and has called for some subtlety of dramatic means to convey it. The two most sympathetic characters in the drama give the "code" itself their active endorsement. It is not for instance suggested that Wilson, in acting as second in the duel, does so with any self-dissociating reservations or reluctance, and he rebukes Tom for not telling his uncle about the kicking and "letting him have a gentleman's chance": "if I had known the circumstances," he says, "I would have kept the case out of court until I got word to him and let him have a gentleman's chance."

> "You would?" exclaimed Tom, with lively surprise. "And it your first case! And you know perfectly well there would never have *been* any case if he had got that chance, don't you? And you'd have finished your days a pauper nobody, instead of being an actually launched and recognized lawyer to-day. And you would really have done that, would you?"
>
> "Certainly."
>
> Tom looked at him a moment or two, then shook his head sorrowfully and said:
>
> "I believe you—upon my word I do. I don't know why I do,

but I do. Pudd'nhead Wilson, I think you're the biggest fool I
ever saw."

This reminder of the circumstances of the rebuke will serve to enforce
the point that Wilson, the poised and preeminently civilized moral center of
the drama, whom we take to be very close in point of view to Mark Twain,
is not, all the same, to be identified with him. Wilson *is* an actor in a dramatic
whole that conveys its significances dramatically. The upshot of the drama
is to set a high value on the human qualities fostered by the aristocratic code:
to endorse the code even as far as Wilson does would be quite a different
matter, and no reader of the book can suppose it to be doing that. Against
the pride and the allegiance to an ideal of conduct that make personal safety
a matter of comparative indifference, we see the ignominy and ugliness of
Tom's complete self-centeredness, which is as unchecked by pride or concern
for any ideal as by imaginative sympathy. Hearing that the Judge, fighting
in *his* cause, has survived the duel, he reflects immediately, with an exasperation untouched by shame, how blessedly all problems would have been
solved had the Judge been killed: the duel has been wasted.

The exposure of human nature in Tom Driscoll has an essential part in
the total astringency of the book. But it will not do to suggest that human
nature, as the book presents it, reduces to Tom. If the Wilson of "Pudd'nhead
Wilson's Calendar" is not the Wilson of the drama, neither does he represent
the imagination and the sensibility that inform this as a conceived and realized
whole. Such utterances of Mark Twain's as this marginal note from a book,
characteristic as they are, mustn't be credited with a kind of conclusive
authority they certainly haven't:

> What a man sees in the human race is merely himself in the deep
> and honest privacy of his own heart. Byron despised the race
> because he despised himself. I feel as Byron did and for the same
> reason.

The exhibition of Tom's viciousness has its convincing force, no doubt,
because *we* recognize in ourselves the potentiality, as Mark Twain did in
*him*self. But it would be misleading to say that we despise Tom; that would
be to suggest an animus that we do *not* feel when we place him, unequivocally,
as contemptible: we are not engaged and involved in that way. The irony
of the work as a whole means a very secure poise, and the poise is secure
because the author has achieved a mature, balanced, and impersonal view
of humanity. He himself is not involved in the personal way that involves
animus in condemning.

The attitude of *Pudd'nhead Wilson* is remote from cynicism or pessimism. The book conveys neither contempt for human nature nor a rejection of civilization. It is concerned with the complexities of both human nature and civilization as represented in a historical community—for Dawson's Landing, it may reasonably be said, is one that, at a given time in actual American history, Mark Twain had intimately known.

We are not, by way of dismissing the suggestion of any general contempt, confined to adducing Wilson himself and the "fine, brave, majestic creatures" who uphold the code of the F.F.V. Most impressively, there is Roxy. It is true that her heroic maternal devotion plays against the extremity of mean heartless egotism given us in Tom. But her significance is not exhausted in that irony. We feel her dominating the book as a triumphant vindication of life. Without being in the least sentimentalized, or anything but dramatically right, she plainly bodies forth the qualities that Mark Twain, in his whole being, most values—qualities that, as Roxy bears witness, he profoundly believes in as observable in humanity, having known them in experience. Although born a slave, she is herself a "fine, brave, majestic creature," whose vitality expresses itself in pride, high-spiritedness, and masterful generosity. Her reckless presence at the duel defines Mark Twain's attitude towards the "code" more decisively than Wilson's participation does. When she proudly tells Tom that he is descended from the best blood of Virginia the effect, for all the irony, is not satiric. And her confident and justified reliance on the loyal comradeship, not only of her fellow "niggers," but also of the officers of the *Grand Mogul*, has its part in the appraisal of human nature conveyed by the book as a whole.

Mr. De Voto makes the point that she represents a frank and unembarrassed recognition of the actuality of sex, with its place and power in human affairs, such as cannot be found elsewhere in Mark Twain. That seems to me true and important. It is an aspect of the general fact, that she is the presence in the book of a free and generous vitality, in which the warmly and physically human manifests itself also as intelligence and spiritual strength. It is this far-reaching associative way in which, so dominating a presence, she stands for—she *is*—triumphant life that gives the book, for all its astringency and for all the chilling irony of the close, its genial quality (to be both genial and astringent is its extraordinary distinction).

How far from satiric the spirit of *Pudd'nhead Wilson* is may be seen in the presentment of the subtleties of conscience and ethical sensibility in Roxy. Consider the episode of the stolen money and the threat to sell the Negro servants down the river. We are no doubt very close to the satiric note in the irony with which the chapter ends—in Percy Driscoll's self-gratulation on his magnanimity: "that night he set the incident down in his diary, so that his son might read it in after years and be thereby moved to deeds of gentleness and humanity himself." But we are remote from satire here:

> The truth was, all were guilty but Roxana; she suspected that the others were guilty, but she did not know them to be so. She was horrified to think how near she had come to being guilty herself; she had been saved in the nick of time by a revival in the colored Methodist Church, a fortnight before, at which time and place she had "got religion." The very next day after that gracious experience, while her change of style was fresh upon her and she was vain of her purified condition, her master left a couple of dollars lying unprotected on his desk, and she happened upon that temptation when she was polishing around with a dust-rag. She looked at the money awhile with a steadily rising resentment, and then she burst out with—"Dad blame dat revival, I wisht it had 'a be'n put off till to-morrow!"
>
> Then she covered the tempter with a book, and another member of the kitchen cabinet got it. She made this sacrifice as a matter of religious etiquette; as a thing necessary just now, but by no means to be wrested into a precedent; no, a week or two would limber up her piety, then she would be rational again, and the next two dollars that got left out in the cold would find a comforter—and she could name the comforter.
>
> Was she bad? Was she worse than the general run of her race? No. They had an unfair show in the battle of life.

In spite of that last phrase, we know that what we have been contemplating is not just an exhibition of Negro traits: "her race" is the human race. These naive and subtle changes and adjustments of conscience and the moral sense we can parallel from our own inner experience. But there is nothing cynically reductive in Mark Twain's study of the moral nature of man; he shows the clairvoyance of a mind that is sane and poised, and the irony that attends the illustration of subtleties and complexities throws no doubt on the reality or the dignity or the effectiveness in human affairs of ethical sensibility.

I have not yet touched on the central irony of the book, the sustained and complex irony inherent in the plot. *Pudd'nhead Wilson* should be recognized as a classic of the use of popular modes—of the sensational and the melodramatic—for the purposes of significant art. The book, I have said, is not faultless, and an obvious criticism lies against the unfulfilled promise represented by the twins—the non-significant play made with them, their history and the sinister oriental dagger. Mark Twain, we can see, had intended to work out some interplay of the two parallel sets of complications: twins and interchanged babies. He abandoned the idea, but didn't trouble to eliminate that insistent focusing of expectation upon the twins. The fault is in a sense a large one, and yet it is not, after all, a very serious one: it doesn't affect the masterly handling of the possibilities actually developed.

The ironic subtleties that Mark Twain gets from the interchange of the babies in their cradles seem, as one ponders them, almost inexhaustible. There is the terrible difference, no more questioned by Roxy than by her master, between the "nigger" and the white. The conventionality of the distinction is figured by the actual whiteness of Roxy, whose one-sixteenth of Negro blood tells only in her speech (with which, indeed, it has no essential relation, as is illustrated later by the inability of "Valet de Chambers," now revealed as the pure-white heir, to shed the "nigger"-speech he learnt in childhood). So awful, ultimate and unchangeable is the distinction that Roxy, as, in order to save her child from the fate hanging over the slave (to be "sold down the river"), she changes the babies in their cradles, justifies herself by the example of God. The rendering is an irresistible manifestation of genius, utterly convincing, and done with a delicate subtlety of ironic significance:

> She flung herself on her bed and began to think and toss, toss and think. By-and-by she sat suddenly upright, for a comforting thought had flown through her worried mind:
>
> "Tain't no sin—*white* folks has done it! It ain't no sin, glory to goodness it ain't no sin! *Dey's* done it—yes, en dey was de biggest quality in de whole bilin', too—*kings!*"
>
> She began to muse; she was trying to gather out of her memory the dim particulars of some tale she had heard some time or other. At last she said—
>
> "Now I's got it; now I 'member. It was dat ole nigger preacher dat tole it, de time he come over here fum Illinois en preached in de nigger church. He said dey ain't nobody kin save his own self—can't do it by faith, can't do it by works, can't do it no way at all. Free grace is de *on'y* way, en dat don't come fum nobody but jis' de Lord; en *he* kin give it to anybody he please, saint or sinner—*he* don't kyer. He do jis' as he's a mineter. He s'lect out anybody dat suit him, en put another one in his place, en make de fust one happy for ever en leave t'other one to burn wid Satan."

There is of course a glance here at the Calvinism of Mark Twain's youth. And it is to be noted that Roxy, while usurping the prerogative of the predestinating Deity, has shown a wholly human compassion, and has invoked a compassionate God in doing so:

> "I's sorry for you, honey; I's sorry, God knows I is—but what *kin* I do, what *could* I do? Yo' pappy would sell him to somebody, some time, en den he'd go down de river, sho', and I couldn't, couldn't, *couldn't* stan' it."

In saving the child from the consequences of the awful distinction that she assumes to be in the nature of things, she demonstrates its lack of any ground but convention; she demonstrates the wholly common humanity of the "nigger" and the white. The father himself cannot detect the fraud: he cannot tell his own child from the other. And—one of the many ironies—it is his cruel, but confidently righteous, severity that imposes the full abjectiveness of slave mentality upon his own child, who becomes the defenseless and rightless servant of the slave's child. On the other hand, Roxy's success in saving Valet de Chambers (the name her proud tribute to an ideal "white" lordliness) from the fate of the slave erects a dreadful barrier between child and mother. Treated as "young Marse Tom," not only does he become that different order of being, the "master"; in Roxy herself the slave attitudes that she necessarily observes towards him find themselves before long attended by the appropriate awe. When at last, outraged by the humiliating and cruel rebuffs that meet her appeal for a little kindness (she is in need) to the old "nigger-mammy," she forgets habit and the ties of motherhood, and pants for revenge, she has to recognize that she has placed him in an impregnable position: no one will believe her tale. A further irony is that, if he has turned out bad, a portent of egocentric heartlessness, that is at least partly due to his spoiling as heir and young master, the lordly superior being.

It is a mark of the poised humanity characterizing the treatment of the themes of *Pudd'nhead Wilson* that, worthless and vicious as "Tom" is, when he has to face the sudden revelation that he is a Negro, we feel some compassion for him; we don't just applaud an irony of poetic justice when he is cornered into reflecting, with an echo of his mother's self-justifying recall of the Calvinistic God:

> "Why were niggers and whites made? What crime did the uncreated first nigger commit that the curse of birth was decreed for him? And why is this awful difference made between black and white?"

Compassion, of course, soon vanishes as the dialectic of utter selfishness unfolds in him. The developments of his incapacity for compassion are done with a convincingness that the creator of Tito Melema would have envied. When Roxy offers to be sold back into slavery in order to save "Tom" from being disinherited, and he, with dreadfully credible treachery, sells her "down the river," the opposite extremes of human nature are brought together in an effect that belongs wholly to the mode of *Pudd'nhead Wilson*, and is equally removed from melodrama and from cynicism. It can hardly be said, when we close the book, that the worst in human nature has not been confronted; yet the upshot of the whole is neither to judge mankind to be contemptible nor to condemn civilization. And it is remarkable how utterly free from animus that astringency is which takes on so intense a concentration in the close:

> Everybody granted that if "Tom" were white and free it would be unquestionably right to punish him—it would be no loss to anybody; but to shut up a valuable slave for life—that was quite another matter.
>
> As soon as the Governor understood the case, he pardoned Tom at once, and the creditors sold him down the river.

It is an irony of the tale that this, the fate to secure him against which Roxana had committed her crime, is, as an ultimate consequence of that crime, the fate he suffers.

J. HILLIS MILLER

First-Person Narration
in David Copperfield
and Huckleberry Finn

David Copperfield (1849–50) and *Huckleberry Finn* (1884), among nineteenth-century English and American novels, are salient examples of masterworks of fiction written as first-person narratives. The first-person novel, in spite of Henry James's distaste for its baggy looseness, is not so much formless as a special case of fictional form. It provides a good example of the interaction of the three aspects of that form.

The distinguishing characteristic of the first-person novel is the fact that the narrator in most cases coincides with the protagonist. This does not mean, however, that in this coincidence the structure of intersubjective relations usual in the third-person novel is truncated or collapsed. Rather, it takes another form. In *David Copperfield* or *Huckleberry Finn* the author attempts to come to terms with his own life by playing the role of an imaginary character who in both cases has obvious similarities to the author himself. This imaginary character, in his turn, retraces from the point of view of a later time the earlier course of his life. The interpersonal texture of both novels is made up of the superimposition of two minds, the mind of the adult David reliving his experiences as a child, the mind of Huck after his adventures are over retelling them from the perspective of the wisdom, if wisdom it is, to which they have led. In both novels the older narrator, from the vantage of a later time, watches his younger self engage himself more or less naively in relations to other people. Behind this double consciousness

From *Experience in the Novel*. © 1968 by Columbia University Press. Originally entitled "Three Problems of Fictional Form: First-Person Narration in *David Copperfield* and *Huckleberry Finn*."

45

may be glimpsed the mind of the author himself, the Charles Dickens who is reshaping the events of his life to make a novel out of them, the Mark Twain who is present in the irony which runs through *Huckleberry Finn* as a pervasive stylistic flavoring. This stylistic quality results from Huck's inability to understand his experiences, either while they are happening or as he retells them, as well as the reader and the author understand them. From author to narrator to youthful protagonist to other characters—the structure of *David Copperfield* or *Huckleberry Finn* is no less than that of *Pride and Prejudice* (1813), *Middlemarch* (1871–72), or *The Golden Bowl* (1904), a pattern of related minds. In both first-person novels the author may be seen going away from himself into an imagined person living in an imagined world in order to return to himself and take possession by indirection of his own past self and his own past life.

If intersubjective relations and relations of the imaginary and the real are so closely intertwined in these two first-person novels, they both provide classic examples of the incomplete circle or spiral form taken by temporality in fiction. The autobiographical novel has exactly the structure of human temporality. It is a moving toward the future in order to come back to what one has already been, in an attempt to complete one's deepest possibility of being by drawing the circle of time closed and thereby becoming a whole. But the circle of time is complete only with my death. As long as I live I cannot reach that future moment when I shall understand myself completely, coincide completely with the hidden sources of my being. Going forward in time through a recapitulation in language of his experiences in the past, the narrator of a first-person novel returns eventually back through his past to himself in the present, but at a higher level of comprehension, it may be, than he had when he began to tell his story. The insight born of the act of retelling may lead the narrator to an authentic understanding of his life, a recognition of its hitherto hidden patterns. On the basis of this recognition he may then take hold of his past life, accept it in a new way in the present, and come to a resolute decision about the future. This revelation, however, is never complete as long as the narrator lives. The spiral is endless. Huck or David could go around and around the circle indefinitely, bringing their past lives up to the present in the light of the new insight gained by the act of retelling, recapitulating their lives over and over without exhausting them or finding that a new circling repetition had brought them back to exactly the same place.

Even so, the moment of return from a journey through the past to the present, when the two levels of the narrator's mind coincide, is the crucial instant in a first-person novel. It is the moment at the end of *Huckleberry*

Finn, for example, when Huck speaks in the present tense of his present situation. Having gone through his life up to the present, he sees it whole and sums up what he sees in his decision to run away from civilization. Only in this way can he escape from another repetition of his repetitive adventures, adventures which have rhythmically alternated between solitude and disastrous involvement in society, and are about to culminate, as Daniel Hoffman and others have seen, in a recurrence of the involvement most dangerous of all to his integrity: subjection to the loving-kindness of a well-meaning member of respectable society. "But I reckon I got to light out for the Territory ahead of the rest," says Huck, "because Aunt Sally she's going to adopt me and sivilize me and I can't stand it. I been there before."

At the end of *David Copperfield* David, like Huck, returns after a long looping circuit through his past to present-tense speech about the present. He too looks toward the future on the basis of a clear understanding of the past and makes a decision about that future. But how different is his state of mind! How different is his relation to other people, and how different the resolution he takes! David has experienced in childhood, like other Dickensian heroes or heroines, Oliver, Pip, Arthur Clennam, or Esther Summerson, solitude and deprivation, the lack of a satisfactory place within a family or within society. He has been "a somebody too many" "cast away among creatures with whom [he has] had no community of nature." His search through the adventures he retells is for something which will focus his life and give it substance. Throughout his experiences he is troubled by "a vague unhappy loss or want of something." He seeks something to fill the void in his heart. The novel is his "written memory," in which the adult David, as he says, "stand[s] aside, to see the phantoms of those days go by me, accompanying the shadow of myself, in dim procession." *David Copperfield*, like Thackeray's *Henry Esmond* (1852), contains many references to time and memory. These call the reader's attention to the distance between the present condition of the narrator and that of his past self. They interpose between the one and the other "a softened glory of the Past, which nothing could [throw] upon the present time." Retracing the journey which has led him step by step to the present, David seeks to find the source of the cohesive force which associates each detail with the others and gradually organizes them all, as he retells them, into the pattern which constitutes his destiny.

Is it a private power of feeling in David which does this, a subjective energy of association? The many references to the psychology of association suggest that this is the case. Agnes is "associated" in David's mind with "a stained glass window in a church," just as the image of Ham's anguish after little Em'ly runs away "remain[s]," says David, "associated with that lonely waste, in my remembrance, to this hour," or as David says of Steerforth's death: "I have an association between it and a stormy wind, or the lightest mention of a sea-shore, as strong as any of which my mind is conscious." It may be such associations which gather all the events of David's life together and make them one.

On the other hand, the source of the coherence of David's life may be a providential power which has been secretly working behind the scenes to give an objective design to his life. This is suggested by the way the sea, especially in the descriptions of little Em'ly walking on the causeway by the shore and of the storm in which Steerforth and Ham are drowned, becomes a mysterious supernatural reservoir, an external memory and prevision gathering the past and the future together in a time out of time sustained by God. "Is it possible," asks David as he remembers little Em'ly walking so dangerously close to the sea, "among the possibilities of hidden things, that in the sudden rashness of the child and her wild look so far off, there was any merciful attraction of her into danger, any tempting her towards him permitted on the part of her dead father, that her life might have a chance of ending that day?" Later Ham says "the end of it like" seems to him to be coming from the sea. In Steerforth's drowning "the inexorable end [comes] at its appointed time." During the storm which is to wash the body of Steerforth up at his feet, David feels that "something within [him], faintly answering to the storm without, tosse[s] up the depths of [his] memory and [makes] a tumult in them." The personal memory within is matched by a cosmic memory without.

The conflict between these two organizing powers is reconciled when David discovers that Agnes has been all along the secret center of his life, the pivot around which everything else will turn out to have been patterning itself as the circle of his life pervaded by her presence. Agnes is the rock on which he can base himself, the person who will fill the void of his old unhappy loss or want of something. "Clasped in my embrace," says David after his marriage to Agnes, "I held the source of every worthy aspiration I had ever had; the centre of myself, the circle of my life, my own, my wife; my love of whom was founded on a rock!"

In the last chapter of *David Copperfield* the narrator returns, like the narrator of *Huckleberry Finn*, to the present. The young David and the grown-up David coincide, and the narrator speaks for his situation in the present. But far from choosing, like Huck, a solitude which is the only guarantee of an honest life, David has escaped from his solitude into society. He is surrounded by his family and his friends. Far from speaking, like Huck, in the voice of solitude on behalf of the values of solitude, he is now and has been throughout the novel as much the spokesman in the language of the middle-class community for the values of that community as any of the omniscient narrators of Victorian novels told in the third person—the narrators, for example, of *Vanity Fair, Middlemarch,* or *The Last Chronicle of Barset* (1866–67). Though the first-person novel and the third-person novel seem so different, both can become instruments by which Victorian novelists express their sense that authentic life lies in assimilation of the individual mind into the collective mind of society. In marriage to one member of good middle-class society and in a successful career as a writer of novels, like Dickens himself, David has found a way into that society.

Agnes is also for him the mediator of a heavenly light and a promise of heaven. As such, she is the means by which he sees other things and people, judging them according to universal standards. She is the way in which he will rise through society beyond society, not into the solitude of Huck's "Territory," that lonesomeness lacking any vestige of a divine presence, but into the celestial society of Heaven where he can enjoy Agnes's companionship forever.

Huckleberry Finn is an open-ended fiction. Huck's life is not over on the last page of the novel, and his ability to free himself from Aunt Sally and other agents of "civilization" remains in doubt. Dickens, on the other hand, tries to give *David Copperfield* a closed form. He presents the final sentences of David's narrative as a rehearsal of the final moments of his life. The latter will repeat in structure and content the former, realities fading then as memories fade now. The end of the book is an anticipation of the end of David's life, when there will be no more earthly future left. Like Henry Esmond retelling his life as an old man in Virginia, David speaks as if he were writing from beyond time, as if he were writing from the perspective of death:

> And now, as I close my task, subduing my desire to linger yet, these faces fade away. But one face, shining on me like a Heavenly light by which I see all other objects, is above them and beyond them all. And that remains.
>
> I turn my head, and see it, in its beautiful serenity, beside me. My lamp burns low, and I have written far into the night; but the dear presence, without which I were nothing, bears me company.
>
> Oh Agnes, Oh my soul, so may thy face be by me when I close my life indeed; so may I, when realities are melting from me like the shadows which I now dismiss, still find thee near me, pointing upward!

A modern reader may find it difficult to take seriously the image of Agnes "pointing upward," and Dickens himself was in later novels, most subtly in *Our Mutual Friend* (1864–65), to put in question the strategy by which the conflict between two sources of order is resolved in *David Copperfield*. The contrast between Dicken's novel and *Huckleberry Finn*, however, is a striking example of the different cultural and personal meanings which may be expressed within the form of the first-person novel. In Twain's hands the form is used in a masterpiece in the American tradition of ambiguous personal experience which goes from Hawthorne and Melville through Twain to Faulkner, Hemingway, and Bellow.

As many critics have seen, Huck speaks not the language of the community but a pungent vernacular which can thrive only outside society and is the instrument of a devastating criticism of it. *Huckleberry Finn*, however, does more than juxtapose two ways of speaking, one good and one bad. There are three kinds of language in the novel. Each speaks for a different condition of life. Existence within society is again and again dramatized as speaking a false language, playing a role, wearing a disguise, either wittingly or unwittingly perpetrating a fraud. Honest directness of speech, on the other hand, is possible only between Huck and Jim in their ideal society of two on the raft. This openness and lack of guile is the basis of poignancy in the scene in which Huck feels guilty for having fooled Jim into believing he has dreamed events which have really happened during a foggy night on the river. "It was fifteen minutes," says Huck, "before I could work myself up to go and humble myself to a nigger—but I done it, and I warn't ever sorry for it afterwards, neither. I didn't do him no more mean tricks, and I wouldn't done that one if I'd knowed it would make him feel that way." Huck's sin is to have imported into the Eden-like honesty of social relations on the raft the propensity for lies which is characteristic of life on the shore and which is, moreover, Huck's only self-defense when he is there. The colloquial rhythm and idiom of his narrative of his life is speech of the raft society. He does his readers the great honor of speaking to them as if they were in collusion with him against the society of the shore and could share with him his true speech.

There is, however, a third language in the novel, a language belonging neither to good society nor to bad society, but to solitude. This language, and the condition belonging to it, are described in two crucial passages in the novel, one near the beginning, when Huck is still living with Miss Watson, and one just before Huck reaches the Phelps Farm and just after he has made his resolution to steal Jim out of slavery again. The same elements occur in both of these passages: an association of isolation with a state of such desolate "lonesomeness" that Huck wishes for death; so complete an openness to inhuman nature and to the presences of the dead within nature that it is as if Huck were already dead; a transformation of language from a means of communication into silence or into an inarticulate murmur, like the speech of elemental nature. The companionship of the dead is a companionship of mute and incommunicable secrets. These texts are of fundamental importance as clues to the quality of Huck's authenticity. They seem clearly related to Twain's deepest sense of his own existence:

> I felt so lonesome [says Huck in the first such passage] I most wished I was dead. . . . [T]he wind was trying to whisper something to me and I couldn't make out what it was, and so it made the cold shivers run over me. Then away out in the woods I heard that kind of a sound that a ghost makes when it wants to tell about something that's on its mind and can't make itself understood, and so can't rest easy in its grave and has to go about that way every night grieving. I got so down-hearted and scared, I did wish I had some company.

Richard Poirier, in *A World Elsewhere*, has noted how often Huck remains speechless when he is with other people on the shore. He is often a silent watcher and listener who effaces himself as much as possible. This silence is an expression of the onlooking detachment from society which is his natural condition and which is affirmed in his resolution at the end to free himself from civilization. If Huck chooses for silence and solitude, the book allows the reader no illusion about what these mean. They mean loss of language and a kinship with the dead. In solitude one becomes a kind of walking dead man, mute spectator of life. This, however, is preferable to the intolerable falsehood of existence within society.

This stark either/or replaces finally the choice between good society on the raft and bad society on the shore which has apparently structured Huck's narrative. Twain's hesitation before the darker implications of his story may explain that descent to the style of *The Adventures of Tom Sawyer* (1876) in the last episode, so troubling to critics. The Phelps Farm episode, however, plays a strategic role in the progress of the novel. It is the final stage in a gradual contamination of the honest language of the raft by the fraudulent language of the shore. In the end, Huck must choose not between true speech and false speech, but between speech and silence.

If the temporal structure of the novel brings Huck back to himself in the present and to the need for a decision there, the terms of this decision may be identified in its intersubjective structures. In *Huckleberry Finn* Twain plays the role of Huck in order to speak indirectly to the real society of his day, just as he took a pseudonym for his writing, so confronting his readers in disguise. In this novel he is Samuel Clemens pretending to be Mark Twain pretending to be Huckleberry Finn. This playing of roles is also fundamental to the inner structure of the novel, within the mirror-world its words create. Nothing is more natural to Huck, or more necessary, than lying. Repeatedly he leaves the "free and easy and comfortable" life on the raft to involve himself in life on the shore. As soon as he meets someone there he spontaneously makes up a whole history for himself, a name, past life, present situation and intention. Only in this way can he protect Jim and that separate part of himself which can hear ghosts and understands what it would be like to be dead. When he enters society he must enter it in disguise, reborn as someone else. To be within the community is to be a fraud, to pretend to be another person, just as in writing the novel Clemens plays the role of Huck. Even the truth must be spoken by way of fiction. Significantly, Huck's final incarnation is as Tom Sawyer, for his greatest danger is that he will become, like Tom, someone who lives his life as a play and is entirely subjected to one form of fiction: the false idols of society and its romantic traditions.

This pattern of person within person, or of person confronting person by way of a disguise, is also a pattern of imaginary and real. If the novel is a fiction by which Twain attempted to approach his childhood and therefore to reach his own inmost reality, the story itself is constructed as a design of fictions within fictions—the fictions of Huck's lies and disguises, the fictional world taken from novels and historical romances within which Tom Sawyer lives, the no less fictional structures of religious and social beliefs which entrance the Mississippi communities, the frauds perpetrated by the duke and the king. In the travesties of *Hamlet* and *Romeo and Juliet* by the latter, they pretend to be a king and a duke pretending to be the famous actors Garrick and Kean pretending to be Shakespearean characters. These fictions within fictions keep before the reader a picture of interpersonal relations as a complex system of deceit within deceit in which every man lies to his neighbor.

The theme of lies leads back to the paradox of Huck's own language. As Ernest Hemingway, T. S. Eliot, and others have said, Huck's speech is the basis of the book's authenticity. He uses a rich vernacular idiom, couched in indigenous American rhythms, vocabulary, and syntax. His speech grows out of the way of life of a people in a place, and therefore is rooted in reality in a way no abstract language can be. At the same time the novel is full of demonstrations of the hollowness of the language spoken by people around

Huck. This is most apparent in the vigorous satires of religious language, but it is also present in the satire of Southern romanticism in the references to Sir Walter Scott and *Lalla Rookh* (both names of steamboats in the novel). A similar theme is expressed in the imprisonment of the Grangerfords and Shepherdsons in linguistic molds which keep their absurd feud going from generation to generation. To belong to Mississippi Valley society is to be unable to speak the truth, to use one form or another of a fantasy language which justifies the greatest cruelties and injustices—slavery, economic exploitation, and the arrogant self-righteousness and psychological cruelties practiced, in Twain's view, in the name of Protestant Christianity.

Though Huck's language is a speech within the community speech, one based partly on the folklore and linguistic vigor of children and Negroes, nevertheless it has grown out of the community language and remains part of it. If it has drawn its strength from its source, it must share also the weaknesses of its origin. Huck's style comes from the popular culture of the Mississippi, but the novel is the exposure of that culture by way of its imitation in its own words. This use of the destructive power of imitative language reveals the silent presence of Twain behind Huck, of the lonesome and silent Huck behind his participation in his culture.

When Huck speaks he too gets caught in the speech patterns of his society. This is apparent in the irony of those many places where the reader can glimpse Twain judging Huck, deploring his enslavement to a false rhetoric. An example is the famous passage in which Huck, in response to a question about whether anyone was killed in a steamboat explosion, says, "No'm. Killed a nigger." The poignant ambiguity of the crucial text in which Huck decides to rescue Jim from slavery lies in the fact that he is forced to express his decision in the language of the culture surrounding him. He must use religious and social terms which reverse Twain's judgment of good and bad in the situation. Worse yet, he is forced to experience the feelings appropriate to the rhetoric of the language he must use because he has no other. As long as he is within society he remains trapped in its language. However he acts, his actions are defined in the community's terms.

Twain and his readers may see in Huck's resolve a heroic act of moral improvisation, an intuition of the truth like that described in W. E. H. Lecky's *History of European Morals from Augustus to Charlemagne* (1869), a book Twain admired. Such a reading sees in Huck the courage to act in accordance with an intuitively perceived moral truth even though it goes counter to the rules of a bad society. Huck, however, does not see it that way at all. He sees his decision to free Jim as the victory of his innate evil over the good teaching of society. It is a conscious choice of damnation. To him it is not the creation of a just moral order in place of the evil one supported by society. His decision to "take up wickedness again" is reprehensible defiance of community laws defending religious right and the sanctity of private property. His act is not a "yes" in obedience to a higher ethical law but a "no" to the yes of a community which he continues to accept. "I was a trembling," says Huck, "because I'd got to decide, forever, betwixt two things, and I knowed it. I studied a minute, sort of holding my breath, and then says to myself: 'All right, then, I'll *go* to hell.' "

Even if Huck succeeds in freeing Jim, this freedom is still a social condition. As the concluding episode of Tom's "evasion" of Jim shows, Jim is as much subject to the sham of his society when he is free as when he is a slave. Only complete isolation is freedom. This is the meaning of the absurdity of Tom's freeing Jim when he is already legally free. Free man or slave, he is still enslaved, like Tom, Aunt Sally, and the rest, by the linguistic and cultural patterns of his society. To negate these is still to remain within them, and so to affirm them indirectly. Whenever Huck speaks he is necessarily subject to this inexorable law. To speak at all he must speak lies, not only because his situation forces him to deception, disguise, play-acting, but because the language of his community is inevitably the instrument of lies. The truth cannot be spoken directly in it, as Huck proves in the soliloquy of his decision to rescue Jim. The choice Huck faces is therefore between false language and no language at all. And this corresponds to the choice between participation in a false society and an isolation from other people which is like death. Society is always imaginary. Solitude is the way to the real. Huck's final resolution, his final integrity, is a choice of lonesomeness and the silence which goes with it: "[S]o there ain't nothing more to write about, and I am rotten glad of it, because if I'd a knowed what a trouble it was to make a book I wouldn't a tackled it and ain't agoing to no more." Then follows his decision to "light out for the Territory ahead of the rest."

To explore in a given novel temporal, interpersonal, and representational structures will lead to an identification of the specific shaping energy which generates form and meaning in the novel in question: the reaffirmation in *David Copperfield*, against alternative possibilities, of a traditional transcendentalism, or the rejection of society and its languages which in *Huckleberry Finn* prepares for the more overt nihilism of Satan's scorn for the "moral sense" in *The Mysterious Stranger* (1916).

ROBERT PENN WARREN

Mark Twain

Everybody knows that a profound incoherence marked the life of Samuel Clemens, whose very existence was one long double take and who lived with a double that he had summoned into existence in order, himself, to exist at all. His feelings on any subject, but especially on the subject of himself, were violently divided; his humor was the cry of despair of a man incapable of feeling himself worthy of love. In his last coma, out of the old obsession and a self-knowledge that had never, however, proved deep enough to be redemptive, he spoke of a dual personality and of Dr. Jekyll and Mr. Hyde.

We know, too, that there was an especially bitter division of feeling in relation to the backward region of Clemens's birth and the great world of thriving modernity that he went out so successfully into, and between the past and the present—or rather, the future. When the little band of Confederate irregulars to which Sam Clemens belonged dissolved without firing even one shot in anger, Sam simply cut himself off from his Southern heritage, his father's ill-grounded pride in high Virginia lineage, and the aura of glory about the mahogany sideboard brought from Kentucky. He resigned, in a sense, from history, which he indifferently left in the hands of Confederate or Yankee heroes, and headed West, where the future was all. Later he was to regard Sir Walter Scott as the source of the Southern disease whose contagion he had thus fled and was, in *A Connecticut Yankee at King Arthur's Court*, to equate chivalry with the barbarous irrationality that the rational Yankee tries to redeem. But though the young Sam did repudiate the his-

From *Southern Review* 8, no. 3 (July 1972). © 1972 by Robert Penn Warren.

torical past, he did not, or could not, repudiate the personal past and for his
doppelgänger Mark Twain, the story of that past became the chief stock-in-
trade.

What is equally significant is the complex of feelings that went into the
telling of that tale. Twain knew the hard facts of his world. He knew that
Hannibal, Missouri, had its full quota of degradation and despair. He knew
that the glittering majesty of the steamboat was not much more than a cross
between a floating brothel richly afflicted with venereal disease and a gambling hell full of stacked decks and loaded dice. Indeed, in cold print both
Hannibal and the South were to get their realistic due, and in 1876, writing
to one of the erstwhile boys of Hannibal, Twain chides his old companion's
nostalgic yearnings:

> As for the past, there is but one good thing about it, . . . that it
> is past. . . . I can see by your manner of speech, that for more
> than twenty years you have stood dead still in the midst of the
> dreaminess, the romance, the heroics, of sweet but happy sixteen.
> Man, do you know that this is simply mental and moral mastur-
> bation? It belongs eminently to the period usually devoted to
> *physical* masturbation, and should be left there and outgrown.

In the wilderness of paradox and ambivalence in which he lived, Twain,
during the first days of his happy marriage, enjoying a mansion and a solid
bank account, could yet write to another companion:

> The old life has swept before me like a panorama; the old days
> have trooped by in their glory again; the old faces have looked
> out of the mists of the past; old footsteps have sounded in my
> listening ears; old hands have clasped mine; and the songs I loved
> ages and ages ago have come wailing down the centuries.

In all the new splendor and bliss of mutual love, Twain discovered the poetry
of the old life and, in fact, certain restrictions of the new that, before many
years had passed, would make him look back on the time when he had been
a demigod in the pilothouse watching the stars reflected in the mysterious
river and declare nostalgically that the pilot was "the only unfettered and
entirely independent human being that lived upon the earth." And make
him, in a letter to the widow of another boyhood companion, declare: "I
should greatly like to relive my youth . . . and be as we were, and make
holiday until fifteen, then all drown together."

But Sam Clemens did not drown. He went out into the world and became Mark Twain, with his head chock-full of memories of Hannibal, his ears ringing with the language of that village, and his heart torn in a tumult of conflicting feelings.

In spite of such doublenesses and incoherences in life, there is an extraordinary coherence in the work of the *doppelgänger* of Sam Clemens, the most obvious example being the use of the personal incoherence to provide the dramatic tension of creation. This internal coherence of motivation suggests also a coherence of relation among the individual works, a dynamic of growth by which everything, good and bad, could be absorbed into the master works and by which all subsequent works appear as exfoliations and refinements. In turn, the internal coherence is suggested by the key image of Twain's work, that of the journey. For if Twain were a wanderer who, with no address ever definitely fixed, founded our "national literature," the key image we refer to here is not a record of his surroundings back and forth over two continents but of the journey into the darkest of all continents— the self. In *A Connecticut Yankee*, the explorer gets as close to the heart of darkness as he ever could—or dared—get, and all subsequent works represent merely additional notes and elaborations of detail of that shocking experience.

It may be useful to remind ourselves what discoveries in earlier works led to the creation of the big fulfilling books, *Adventures of Huckleberry Finn* and *A Connecticut Yankee*.

In *Innocents Abroad* (1869) Twain discovered what kind of book he could write. First, he came upon the image of the journey, obviously a simple objective journey but not quite so obviously a journey in which the main character is ruefully or outrageously puzzled by the lunacies of the world through which he travels. Second, the book represents a double vision—in this early instance rather simple and schematic, a travel book that is at the same time a parody of travel books. Third, Mark Twain-actor playing the role of Mark Twain on the lecture platform is here transformed into Mark Twain-author writing a book in which Mark Twain is the main character. Fourth, the book represents Twain's discovery of the rich new middle class of the Gilded Age in America, the class into which he was to marry, by whose standards he would live, whose tyrannies he would fret against, and whose values he would loathe, here for the first time experiencing an ambivalence that was to become more bitter and significant. Fifth, Twain here struck upon a method that was to stand him in good stead. He learned how to make the method of the lecture platform into a book. He once said that his characteristic lecture (derived from the oral anecdote of frontier humor, full of turns and booby-traps) was like a plank with a line of square holes into which he could put plugs appropriate for a particular moment or a particular audience, and this structure persisted, for better and worse, through later work though, with increasing sophistication, often played against the developmental structure of fictional action and theme.

Mark Twain's second book, *Roughing It* (1872), also took a journey for its "plank," but where the narrator of *Innocents Abroad* had been static, simply the "lecturer" transferred from platform to book, now the narrator is in motion, is undergoing step by step the "education of the West," is being forced to submit his romantic illusions to the shock of reality. When the book ends he is a new man, and Twain has discovered his version of the great American theme of initiation that is to be central for his finest work. But there is another important development. On board the *Quaker City* the narrator had merely faced, in his traveling companions, individual examples of a world, selected more or less at random, but now in *Roughing It* he must create a world. This movement toward fiction is more importantly marked, however, in the fact that the narrator himself is more of a creation, and we have now observed the first step in the process by which the author will find fictional identification with Huck or Hank.

In his first novel, *The Gilded Age* (1873), which was to give the epoch its name, Twain again, though less explicitly, used both the image of a journey and the plank-and-plug technique. Both the image and the technique were, however, of a sort to compound rather than correct the hazards of a collaboration—and this was, of course, a collaboration—with Charles Dudley Warner who, as one of the breed of novelists battening on the new middle class, was supposed to provide the fictional know-how for the inexperienced Twain. Though scarcely more than a huddle of improvisations, *The Gilded Age* did its own part in preparing the way for Twain's greatness. Here, for the first time, he created a fully rounded fictional character. Colonel Beriah Sellers— "*the* new American character," as William Dean Howells called him—was a gaudy combination of promoter and bunkum artist, dreamer and con man, idealist and cynic, ballyhoo expert, and vote-broker; and, in the Reconstruction world, an expert in bribery, the old Confederate learning the way of new Yankeedom and collaborating with a good Unionist to get rich at the public expense while ostensibly trying to elevate the black freedman: "Yes, sir, make his soul immortal but don't touch the nigger as he is."

Beyond Colonel Sellers, however, and perhaps of more significance, Twain here pictured for the first time the little towns and lost villages of backcountry America. Now they are done with grim realism; but in the same novel, for the first time in print, Twain was also exploring the world of luxury, greed, self-deception, pharisaism, and cold hypocrisy, the contempt for which was to force him to take refuge in the dream version of rural

America that was to find its image in mythical Hannibal. The ambivalence about both the world of rich modernity and that of the old backcountry had already (though not in literature) been emerging, for instance, as we have seen, in the very first days of his happy marriage into the world of wealth.

With "Old Times on the Mississippi," which he undertook for the *Atlantic* in 1874, Twain developed the poetry of old America—the Edenic dream, the vision of a redemptive simplicity that haunts the tenderfoot going West, the apprentice pilot on the texas deck, and Huck on his raft, a poetry antithetical to the grim realism that had begun with *The Gilded Age* and was to continue as one pole of later work. Specifically, with "Old Times" we enter the world of Hannibal and the river in which Tom Sawyer and Huck Finn were to come to immortal life. But at a thematic level, both "Old Times on the Mississippi" and *Life on the Mississippi* are more deeply prophetic of *The Adventures of Tom Sawyer* and *Adventures of Huckleberry Finn*. As the tenderfoot in *Roughing It* learns the West, so the landlubber learns the river, and here, as before, the story of initiation concerns the correction of illusion by the confrontation of reality. Here the illusion is explicit only in its aesthetic dimension: to the uninitiated observer the river is a beautiful spectacle, but to the old pilot it is a "wonderful book." Though a "dead language to the uneducated passenger [who] . . . saw nothing but all manner of pretty pictures," the same objects "to the trained eye were not pictures at all but the grimmest and most dead-earnest of reading matter." In other words, Twain is dealing with an image (and a narrative) of innocence and experience, a theme that was to prove deeply central in both *Tom Sawyer* and *Huckleberry Finn*, considered either individually or in contrast to each other. For with *Tom Sawyer* (1876) we have, as Twain declared, "simply a hymn, put into prose to give it a worldly air"—that is, we have the Edenic dream of innocence which the mystic journey of Huck will put to various tests.

In the complexity of his inspiration, *Tom Sawyer* goes back, as we have suggested, to the first days of Twain's marriage when an early draft of what was later to be Tom's courtship of Becky Thatcher, known as the "Boy's Manuscript," was (as a matter of fact) composed. And in its early form, something of the same impulse carried over into *Huckleberry Finn*, which was begun while Twain was reading proofs on *Tom Sawyer* and which he then regarded as a companion volume. But this new book did not get beyond the ramming of the raft by the steamboat before he laid it aside. Over the years he added to it, but it was not until the stimulus of writing *Life on the Mississippi* (1883) that he was able to push it through. The book was published in 1885, after an overwhelming advertising campaign and a series of lecture-readings by the author himself. The results of the advertising campaign were gratifying

even to the avarice of Mark Twain, although reviewers were inclined to find
the book crude, irreverent, and even vicious.

Let us rehearse the simple facts of the story. With the treasure that he
now shares with Tom as a result of earlier adventures, Huck has been adopted
into the respectable world of St. Petersburg under the tutelage of Widow
Douglas and Miss Watson. He misses his old freedom, but begins to accept
the new regime of spelling, soap, and prayers. His father reappears to claim
Huck, but when in a drunken rage the old man threatens his life, Huck
escapes to the island after making it seem that he has been murdered by a
robber. Here he is joined by Nigger Jim, the slave of Miss Watson who, in
spite of her piety, is being tempted to sell him downriver. Huck, disguised
as a girl, makes a scouting expedition to shore and finds that the island is
not safe from slave-catchers, and he and Jim take to the river. Huck is troubled
by his conscience at thus depriving Miss Watson of her property, but follows
his natural instinct. The plan to escape to freedom in a Northern state fails
when they miss Cairo, Illinois, in a fog. Then the raft is sunk by a steamboat
and the two, barely escaping with their lives, are separated.

Huck is taken in by the Grangerford family, aristocratic planters, and
enjoys their hospitality until a slaughterous outbreak of their bloody feud
with the Shepherdsons puts him on his own again. He manages to rejoin
Jim, and the growth of his human understanding of the slave constitutes the
psychological action, which concludes when Huck decides that if saving Jim
may get him damned, he'll just have to go to hell.

Meanwhile, the pair pass through various adventures that exhibit the
irrationalities of society and the cruelties possible to human nature. The life
on the river comes to an end when the vagabond "King" and "Duke," the
rogues whom they have befriended, betray Jim for a share in a presumptive
reward and Jim is held captive on the downriver plantation of the Phelps
family, kin of Tom Sawyer. When Huck goes to the plantation with the idea
of rescuing Jim, he is taken for Tom who is expected on a visit. To save
Jim, he accepts the role and when the real Tom appears, Tom accepts the
role of Sid, another boy in the family connection. Tom institutes one of his
elaborate adventures to rescue Jim, with Huck participating in the nonsense
to placate Tom. After Jim's rescue, during which Tom gets shot in the leg,
Jim stays with him and is recaptured; but all comes out happily, for as is
now explained, Miss Watson on her deathbed had long since freed Jim, and
Tom had withheld this information merely to enjoy a romantic adventure.
Huck is now taken in by the Phelps family to be civilized, but he is thinking
of escape to the Indian country.

The story, or rather Twain's treatment of the story, has provoked a vast body of criticism and various interpretations. The most simple view is to regard *Huckleberry Finn* as merely a companion piece to *Tom Sawyer*—more of the same tale of what it was like to be a boy in mythical Hannibal. As far as it goes, this view is valid. But it does not accommodate certain features of the book that are undeniably there.

The book is, indeed, a series of boyish adventures, but these adventures take place in an adult world, and the journey on the raft is, as the critic Bernard De Voto has put it, a "faring forth with inexhaustible delight through the variety of America." The "faring forth" gives, "objectively and inwardly, a panorama of American life, comic and serious, or with the comic and serious intertwined, all levels, all types of that life."

We must remember, however, that here we refer to the objective world of the novel and to the "inwardness" of that world. But what of the "inwardness" of the observers of that adult world? With this question we engage the central issue of the novel, for whenever the boyish world of Huck and Jim touches the adult world—the "shore" world—something significantly impinges upon the "river" idyl. If the basic fact of the novel is that it is a journey, we must think not only of the things seen on the journey but also of who sees them and the effect of the seeing. The journey, in fact, has begun with inward motives of great urgency; both Huck and Jim are more than footloose wanderers—they are escaping from their respective forms of bondage, forms imposed by society. To flee they give themselves to the river; and it is not illogical to agree with the poet T. S. Eliot and the critic Lionel Trilling that the river may be taken to have a central role. As Eliot implies when he says that the river has no clear point of beginning and fades out into its delta toward the sea, the river seems to be an image of a timeless force different from the fixed order of the dry land, an image of freedom and regeneration; or as Trilling puts it, the river is a god to which Huck can turn for renewal.

In any case, the river provides not only a principle of structural continuity but also a principle of thematic continuity. The experience on the river, with its special tone of being, is set against that on land. Huck says: "It was kind of solemn, drifting down the big, still river—looking up at the stars, and we didn't ever feel like talking loud, and it warn't often we laughed." Not only does the river teach a feeling of awe before the universe, but also a kind of human relationship at odds with the vanity, selfishness, competitiveness, and hypocrisy of society: "What you want, above all things, on a raft is for everybody to be satisfied, and feel right and kind toward the others."

But society—in which people are not "satisfied"—pursues the fugitives even on the river; the steamboat runs down the raft. When Huck and Jim escape by diving deep into the bosom of the river beneath the murderous paddle-wheel, this event—like the dive that Frederick Henry, in *A Farewell to Arms*, takes into the Tagliamento River to escape the Italian battle-police and the insanity of the world of institutions—is a baptism that frees them, now fully, into the new life.

If we are to understand the significance of Huck's baptism we must understand Huck himself, for Huck is the carrier of the meaning of the novel. The focal significance of Huck is emphasized by the fact that as early as 1875, Twain, in considering a sequel to *Tom Sawyer*, said to Howells (who had urged him to make Tom grow up in another book) that Tom "would not be a good character for it." He was, he said, considering a novel that would take a boy of twelve "through life," and added that the tale would have to be told "autobiographically—like *Gil Blas*." If the wanderings of the new picaroon are to be "through life," we expect the wanderer to learn something about life, and if, as Twain declared, the tale must be told as autobiography (it would be "fatal" otherwise, he said to Howells), the reason must be that the personality of the learner is crucially important.

In other words, Twain needed a hero who would be sensitive enough to ask the right questions of his adventures in growing up, and intelligent enough to demand the right answers. Furthermore, if Twain was to make the process of learning dramatically central to the tale, he could not well trust it to a third-person narrator, as in *Tom Sawyer*. The hero would have to tell his own tale with all its inwardness, and in his own telling, in the language itself, exhibit both his own nature and the meaning of his experience.

In Huck's language—"a magnificent expression," as De Voto puts it, "of the folk mind"—Twain found a miraculous solution. It is no less miraculous for springing from a well-defined tradition, or rather, from two traditions. The first, of course, was that of the frontier humorists from Augustus Baldwin Longstreet, Davy Crockett, and the anonymous writers of the Crockett almanacs on to George Washington Harris and his *Sut Lovingood*, a tradition that had fed the humor of lecturers and journalists like Artemus Ward and the early Mark Twain. The second was that of the early writers of the local color school, such as James Russell Lowell, Harriet Beecher Stowe, and Bret Harte. But the use of dialect by writers had become more and more cumbersome and mechanical; it set up a screen between the language and the meaning. Furthermore, the dialect itself was a mark of condescension. The writer and the reader, proud of superior literacy, looked down on the dialect and the speaker.

What Twain needed was a language based on colloquial usage and carrying that flavor, but flexible and natural, with none of the mechanical burden of dialect writing. At the same time, even if the speaker were of inferior literacy, his language had to be expressive enough to report subtleties of feeling and thought. In achieving this, Twain established a new relation between American experiences as *content* and language as a direct *expression*—not merely a *medium of expression*—of that experience. The language, furthermore, implied a certain kind of fiction, a fiction that claimed a certain relation to the experience it treated. That Mark Twain was aware of this situation is indicated at the very beginning of the novel: "You didn't know about me without you have read a book by the name of *The Adventures of Tom Sawyer*; but that ain't no matter. The book was made by Mr. Mark Twain, and he told the truth, mainly." Here Huck asserts himself as the literal subject about which Mr. Mark Twain had written in *Tom Sawyer*; but now he himself is to tell his own tale. He is, then, freestanding in his natural habitat outside of both "Mr. Mark Twain's" book and his own, insisting on a special veracity about experience. Actually, Huck Finn is only another fictional dramatization, but a dramatization validated by the language that springs directly from the world treated. The invention of this language, with all its implications, gave a new dimension to our literature. As Hemingway says in *The Green Hills of Africa* (a book which directly descends from Mark Twain's travel books), "All modern American literature comes from one book by Mark Twain called *Huckleberry Finn*."

Huck's language itself is a dramatization of Huck. On one hand, it reaches back into the origins of Huck as the son of the whiskey-sodden Pap sleeping it off with the hogs; it was a language Pap could speak. It is indicative of the world of common, or even debased, life from which Huck moves to his awakening; but as we have said, it is a language capable of poetry, as in this famous description of dawn on the river:

> Not a sound anywhere—perfectly still- –just like the whole world was asleep, only sometimes the bull-frogs a-cluttering, maybe. The first thing to see, looking away over the water, was a kind of dull line—that was the woods on t'other side—you couldn't make nothing else out; then a pale place in the sky; then more paleness, spreading around; then the river softened up, away off, and warn't black any more, but gray; you could see little dark spots drifting along, ever so far away—trading scows and such things; and long black streaks—rafts; sometimes you could hear a sweep screaking; or jumbled up voices, it was so still, and sounds come so far; and by-and-by you could see a streak on the water

which you know by the look of the streak that there's a snag there
in a swift current which breaks on it and makes that streak look
that way; and you see the mist curl up off of the water, and the
east reddens up, and the river, and you make out a log cabin in
the edge of the woods, away on the bank on t'other side of the
river, being a wood-yard, likely, and piled up by them cheats so
you can throw a dog through it anywheres; then the nice breeze
springs up, and comes fanning you from over there, so cool and
fresh, and sweet to smell, on account of the woods and the flowers;
but sometimes not that way, because they've left dead fish laying
around, gars, and such, and they do get pretty rank; and next
you've got the full day, and everything smiling in the sun, and
the song-birds just going it!

The first thing we notice here is what Leo Marx has called a "powerful
pastoral impulse." But Huck's poetry represents more than that. It is a
dramatic poetry, a poetry concerned with the human condition, and this is
presumably what Howells meant when he said, in 1901, that the book was
"more poetic than picaresque, and of a deeper psychology." It is the interfusion of the style with the "deeper psychology" that makes *Huck Finn* truly
revolutionary and that made the discovery of Huck's personal style the base,
subsequently, of Twain's own style and of the style of many writers to come.
Howells called Twain the Lincoln of our literature, and we may interpret
this by saying that as Lincoln freed the slave, Twain freed the writer.

In the light of the general implications of Huck's style, let us return to
what it signifies about him. When we find a language capable of poetic force,
we must remember that it is spoken by a speaker, and a speaker capable of
poetic thought and feeling. The language derives from Pap's world, but it
indicates a most un-Paplike sensibility, and this sensibility, even in its sim-
plest poetic utterances, prepares us for Huck's moral awakening as, bit by
bit, he becomes aware of the way the world really wags. The language of
Huck is, then, an index to the nature of his personal story—his growing up.

Tom Sawyer, it is true, is also the story of growing up, but there is a
crucial difference between the two versions. Huck's growing up is by the
process of a radical criticism of society, while Tom's is by a process of
achieving acceptance in society. Tom's career is really a triumph of conventionality, and though Tom is shown as the "bad" boy, we know that he is
not "really bad." He is simply a good healthy boy making the normal experiments with life, and we know, from our height of indulgent condescension, that in the end all will be well.

And all is well. Tom is accepted into the world of civilized and rational St. Petersburg. Even Huck, as an adjunct to Tom, is accepted as worthy to be "civilized," and this, in the light of his deplorable beginnings and generally unwashed condition, is a good American success story, cheering to parents and comforting to patriots.

Huckleberry Finn is a companion piece to *Tom Sawyer*, but a companion piece in reverse, a mirror image; it is the American *un-success* story, the story that had been embodied in Leatherstocking, proclaimed by Thoreau, and was again to be embodied in Ike McCaslin of Faulkner's *The Bear*, the drama of the innocent outside of society. Tom's story ends once he has been re-claimed by society, but Huck's real story does not even begin until he has successfully penetrated the world of respectability and, in the well-meaning clutches of the Widow and Miss Watson, begins to chafe under their min-istrations. Here Mark Twain indicates the thematic complexity of Huck's rebellion by two additional facts. It is not the mere tyranny of prayers, spelling, manners, and soap that drives Huck forth; Tom and Pap also play significant roles in this story.

Tom, in a sense, dominates not only his gang but Huck, too. He is an organizer and has a flair for leadership, but the secret of his power is his imagination: medieval chivalry, brigandage, piracy, treasure hunts, glorious rescues, and wild adventures drawn from his reading fill his head and must be enacted—with Tom, of course, in the major role. Against this world of fantasy and exaggeration, for which he has the name of "stretchers" or plain lies, Huck brings the criticism of fact, and when he can't keep his mouth shut, Tom calls him a "numbskull." Huck rejects this "dream" escape from civilization:

> So then I judged that all that stuff was only just one of Tom Sawyer's lies. I reckoned he believed in the A-rabs and the ele-phants, but as for me, I think different. It had all the marks of a Sunday-school.

In repudiating romantic adventure and criticizing the romantic view of life, Huck is simply doing what Mark Twain had done in *Roughing It* and was to do in *Life on the Mississippi*, with its criticism of his own nostalgic memories and the Southern legend, and more specifically (and more lethally) in *A Connecticut Yankee*. It is not merely that the romantic lies offend Huck's realistic sense. They offend his moral sense, too; for it is behind the facade of such lies, rationalized and justified by them, that society operates, and we notice that he concludes the remark on Tom's fantasy by saying, "It had all the marks of a Sunday-school"—Sunday school, and religion in general, being the most effective facade behind which society may carry on its secular operations. The equating of Tom's romantic lies with the lies of Sunday school tells us that Tom, in his romantic fantasies, is merely using his "stretchers" to escape from society's "stretchers"—lies as a cure for lies. And the repudiation of Tom's lies prepares us for the bitter unmasking of society's lies that is to occur on the journey downriver.

We have said that Huck has sensitivity and a poetic sense; so we must ask how this squares with his repudiation of Tom's imagination. Tom's brand of imagination is basically self-indulgent—even self-aggrandizing—in its social dimension; for instance, it makes Tom the leader, and more broadly considered, it justifies the injustices of society. But Huck's imagination, as we learn on the journey, has two distinct differences from this brand. First, it is a way of dealing with natural fact, of relating to fact, as in the night scene on the raft or the description of dawn; the poetry here derives from a scrupulously *accurate* rendering of natural fact. Second, it is a way of discovering and dealing with moral fact, a poetry that, as we have said, is concerned with the human condition and as such is the root of his growth; and this distinction comes clear in the end when Tom, on the Phelps plantation, is willing to put Jim through the rigamarole of the rescue just to satisfy his romantic imagination, when he could easily free him by reporting the facts of Miss Watson's deathbed manumission. To sum up, the repudiation of Tom's imagination is of deeper significance than the flight from the Widow's soap and Miss Watson's "pecking."

Pap's role in preparing for Huck's flight is more complex than Tom's. When he reappears, he seems at first a means of escape from civilization—from prayers, spelling, manners, and soap into the freedom of nature. Certainly Pap has little contact with civilization at this level, and for one moment he does seem to be the free "outsider." But he is an "outsider" only insofar as he is *rejected*; he is the offal of civilization, a superfluous and peculiarly filthy part and parcel of civilization. His outsideness means no regeneration, for in his own filthiness he carries all the filth of civilization, as is clearly illustrated by his railing against the free Negro and his talk about the government and his vote. Pap is an outsider only by vice and misfortune—in contrast to the outsider by philosophy, which is what Huck is in the process of becoming. Pap, Tom, and the Widow, that apparently ill-assorted crew, all represent aspects of bondage and aspects of civilization from which Huck flees.

Huck, moreover, is fleeing from Pap to save his quite literal life, for whether or not Pap is the "natural" man, he is a most unnatural father bent on carving up his son with a clasp knife. This literal fact symbolically underscores the significance of the journey. The escape from Pap is symbolically, as Kenneth Lynn puts it in *Mark Twain and Southwestern Humor*, a murder. Literally, Huck has had a gun on Pap all night, clearly prepared to pull the trigger if he goes on another rampage; and later, when to fool Pap about his flight he kills a pig and sprinkles the blood about the shack, the pig is a surrogate for Pap, who sleeps with the pigs—who is, therefore, a pig. But the blood is to indicate that Huck himself has been murdered, and so we have, symbolically, not only a murder but a suicide; Huck "murders" the piglike past and himself "dies" into a new life—a theme restated by the later baptism in the river.

This episode has, in fact, an additional dimension; to grow up implies the effort of seeking individuation from society and from the father—that is, from the bond of the group and from the bond of blood. So Huck, now free from both society and his father, goes forth to find the terms on which his own life may be possible. We have here a journey undertaken, at the conscious level, as a flight, but signifying, at the unconscious level, a quest; and this doubleness is precisely what we find in the psychological pattern of adolescence.

To speak of the journey as a quest, as the stages in the movement toward freedom, we refer to the fact that Huck, episode by episode, is divesting himself of illusions. Illusion, in other words, means bondage: Tom's lies, the lies of Sunday school, all the lies that society tells to justify its values and extenuate its conduct, are the bonds. For Huck the discovery of reality, as opposed to illusion, will mean freedom. And here we may note that the pattern of the movement from illusion to reality follows that of *Roughing It* and of *Life on the Mississippi*. The main action of *Huckleberry Finn*, in fact, may be taken as the movement toward reality after the Edenic illusion of *Tom Sawyer*—i.e., Mark Twain's revision of his own idyllic dream of boyhood and Hannibal after his return to that world preparatory to writing *Life on the Mississippi*. And the contrast between illusion and reality is, of course, central to Twain's work in its most serious manifestations; it is at the root of his humor, as well.

To return to the theme of the quest, Huck's voyage toward spiritual freedom is counterpointed structurally by Jim's search for quite literal freedom. This contrapuntal relationship is complex, but the most obvious element is that many of the lies of society have to do with the enslavement of Jim. Miss Watson, though a praying woman, will sell him downriver. The woman who receives Huck in his disguise as Sarah Mary Williams will be kind to him and protect him, but when it comes to catching Jim for the reward, she innocently asks, "Does three hundred dollars lay round every day for people to pick up?" And in Pap's drunken tirade about the "free nigger" with his fine clothes and gold watch and chain, we see a deeper motivation than greed, the need of even the lowest to feel superior to someone.

Not that all of the evils of society have to do directly with Jim. There are the men on the river who would let a raft with a dying man drift on because they are afraid of smallpox. There are the Grangerfords with their bloody code of honor, and Colonel Sherburn's cold-blooded gunning down of Boggs. There is the mob that under the guise of administering justice would gratify its sadism and envy by lynching Sherburn, but will turn coward before him and then, right afterwards, go to the circus; and the mob that, justly, takes care of the rascally King and Duke, but in doing so becomes, for Huck, the image of human cruelty. Even so, all the lies, as we have observed, are forms of bondage, and the dynamic image for this theme is the slave; and this dominant image implies the idea that all lies are one lie, that all evil springs from the same secret root.

This idea of the fusion of evil with evil leads to a fundamental lesson that Huck learns in his continuing scrutiny of society: as one evil may fuse with another, so good may fuse with evil, and neither good nor evil commonly appears in an isolable form. Society is a mixture and the human being is, too. The woman who would catch Jim for three hundred dollars is a kind woman. The men on the river (chasing runaway slaves, in fact) who are afraid of smallpox do have a human conscience, at least enough of one to make them pay two twenty-dollar gold pieces as conscience money. The Grangerfords, even with their blood-drenched honor, are kind, hospitable, dignified, totally courageous, and even chivalric in their admiration of the courage of the Shepherdsons. Sherburn, too, is a man of intelligence and courage.

The discovery of the interfusion of evil with good marks a step toward Huck's growing up, but he has reached another stage when he learns that the locus of the problem of evil is his own soul. And here the relationship with Jim is crucial; for it is this relationship that provides a specific focus for the general questions raised by the scrutiny of society. Coming down the river, Huck has more and more freed himself from the definition of Jim that society would prescribe: an inferior creature justly regarded as property. Huck even comes to "humble" himself before a "nigger" and apologize to him. The climax of this process comes in the famous chapter 31 when Huck's "conscience" dictates that he write to Miss Watson and turn Jim over to her. Having written the letter, he feels cleansed, "reformed," saved from the danger of hellfire. But the human reality of Jim on the raft, of Jim's affection for him, undoes all Huck's good intentions, and in a moment of magnificently unconscious irony, he bursts out, "All right, then, I'll go to hell," and tears up the letter.

Here, of course, Twain is concerned with the inherited doctrine of conscience as "revelation," in contrast with the notion of conscience as merely the voice of the particular society in which a person has been born. For him conscience was, as he put it in his *Notebook*, "a mere machine, like my heart— but moral, not physical . . . merely a *thing*; the creature of *training*; it is what- ever one's mother and Bible and comrades and laws and system of government and habitat and heredities have made it." In such a question, Twain, con- stantly and pathologically tormented by guilt and conscience, might well find the dynamic emotional center of his work. One escape from his suffering was in the idea of determinism; if he could regard man as "merely a machine, moved wholly by outside influences," then he was guiltless; and if conscience could be regarded (as a corollary) as "a mere machine . . . merely a thing," then its anguishing remarks were meaningless.

In Huck, then, Twain is exploring another possibility of alleviating his torments of conscience, a way which would also relieve him from the grip of an iron determinism. Against the conscience of revelation Huck would set, not the relief of determinism, but the idea of what we may call a "free consciousness" forged by the unillusioned scrutiny of experience. Huck wants to look at the world directly, with his own eyes, and this desire and talent is the reward for being outside society, having no stake in it. When on the Phelps plantation, in the plot with Tom to rescue Jim, Huck objects to some of Tom's romantic irrelevancies, Tom says: "Huck, you don't ever seem to want to do anything regular; you want to be starting something fresh all the time." Huck is, in short, a moral pragmatist; he wants to derive his values "fresh," to quarry them out of experience, to create his own moral consciousness.

In his creation of Huck, Twain, in a revolutionary and literally radical way, is undercutting impartially both conventional society and religion, and the tradition of antinomianism in America. Twain was simply against all notions of revelation and to him the "higher law," the idea that one with God is a majority, and an encyclical all looked alike; any quarrels among Mrs. Grundy, Henry David Thoreau, Theodore Parker, the Pope of Rome, and a certified case of paranoia were, according to Twain's theory, strictly intramural.

Huck is an antinomian, to be sure, but his antinomianism is of a root- and-branch variety, and one mark of it is in emotional attitude: he is as much against the arrogance of an antinomian who would take his conscience as absolute as against that of any established order. Huck's free consciousness comes, not from any version of revelation, but from a long and humble scrutiny of experience; humility is the mark of Huck's mind. Furthermore, if Twain recognizes that conscience is conditioned, is a historical accident, he would recognize the corollary that more things than society may do the conditioning and that the appeal to "conscience," the "higher law," or to revelation from on high may simply be an expression of the antinomian's deep psychic needs, not necessarily wholesome or holy.

Huck is, in short, an antinomian of an educable "consciousness," not of the absolute "conscience." As an antinomian, he is much closer to the naturalist William James than to the idealist Emerson; he would recognize, even in the moment when he violates "conscience" and follows the dictates of "consciousness," putting his soul in jeopardy of hellfire, that a crucial decision is always a gamble (the awareness that there is no absolute standard by which a choice is to be judged). Furthermore, if the consciousness has been educated to the freedom of choice, the process has also been an education in humility—not only humility but charity—and this aspect of Huck's development comes into focus (there are many other aspects of it) when he learns to recognize and accept the love of a creature for whom he had had only the white man's contempt, however amiable, and whose company he had originally accepted only because of an animal loneliness. And here we may recall that if Jim comes to Huck originally in the moment of loneliness, it is significant that when Huck goes to seek Jim after his reported capture, the description of the Phelps plantation is centered on the impression of loneliness: "then I knowed for certain I wished I was dead—for that the distant wail and hum of a spinning wheel is the lonesomest sound in the whole world."

The forging of Huck's free consciousness has, indeed, many aspects. With the flight from society, with the symbolic patricide, the symbolic suicide, and the symbolic baptism, Huck has lost his old self. He must seek a new self; and so we see emerging the psychological pattern in which, with every new venture back to shore—that is, to society—Huck takes on a new role, has a new personal history to tell, a new "self" to try on for size. In every instance, there is, of course, a good practical reason for this role-playing, but beyond such reasons the act represents a seeking for identity; such an identity will, presumably, allow him to achieve freedom in contact with society (and role-playing is, we should remind ourselves, characteristic of the process of growing up). Huck is not, in other words, seeking to exist outside society—to be merely an outcast, like Pap; for we must remind ourselves that at the beginning of the journey and at the Phelps farm he can suffer loneliness. What Huck is seeking, then, is simply a new kind of society, a kind prefigured by the harmony and mutual respect necessary on a raft. But Huck is also seeking a new kind of father, and here is where Jim assumes another dimension of significance; Jim is the "father" who can give love, even when the son, Huck, is undeserving and ungrateful. The role of Jim finds its clearest definition and confirmation in chapter 31 when Huck thinks back upon the relationship, but it has a subsidiary confirmation in the fact that Jim on the raft is the father deprived of his blood children (whom he intends to buy once he has his own freedom) who now needs to find a "son" to spend his love on.

To sum up: Though on the negative side the novel recounts the discovery of the "lies" in society and even in the "conscience," it recounts, on the positive side, the discovery of a redemptive vision for *both society and the individual*. It is a vision of freedom to be achieved by fidelity to experience, humility, love, charity, and pity for suffering, even for the suffering of those who, like the King and the Duke, are justly punished. This is not to say that such a vision is explicitly stated. It is implied, bit by bit, as Huck drifts down the river; it is, we might say, the great lesson inculcated by the symbolic river—the lesson that men can never learn on shore.

But what is the relation between this vision and the world of reality on shore?

In the last section of the novel, Huck does come back to shore, and the crucial nature of the return is signaled by the question that Mrs. Phelps asks him when he tells his lie about the blowing up of a cylinder head on the steamboat that never existed:

> "Good gracious! anybody hurt?"
> "No'm. Killed a nigger."

So with his answer Huck has fallen back into society and society's view that a "nigger" is not human, is not "anybody"—this in the very moment when he has come ashore to rescue Jim.

This moment signals, too, the issue that has provoked the most searching critical debate about the novel. According to one side of the debate, the last section undercuts all the meaning developed in the main body of the novel, and the working out of the end is, as Hemingway puts it, "just cheating."

Here we see the repetition of the old situation in which Huck had been reared, the "good" people, now Silas Phelps and Aunt Sally, holding Jim for a reward; but this fact, which earlier, on the raft, would have been recognized as one of the "lies" of society, is now quite casually accepted. Even the rescuing of Jim is presented to the reader not in terms of Huck's values as earned on the river—even though he is still the narrator—but in terms of Tom's, as a comic game. Huck's role now is simply to underscore the comic point of this game, by giving the same realistic criticisms of Tom's romantic fancies that we have known from long back.

These "land-changes" that the novel undergoes imply other, more important ones. Huck is no longer the central character, the focus of action and meaning, but now merely the narrator; and indeed he has regressed to the stage of limited awareness exhibited in *Tom Sawyer*. Associated with this regression is a change in the role of Jim: Huck no longer recognizes him as the surrogate father (whose love had been the crucial factor in his own redemptive awakening), and now simply regards him as a thing (a chattel slave is, legally, a "thing"); and so the reader is presumed to accept him as that, a counter to be manipulated in the plot and a minstrel show comic.

All of the changes that we have listed are associated with a basic change of tone. We are back in the world of *Tom Sawyer*, with a condescending and amused interest in the pranks and fancies of boyhood; and even the rescue of Jim becomes merely a lark, a charade, not to be taken seriously, for at the end we learn that Jim was free all the time, and presumably we are to accept as a charming stunt the fact that Tom has withheld this information in order to have his "adventure."

The third section simply does not hang together, and our first impulse is to ask what brought Twain to this pass. Clearly, during the process of writing the book, he was feeling his way into it, "discovering" it, and when he got to the end of the second section, he did not know where to go. Henry Nash Smith, in "Sound Heart and a Deformed Conscience" (a chapter in his *Mark Twain: The Development of a Writer*), holds that Twain finally took refuge in the tradition of backwoods humor. It is true that the novel has been, from the start, a "hybrid"—"a comic story in which the protagonists have acquired something like a tragic depth"—and so there was a certain logic in choosing the comic resolution, which would, by returning to the tone of the beginning, establish a structural symmetry and which would solve the main plot problem by getting Jim legally freed. In one sense, the trouble was that Twain, in the river journey, had wrought better than he knew and differently from his original intention, and the "tragic depths" he had opened up were not now to be easily papered over. Twain was, apparently, aware that he hadn't been quite able to paper things over, and so at the end does try to fuse the serious elements of the novel with the comic. First, he gives a flicker of the old role of Jim in having him stay with the wounded Tom, in that act reconverting him from "thing" to man and echoing Jim's old role in relation to Huck. Second, Twain tacks on the last few sentences—to which we must return.

From the foregoing account, it would seem that the last section is, indeed, "cheating." But, on the other side of the debate, we find, for example, the critic Lionel Trilling and the poet T. S. Eliot. Trilling follows much the same line of thought as Smith in commenting on the "formal aptness" that returns us at the end to the world of Tom Sawyer, but finds this grounding of the arch much more satisfying than does Smith, seeming to feel that the problem of the "tragic depths" is thus exorcised. T. S. Eliot goes further, and in addition to recognizing a formal aptness in that the "mood of the end should bring us back to that of the beginning," argues that since the river, with its symbolic function of a life force, has "no beginning and no end," it is "impossible for Huck as for the River to have a beginning or end—a *career*." The novel, that is, can have no form more significant than the mere closure in tonal repetition. If this is not the right end, what, Eliot asks, "would have been right?" And he adds that no book ever written "ends more certainly with the right words"—the statement of Huck that he can't stand to be adopted and "sivilized" as Aunt Sally now threatens to do: "I been there before." He is about ready to cut out for the "territory."

Let us, however, explore what might be involved in a "right" ending for the novel. Clearly, such an ending would have to take into account the main impulse of meaning through the second section; it would, in other words, have to accommodate the new Huck. This does not imply that the story should have a happy ending—i.e., Huck in a society embodying the values of the vision on the river. Such an ideal society never existed, nor is ever likely to exist; as Bertrand Russell has remarked, the essence of an ideal is that it is *not* real. But there are different degrees in which a society may vary from the ideal; there are more acceptable and less acceptable compromises, and the new vision gained by Huck would certainly preclude the easy acceptance of the old values exemplified on the Phelps plantation and by the whole action of the third section. The compromise here simply isn't good enough. We want *both* the "formal satisfaction" of returning the arch of narrative to the firm grounding in the original world of Tom Sawyer (that is, in the "real" world) and a "thematic satisfaction."

Here we must emphasize that the novel is not, ultimately, about a literal Huck (though he is literal enough, God knows) and the possibility of a final perfection in the literal world. Imagine, for example, an ending in which land-society, like that on the raft, would become a utopia, with all tensions resolved between man and man, man and society, and man and nature. Such an ending would be totally irrelevant to the novel we now have. What the present novel is about is, rather, the eternal dialectic between the real and the ideal. It is, more specifically, about the neverending effort in life to define the values of self-perfection in freedom. But if the distinction made earlier between "conscience" and "consciousness" be followed to its logical conclusion, the freedom would be one in which man, even in repudiating the "lies" of society, would not deny the necessity of the human community and would assume that the "dream" of such a "freedom" would somehow mitigate the "slavery" of the real world.

Or should the novel be taken to deny the necessity of community? Does it suggest that the human community is not only beyond redemption in the ideal, but beyond hope in the slow, grinding amelioration perhaps possible in the real process of history, and that, therefore, the only integrity to be found is in the absolute antinomianism of "flight"—literal or symbolic—to the "territory"? But even if Huck must take flight from society, is the flight negative or positive in its motivation? Does Huck—or will Huck—flee merely in protest against the real world, or in the expectation that in the "territory" he will find the ideal community? The original flight from Pap and Miss Watson was, of course, negative—simply "flight from." What about the possibility now envisaged in the end? Even if one professes to be uncertain about Huck's expectations, there can be no uncertainty about Twain's. He knew all too well what Huck, however far West he went, would find—a land soon to be swept by buffalo-skinners, railroad builders, blue-coated cavalry, Robber Barons, cold deck artists, miners, whores, schoolteachers, cowhands, bankers, sheep raisers, "bar-critters," and a million blood brothers of Old Pap and a million blood sisters of Miss Watson. Or, to treat the flight West as symbolic rather than literal, Twain knew that there is no escaping the real world—not even by dreaming of Hannibal or the Mississippi in moonlight, viewed from the texas deck.

Considering all this, we might take Huck as the embodiment of the incorrigible idealism of man's nature, pathetic in its hopeful self-deception and admirable in its eternal gallantry, forever young, a kind of Peter Pan in patched britches with a corncob pipe stuck in the side of his mouth, with a penchant for philosophical speculation, a streak of poetry in his nature, and with no capacity for growing up.

But thus far we have been scanting one very important element that bears on interpretation—the function of Jim. His reduction, in the third section, from the role of father seems to be more than what we have been taking it to be—merely one of the sad aspects of the land-world. To go back, we remember that he had assumed that role after the symbolic patricide performed by Huck, and that the role was central to the development of Huck on the journey downriver. But once he and Huck are ashore, the relationship ends; Huck loses the symbolic father. But—and we must emphasize this fact—he also loses the literal father, for now Jim tells him that Old Pap is, literally, dead. So, to translate, Huck is "grown up." He has entered the world, he must face life without a father, symbolic or literal, the "good" father of the dream on the river or the "bad" father of the reality on shore.

In this perspective of meaning *Huckleberry Finn* is, in addition to whatever else it may be, a story of growing up, of initiation—very similar, for instance, to Hawthorne's "My Kinsman, Major Molineux" and Katherine Anne Porter's "Old Mortality." Jim's report of the death of Pap clinches the fact that Huck must now go it alone and, in doing so, face the grim necessity of re-living and re-learning, over and over, all the old lessons. The world has not changed, there will be no utopia, after all. Perhaps, however, Huck has changed enough to deal, in the end, with the world—and with himself. Or has he changed enough? If he lights out for the territory will that mean that he has grown up? Or that he has not? Is the deep meaning of the famous last sentence so clear, after all? It often seems clear—but—

And here we may recall that the two great stories by Hawthorne and Katherine Anne Porter are open-ended—are stories of the dialectic of life.

There are, indeed, incoherences in *Huckleberry Finn*. But the book survives everything. It survives not merely because it is a seminal invention of a language for American fiction, nor because Huck's search for a freedom of "consciousness" dramatizes the new philosophical spirit which was to find formulation with William James; nor because it is a veracious and compelling picture of life in a time and place, or because Huck is vividly alive as of that time and place; nor because, in the shadow of the Civil War and the bitter aftermath, it embodies a deep skepticism about the millennial dream of America, or because it hymns youthful hope and gallantry in the face of the old desperate odds of the world. All these things, and more, are there, but the book survives ultimately because all is absorbed into a powerful, mythic image.

That mythic image, like all great myths, is full of internal tensions and paradoxes, and it involves various dimensions—the relation of the real and the ideal, the nature of maturity, the fate of the lone individual in society. In its fullness, the myth is not absorbed formally into the novel. It bursts out of the novel, stands behind the novel, overshadows the novel, undercuts the novel. Perhaps what coherence we can expect is not to be sought in the novel itself, in formal structure, plot, theme, and so on. Perhaps it resides in the attitude of the author who, as novelist facing the myth he has evoked, finally throws up his hands and takes refuge, cynically if you will, in the tradition of backwoods humor, repudiating all sophisticated demands and norms. He throws up his hands, however, not merely because he cannot solve a novelistic problem (which is true), but because the nature of the "truth" in the myth cannot be confronted except by irony—perhaps an irony bordering upon desperation—an irony that finds a desperately appropriate expression in the refuge in a reductive, primitive form that makes a kind of virtue of the inability to control the great, dark, and towering genii long since and unwittingly released from the bottle.

And so we may find in the ending of *Huckleberry Finn* a strange parallel to Twain's manner on the lecture platform, as described by an early reviewer. According to that report, he would gaze out of his "immovable" face, over "the convulsed faces of his audience, as much as to say, 'Why are you laughing?' " Now, at the end of *Huckleberry Finn*, having released the dark genii from the bottle, he turns his "immovable" face on us, his audience, and pretends there is no genii towering above us and that he has simply been getting on with his avowed business of being the "funny man."

But with this very act, he has taken another step toward the dire time when he will "never be quite sane at night."

In *The Prince and the Pauper*, a children's book laid in Tudor England, Mark Twain had, in 1881, taken his first excursion into historical fiction. This work, which interrupted the composition of *Huckleberry Finn*, was nothing more than a piece of sentimental junk cynically devised to captivate his own children, clergymen of literary inclinations, nervous parents, and genteel reviewers, but it broke ground for *A Connecticut Yankee*. That work, however, was on the direct line of Mark Twain's inspiration; it was connected with the grinding issues of his nature, and it drew deeply on earlier work. Laid in the sixth century, in Arthurian England, it put the new American mind in contrast with feudal Europe, the remains of which the "Innocents" of the *Quaker City*, and their chronicler, had had to face on their tour. But *A Connecticut Yankee* also harks back to the contrast between the "feudal" South and the "modern" North that looms so large in *Life on the Mississippi*; it embodies not only the spirit of social criticism found in *Huckleberry Finn*, but something of Huck's pragmatic mind that always wanted to start things "fresh"; and in a paradoxical way, after it celebrates the new Yankee order of industry, big business, and finance capitalism, it also returns to the Edenic vision of Hannibal and the river found in *Tom Sawyer* and *Huckleberry Finn*.

Most deeply, however, *A Connecticut Yankee* draws on the social and personal contexts of the moment in which it was composed. At this time Mark Twain was totally bemused by one James W. Paige, the inventor of a typesetting machine which Twain was trying to organize a company to manufacture, and by which he dreamed of becoming a financial titan. Behind

Hank Morgan, the Yankee, stands Paige. And, we may add, stands Twain himself, for if Hank (a superintendent in the Colt Arms Company) is an inventor (he claims that he can "invent, contrive, create" anything), he quickly becomes the "Boss"—a titan of business such as Twain dreamed of becoming.

The medieval values that Hank confronts were not confined to Arthurian Britain. For one thing, there was also present-day England, for whatever remnants had remained of an Anglophilia once cherished by Twain were now totally demolished by Matthew Arnold who, after a visit to America, had declared, in "Civilization in the United States," that the idea of "distinction" in this country could not survive the "glorification of 'the average man' and the addiction to the 'funny man.' " In his outraged patriotism and outraged *amour propre*, Twain, a "funny man," tended to merge the England of Arthur with that of Victoria.

In addition, the Romantic movement had discovered—or created—the Middle Ages, and made them current in nineteenth-century thought and art. Tennyson's *Idylls of the King* ranked in the esteem of the pious only a little lower than the New Testament, and James Russell Lowell's "The Vision of Sir Launfall" was a close contender for the popularity prize with the Book of Common Prayer. The poetry of William Morris and the painting of the Pre-Raphaelites, with Ruskin's Gothic aestheticism and the related social theories that pitted medieval spirituality and happy craftsmanship against the age of the machine, had great vogue in the United States, a vogue that found its finest bloom in Henry Adams and Charles Eliot Norton, who wistfully pointed out to his students at Harvard that there were in America no French cathedrals.

This cult of medievalism had a strongly marked class element; usually it was cultivated by persons of aristocratic background or pretensions, often with an overlay of sentimental Catholicism. It was also associated with wealth, but with inherited wealth as contrasted with that, usually greater, of the new kind of capitalist; for inherited wealth, untainted by immediate contact with the crude world of business, was "genteel." It was only natural, then, that a poem like Sidney Lanier's "Symphony" and the early novels attacking business should use the aristocratic feudal virtues as the thongs with which to scourge the business man. So when Hank guns down Malory's knights in armor with his six-shooters, he is also gunning down Tennyson, Ruskin, Lowell, Lanier, et al. *A Connecticut Yankee* is, in fact, the first fictional glorification of the business man.

But Hank is arrayed not only against Sir Sagramar le Desirious and Alfred Lord Tennyson and their ilk, but also against the spectral legions of Lee, abetted by the ghost of Sir Walter Scott. It was highly appropriate that

Twain should have given a first public reading of *A Connecticut Yankee* (an early version) to an audience in which sat General William Tecumseh Sherman, for if anybody was equipped to understand Hank's kind of warfare, it was the gentleman who, as first president of the Louisiana State University, had remarked to a Southern friend that "In all history no nation of mere agriculturalists had ever made successful war against a nation of mechanics," and who, a little later, was to lift the last gauzy film of chivalric nonsense to expose the stark nakedness of war.

If the anachronistically slaveholding society of Britain is an image of the Old South and if Hank's military masterpiece, the Battle of the Sand Belt, in which, after the explosion of Hank's mines, the air is filled with the ghastly drizzle of the atomized remains of men and horses, is an image of the Civil War (the first "modern" war), then Hank's program for Britain is a fable of the Reconstruction of the South and the pacification of that undeveloped country. Furthermore, in being a fable of that colonial project, this is also a fable of colonialism in general and of the great modern period of colonialism in particular, which was now well under way from the Ganges to the Congo; thus to Hank, Britain is simply something to develop in economic terms—with, of course, as a paternalistic benefit to the natives, the by-product of a rational modern society. In this context *A Connecticut Yankee* is to be set alongside Conrad's *Nostromo* and *The Heart of Darkness* and the works of Kipling.

There is, however, another and more inclusive context in which to regard it. More and more in our century we have seen a special variety of millennialism—the variety in which bliss (in the form of a "rational" society) is distributed at gunpoint or inculcated in concentration camps. So in this context, *A Connecticut Yankee* is to be set alongside historical accounts of Fascist Italy, Nazi Germany, or Communist Russia. This novel was prophetic.

The germ of *A Connecticut Yankee* was, however, much more simple than may have just been suggested. An entry from 1884 in Mark Twain's notebook read:

> Dream of being a knight errant in armor in the middle ages. Have the notions and habits of thought of the present day mixed with the necessities of that. No pockets in the armor. No way to manage certain requirements of nature. Can't scratch. Cold in the head—can't blow—can't get a handkerchief, can't use iron sleeve. Iron gets red hot in the sun—leaks in the rain, gets white with frost and freezes me solid in winter. Suffer from lice and fleas.

Make disagreeable clatter when I enter church. Can't dress or
undress myself. Always getting struck by lightning. Fall down,
can't get up. See Morte d'Arthur.

What Twain began with was burlesque, merely the torpedoing of high
falutin' pretensions. But within a year after the first entry, there is a note
for a battle scene "between a modern army with gatling guns (automatic)
600 shots a minute . . . torpedos, balloons, 100-ton cannon, iron-clad fleet &
Prince de Joinville's Middle Age Crusaders." Thus we have what we may
take as the poles of Mark Twain's inspiration for the book, on the one hand
the satirical burlesque and on the other the sadistic and massive violence
motivated by a mysterious hatred of the past.

The body of the work has to do with Hank's operations from the moment
when he decides that he is "just another Robinson Crusoe," and has to
"invent, contrive, create, reorganize things." The narrative proceeds in a
two-edged fashion: there is the satirical exposure of the inhuman and stul-
tifying life in Arthur's kingdom, with the mission for modernization and
humanitarian improvement, but there is also the development of Hank's
scheme for his economic and political aggrandizement, his way of becoming
the "Boss." By and large, it seems that the humanitarian and selfish interests
coincide; what is good for Hank is good for the people of Britain, and this
would imply a simple fable of progress, with the reading that technology in
a laissez faire order automatically confers the good life on all. There is no
hint, certainly, that Twain is writing in a period of titanic struggle between
labor and capital, a struggle consequent upon the advent of big technology.
In the new order in Britain there are no labor problems. The boys whom
Hank had secretly recruited and instructed in technology are completely
loyal to him, and as his Janissaries, will fight for him in the great Armageddon
to come, enraptured by their own godlike proficiency; if they represent labor
they have no parallel in the nineteenth-century America of the Homestead
strike and the Haymarket riot.

In the fable there are, indeed, many lags and incoherences that, upon
the slightest analysis, are visible. Twain had not systematically thought
through the issues in his world, or his own attitudes, and he did not grasp,
or did not wish to grasp, the implications of his own tale. During the course
of composition he had written—in a letter of either cynical deception or
confusion of mind—that he had no intention of degrading any of the "great
and beautiful characters" found in Malory, and that Arthur would keep his
"sweetness and purity," but this scarcely squares with the finished product.
Again, though the narrative, once finished, shows no hint of the tensions in

the world of the new capitalism, Twain most inconsistently could, when the socialist Dan Beard illustrated the first edition and made the fable apply to contemporary persons and abuses, enthusiastically exclaim, "What luck it was to find you!" And though Twain, now reading Carlyle's *French Revolution*, could proclaim himself a "Sansculotte," he was at the same time dreaming of his elevation to the angelic choir of Vanderbilt, Rockefeller, and other Bosses. And most telling of all, though *A Connecticut Yankee* was rapturously received, even by such discerning readers as Howells, as a great document of the democratic faith, and though Twain himself, sometimes at least, took it as such, Hank is not ethically superior to Jay Gould or Diamond Jim Brady in many of his manipulations. What Hank turns out to be is merely the "Boss," more of a boss than even Boss Tweed ever was, something like a cross between a Carnegie and a commissar.

There are various other logical confusions in *A Connecticut Yankee*, but one is fundamental. If the original idea of the book had been a celebration of nineteenth-century technology, something happened to that happy inspiration, and in the end progress appears a delusion, Hank's modernization winds up in a bloody farce, and Hank himself can think of the people whom he had undertaken to liberate as merely "human muck." In the end Hank hates life, and all he can do is to look nostalgically back on the beauty of pre-modern Britain as what he calls his "Lost World," and on the love of his lost wife Sandy, just as Twain could look back on his vision of boyhood Hannibal.

What emerges here is not only the deep tension in Twain, but that in the period. There was in America a tension concerning the Edenic vision, a tension between two aspects of it: some men had hoped to achieve it in a natural world—as had Jefferson—but some had hoped to achieve it by the conquest of nature. The tension, in its objective terms, was, then, between an agrarian and an industrial order; but in subjective terms the tension existed, too, and in a deep, complex way it conditioned the American sensibility from *Snow-Bound* through *A Connecticut Yankee* and Henry Adams's idea of the Virgin versus the dynamo, on through the poetry of T. S. Eliot and John Crowe Ransom, to the debased Rousseauism of a hippie commune.

The notion of the Edenic vision reminds us of *Huckleberry Finn*, for thematically *A Connecticut Yankee* is a development of that work—and the parallel in the very names of the heroes suggests the relation: *Huck/Hank*. Huck journeys through the barbarous South, Hank through barbarous Britain, both mythic journeys into a land where mania and brutality are masked by pretentions of chivalry, humanity, and Christianity. After each encounter with a shocking fact of the land-world, Huck returns to his private Eden on the river and in the end contemplates flight to an Edenic West. In other words, Huck belongs to the world of Jefferson's dream, in which man finds harmony with man in an overarching harmony of man in nature. Hank, however, is of sterner stuff. When he encounters a shocking fact he undertakes to change it—to conquer both nature and human nature in order to create a rational society.

Both Huck and Hank come to a desperate collision with reality, Huck on the Phelps farm and Hank at the Battle of the Sand Belt; but the end of the project of regeneration through technology and know-how is more blankly horrible than life on the Phelps farm, with not even a facade of humor but only the manic glee of the victors exalted by their expertise of destruction. The "human muck" has refused the rule of reason—and the prophet of reason has done little more than provide magnificently lethal instruments by which man may vent his mania.

When the book was finished, Twain wrote to Howells: "Well, my book is written—let it go. But if it were only to write over again there wouldn't be so many things left out. They burn in me. . . . They would require a library—and a pen warmed up in hell." But the pen had already been warmed enough to declare that dark forces were afoot in history and in the human soul to betray all aspiration, and with this we find, at the visceral level of fable, the same view of history later to be learnedly, abstractly, and pitilessly proclaimed by Henry Adams and dramatized in (to date) two world wars.

As for Mark Twain himself, the shadows were soon to gather. The metaphysical despair of *A Connecticut Yankee* was shortly to be compounded by personal disasters, bankruptcy (from which, with an irony worthy of his own invention, he was to be rescued by one H. H. Rogers, of the Standard Oil trust, one of the more ruthless of the Barons), the death of Livy (by which was added to grief his guilt of having robbed her of the Christian faith), the deaths of the adored Suzy and of a second daughter, Jean, the deaths of friends, and what seems to have been a struggle against madness. His fame continued; he walked up and down Fifth Avenue in his eye-catching white suit that advertised his identity; he consorted with the rich and great, and once Andrew Carnegie even addressed him in a letter as "Saint Mark"; he played billiards to the point of exhaustion; he received an honorary degree from Oxford, which mollified the Anglophobia that had been enshrined in *A Connecticut Yankee*; he railed at the degeneracy of the age and the abuses of wealth and power and at American imperialism in the Philippines and at Belgian imperialism in the Congo, and greeted Gorky, on his visit to the United States, as an apostle of Russian democracy. But nothing really helped much, as he was never, as he put it, "quite sane at night."

Nothing helped much, that is, except writing. He kept on wielding his pen "warmed up in hell," with flashes of genius, as in *Pudd'nhead Wilson* (1894), "The Man That Corrupted Hadleyburg" (1899), and *The Mysterious Stranger* (published posthumously), in work that obsessively rehearsed, in various disguises, his own story and his own anguish. He took refuge in a massive autobiography, in which chronology is replaced by association as a principle of continuity and as a method for mastering his own experience and plumbing his own nature; he was trying to achieve truth by thus recording a voice to speak from the grave.

But perhaps there was no truth to be achieved. Perhaps there was only illusion, after all, as he put it in the unfinished story called "The Great Dark" and in a letter to Sue Crane, his sister-in-law:

> I dreamed that I was born and grew up and was a pilot on the Mississippi and a miner and a journalist in Nevada and a pilgrim in the *Quaker City*, and had a wife and children and went to live in a villa at Florence—and this dream goes on and on and sometimes seems so real that I almost believe it is real. But there is no way to tell, for if one applied tests they would be part of the dream, too, and so would simply aid the deceit. I wish I knew whether it is a dream or real.

JUDITH FETTERLEY

The Anxiety of Entertainment

Toward his "alternate career" as a professional entertainer, Mark Twain was consistently ambivalent. From his triumphant note to Livy on the success of his toast to "The Babies" at the Grant reception to his grovelling recantation after the "fiasco" of the Whittier Birthday speech, the arcs of his emotional pendulum swung between the twin poles of exultation and disgust. As Lorch, Fatout, and others have demonstrated, Mark Twain was highly self-conscious about the art of public performance, more so than he was about the art of writing. Often sloppy when it came to revising manuscripts, he would spend hours polishing a lecture or analyzing a performance down to the last detail, and "How To Tell A Story" is perhaps his major aesthetic document. It is not, therefore, surprising that while his fictions present virtually no portraits of the artist as writer, they are filled with portraits of the artist as performer, entertainer, showman, storyteller. Indeed, seen in this light, they present a complex and interesting study of the artistic self, analogous in some respects to that provided by the works of that most self-conscious of artists, Henry James. By and large, the portrait of the entertainer that emerges from Mark Twain's fiction is a negative one: it is a portrait flooded with anxiety, rage, contempt, and disavowal; one which works in constant counterpoint to the tone of exultation and triumph frequently revealed in the autobiographical dictations and letters; and one which illuminates the sources of his ambivalence.

Despite the air of detachment, permitted by virtue of his speaking from

From *The Georgia Review* 33, no. 2 (Summer 1979). © 1979 by the University of Georgia. Originally entitled "Mark Twain and the Anxiety of Entertainment."

the grave, Mark Twain's autobiographical projection of himself as the sole survivor in the "cemetery" of American humor reveals considerable anxiety about the profession of entertainer and suggests that the central quality which defined that profession for him was the sense of risk. That risk should characterize entertainment is not surprising for, although Mark Twain describes his failed contemporaries as "merely humorists" and attributes his survival to his seriousness, in fact successful entertainments are more difficult to accomplish than successful sermons. The expectation of pleasure is a harder taskmaster than the promise of information, and the fear of failure in the service of pleasure is aggravated by the knowledge that proof of success or failure is immediate, tangible, and irrefutable: the audience laughs or it doesn't. Further, success at entertainment, while it brings a momentary triumph, generates a demand for ever greater effects. The achievement is fragile; it cannot survive repetition or competition—a perception reflected in the fact that all of Mark Twain's entertainers are solitary figures.

In Mark Twain's work, however, the anxieties surrounding the failure of entertainment are equalled, if not exceeded by, the anxieties attendant upon success. If the entertainment is successful, then the entertainer is forced to confront certain fears about the nature of entertainment. Primary among these is the fear that the entertainment is without substance and that the entertainer is a fraud, an impostor, a thief (Mark Twain often "jokingly" referred to lecturing as robbery)—a taker rather than a giver. The autobiographical explanation of his success as a humorist reflects this fear of not being sufficiently serious, of not providing the audience with "food for thought." However, the most interesting treatment of this particular performance anxiety is the infamous Whittier Birthday speech. In this sketch, Mark Twain implicitly accuses Emerson, Holmes, and Longfellow of imposing on the public and getting food, lodging, and clothing for nothing. The poets are robbers who steal the miner blind; in return for his beans and boots, they offer only words. While on one level the sketch makes a distinction between the value of the serious genteel New England poets and the wild Western humorist (in favor, of course, of the latter), the complexities of impersonation which provide its structure link Mark Twain with the poets under the larger aegis of entertainer, one who makes a living playing with words. Thus, at the end of the speech, Mark Twain puts to himself the question which not only the speech itself but the lavish *Atlantic Monthly* dinner given in honor of entertainers could not help but raise: "Ah! impostors, were they? Are you?" What return for *your* beans, Mark Twain?

A second fear attendant upon the successful entertainment is the logical corollary, given the nature of anxiety, of the first—not that entertainment is without substance but that its substance is suspect. That entertainment is aggression and the entertainer engaged in an act of hostility against the audience was a perception both close to the surface of Mark Twain's consciousness, as is evidenced by his remarks on the response to his toast at the Grant reception or on the proper delivery of "The Golden Arm"; and finally unavailable to him for analysis, as his frantic apologies for and denials of the Whittier Birthday speech make clear. In his fictions, however, Mark Twain could undertake this analysis; the hostile relationship, whether implicit or explicit, of the entertainer and the audience is a constant element in his portraits of entertainments. His books are filled with aggressive entertainers: the returned crusader of the spoof on legends in *Innocents Abroad* who enters the castle disguised as a harlequin and exterminates his audience; Tom Sawyer, whose staging of his own funeral involves the potential humiliation of all of St. Petersburg; the Duke and the King, whose Royal Nonesuch is a common rip-off; Hank Morgan, whose entertainments cause his audience to collapse by platoons; Dave "Pudd'nhead" Wilson, who enters his world with a hostile joke whose intention he ultimately fulfills by killing his half of the social dog. And they are filled with "sold" audiences: the narrator of "The Jumping Frog," the "innocent" abroad, the attendants at Tom Sawyer's "funeral," the viewers of the Royal Nonesuch. And they are filled with entertainers under attack: the aging singer in *Innocents Abroad* whom the audience torments mercilessly; the Duke and the King, tarred and feathered and ridden out of town on a rail; Hank Morgan sold into slavery as a result of one of his entertainments; Tom Driscoll kicked into a crowd of drunks and tossed from row to row because of a joke. Clearly, the impulse to entertain has its dangerous side, and entertainment is, not surprisingly, associated with anxiety.

Tom Sawyer is central to St. Petersburg because he is an entertainer. Tom's centrality defines his world: in St. Petersburg entertainment is the most significant human activity. The human condition in St. Petersburg is boredom; thus entertainment is not simply relief, it is survival. The Widow Douglas is saved from the vengeance of Injun Joe by reading. In St. Petersburg everything is converted to entertainment—funerals, murders, trials; the need for entertainment takes precedence over justice, even safety—Tom risks his life and the lawyer risks Injun Joe's escape in order to make theatre of Tom's testimony.

Tom is the power in St. Petersburg because he is a genius of entertainment. He is defined through the whitewash scene as the one truly able to convert *everything* into play; he has the imagination and the irreverence necessary to free people from their boredom and to provide them with the opportunities for acting out their secret fantasies. In a world whose concept of entertainment is suggested by the annual "Examination Evening," Tom is a gift; and he is amply rewarded by attention, glory, and power.

This portrait of the entertainer is remarkably free from anxiety. Tom's entertainments are all successes; they are substantive and liberating; and the relation between Tom as entertainer and St. Petersburg as audience is remarkably symbiotic. They need him and he needs them and everybody gets to be Robin Hood or at least have a nice part in the play.

But there are negative undercurrents to this relationship that derive from what must inevitably be Tom's attitude toward his audience. His power, after all, results from their *lack* of it, and they lack power because they are cowardly and hypocritical. They are as bored in church as he is and are delighted when his bug gets them out, but they submit to church and pretend to like it because they are supposed to. In addition, Tom's entertainments are exposures and as such come perilously close to being acts of aggression. This tension culminates in Tom's appearance at his own funeral, which is timed to produce the maximum exposure, and consequently humiliation, of the audience as sentimental hypocrites. Tom backs off from the hostility implicit in his entertainment and after his "funeral" is reborn as a thoroughly conventional good boy who protects women, accumulates capital, and enforces conformity on rebels such as Huck Finn. But he is no longer an entertainer. When he reemerges as an entertainer in *Adventures of Huckleberry Finn*, Tom is completely aggressive and his concept of fun is cruelty. In his handling of Tom Sawyer, Mark Twain has subtly bonded entertainment and aggression; and the entertainer's contempt for an audience that craves entertainment and then attacks those who provide it—for not being serious or substantial, for being "merely" entertainers—is implicit in this portrait.

Since Huck Finn is in so many ways a reaction against Tom Sawyer, it is not surprising that *Adventures of Huckleberry Finn* reflects a revulsion against viewing life from the perspective of entertainment. Despite his adulation of Tom's style and his enjoyment of the circus, Huck is singularly free from the desire to be either entertainer or entertained. Huck's position outside the drama of entertainment has several implications. It suggests, for instance, that being an entertainer is incompatible with a whole range of significant human qualities—kindness, compassion, humility, innocence; indeed, one might say that the heaviest indictment Mark Twain ever made of entertainment was to define Huck in opposition to it. In addition, Huck's position suggests a radical revision of the functional value of entertainment. Entertainment is salvation in St. Petersburg because it handles boredom, but it can't handle the loneliness and fear which are Huck's conditions. Huck handles his loneliness by joining up with Jim, but the bond between them is threatened when Huck tries to entertain Jim or to entertain himself at Jim's expense. The King Sollermun exchange produces an interaction between Jim and Huck that is palpably different from their previous or subsequent relation; each one concludes that the other is a fool, incapable of reason, and impervious to a differing point of view or frame of reference. It is just possible that Huck's decision in the fog episode shortly thereafter (to act like Tom Sawyer and have fun at Jim's expense) derives from the contempt implicit in the conclusion he drew following his attempt to entertain ("you can't learn a nigger to argue"). Certainly, it is clear that entertainment and companionship are incompatible in *Huckleberry Finn*.

Nor can entertainment handle fear. In *Huckleberry Finn*, entertainment is perceived as the luxury of the safe. The encounter with the wrecked *Walter Scott* (which Huck says Tom would call an "adventure" and would undertake "if it was his last act") and the final "evasion" (note the significance of the title in this context) elaborately staged by Tom amply demonstrate that entertainment is defined by an absence of risk for the entertainer. When Huck tries to convince Jim that landing on the *Walter Scott* was a grand adventure, Jim replies "that he didn't want no more adventures . . . because he judged it was all up with *him* anyway it could be fixed." And at the end of the novel, Tom is safe in bed, but Jim is "in that cabin again, on bread and water, and loaded down with chains, till he's claimed or sold." Indeed, the centrality of entertainment to *The Adventures of Tom Sawyer* is closely correlated with the utter safety of a world in which all dangers are magically sealed up in a cave; entertainment cannot answer to Huck Finn's nightmare world in which all the caves are open. (That entertainment may involve no real risk at all is, perhaps, the ultimate anxiety of the entertainer who thinks of entertainment as risky.)

The denigration of entertainment implicit in Huck's lack of interest in it is made explicit by the portraits of entertainers and entertainments in the novel. In *Adventures of Huckleberry Finn*, the human need for entertainment is embodied in the instantaneous conversion of the shooting of Boggs into theater, with the actor being generously "treated" for his performance. In this context, it is one of the major items in the indictment of the damned human race. In *Tom Sawyer*, the Widow Douglas is saved by entertainment; in *Huckleberry Finn*, Boggs is killed by it, for it is the need for entertainment that makes possible the original performance by Sherburn. The need for entertainment also supports people like the Duke and the King, portraits of the entertainer whose fulfilling of that need simply denigrates it further. The fear that entertainers are impostors and entertainments are "sells" is thoroughly expressed in *Huckleberry Finn* through the Duke and the King and the Royal Nonesuch. Equally explicit is the vision of entertainment as aggression. The audience, which receives because it demands the "sell," gladly turns on the entertainer, and the hostile relation between them is carried to its ultimate conclusion as Huck and Tom encounter the audience of the Royal Nonesuch having fun with the old tar, feather, and rail routine. As Huck says, "human beings *can* be awful cruel to one another." In *Huckleberry Finn*, cruelty is entertainment and entertainment is cruelty: tying pans to dogs' tails; soaking them in turpentine and setting them on fire; screaming at drunks in circuses—"knock him down! throw him out!"; shooting old men; tarring and feathering; acting out in the name of fun the slave's horrified vision of what it means to be sold down the river, deaf to the cry of "but what kine er time is *Jim* havin'?" Only a sadist would take part in it; "it was enough to make a body ashamed of the human race."

A *Connecticut Yankee in King Arthur's Court* continues the denigration of entertainment by associating it with the world of sixth-century Britain, the world which Hank Morgan is bent on reforming and transforming. There are more explicit references to entertainers and entertainments in *A Connecticut Yankee* than in other books—Merlin, Sir Dinadan, the musicians whom Morgan Le Fay hangs, the numerous after-dinner scenes involving dog fights, joke swapping, storytelling; but the cumulative effect of these references is to identify entertainment with the primitive. In Hank's republic of the future, built on the patent and the paper, there is no place for—because there is no need for—entertainment. The fear that entertainment is insubstantial is here reflected in the conviction that it has no part to play in the serious business of converting the sixth century into the nineteenth. In fact, Hank is always dreaming up entertainments to keep the knights occupied and out of the way while the real work goes on.

Entertainment is big in Arthur's Britain because the people are ignorant, superstitious, and mentally and physically enslaved. Entertainment is the signature of a corrupt world based on the system of monarchy, an unjust hierarchy which provides power for the few and slavery for the many. The knights, symbols of that system, are devoted to entertainment; in isolating them as the enemy, Hank defines his attitude toward entertainment. Merlin, another entertainer, is another enemy. Merlin is a fraud who exploits the ignorance of the people and their superstitious need for the sensation of miracles to achieve and maintain a position of power in the kingdom. To the power and attraction of Merlin's entertainments Hank wishes to oppose the power and attractions of technology—the opportunity to change the conditions of one's life. That Hank must disguise his offering in the trappings of entertainment is one of the major ironies of his situation and one of the major sources of his ultimate failure. Hank's performances as a showman are atavistic; they are imitations of the primitive undertaken to gain the power to transform it. But the degree to which he enjoys the role suggests the extent of his own identification with the primitive. The pleasure he takes in being a showman is part of the web that finally traps him in a sixth-century identity. The dangers inherent in entertainment and the anxieties attendant upon success at it are succinctly dramatized in our final view of Hank, dying in the attempt to get up one last "effect."

The desire to be free of the anxieties of entertainment may well be one of the reasons why it has no place in Hank's brave new world. Hank rapidly discovers the fragility and instability of the performer's triumph. One miracle demands another, and Hank finds himself under pressure to produce more and greater sensations. When he responds to this pressure and provides one of his greatest shows, the "miracle" of the Valley of Holiness, its effect is short-lived. Out of commission briefly due to a cold contracted in the line of duty, he reemerges to find that his audience has deserted to a rival and that if he wishes to remain the center of attention, he must quickly come up with yet another "miracle." The fickleness of the public asserts the essential hostility of the relation between audience and entertainer. In a world which responds to Merlins, Dinadans, dog fights, and knights, how can an expert showman find adequate appreciation? When Hank hangs Sir Dinadan for his volume of stale jokes, he is expressing his rage at a public that supports such entertainers and that, by its support, allows Sir Dinadan to assume Hank as *his* audience. The particular joke that produces Hank's rage is revealing; it is the old story "about a humorous lecturer who flooded an ignorant audience with the killingest jokes for an hour and never got a laugh" because "it was all they could do to keep from laughin' right out in meetin'." The entertainer's performance fails because of the stupidity of his audience. Hank's final act of massive aggression, his blowing up of his entire world, is in part the act of a frustrated performer who feels he has not been sufficiently appreciated. This is truly primitive. Freed from the plague of entertainment, the new world might indeed be brave.

The original impulse behind *A Connecticut Yankee in King Arthur's Court* was the desire to transform; annihilation was the court of last resort. By the time of Mark Twain's later works—*Pudd'nhead Wilson, The Mysterious Stranger*—annihilation is the original impulse. This shift, however, provides the context for a restoration of the status of entertainers and a framework for resolving the anxieties attendant upon entertainment. Entertainment is no longer a way into power and therefore suspect to the audience and unnerving to the performer, as it was in *The Adventures of Tom Sawyer* and *A Connecticut Yankee*; rather power manifests itself as entertainment. And entertainment is transformed from the personally invested and potentially hostile act of exposure into the cosmically transcendent act of revelation—of the status of the entertainer and of the nature of reality. Dave Wilson enters Dawson's Landing with a joke that defines the essence of that community and identifies Wilson as one who sees through to that essence. The "comprehensively disagreeable" dog is a metaphor for Dawson's Landing, which kills one half of itself and foolishly believes that the other half can live. Invisible to the community, the dog is visible to Wilson who proceeds in the course of the novel to reveal his vision. While the community rejects both seer and vision and isolates Wilson by calling him a "pudd'nhead," Wilson's isolation signifies not the anxiety of an entertainer unappreciated by his audience but rather his power over them. And that power derives from his knowledge of who they are, systematically acquired through the collection of their signatures in the form of fingerprints. In *Pudd'nhead Wilson*, it is not the entertainer who is an impostor—he is the only one whose identity is what it appears to be; the impostor is the audience, the town of Dawson's Landing, whose communal identity is built upon the myth that black and white are different and distinguishable. Wilson's courtroom performance, reminiscent of Tom Sawyer's, is a revelation of reality that has the potential for reuniting and revivifying the social dog. That it does not do so is the result of the severe pessimism which informs the novel, and it reminds us that the restored status of the entertainer is the result of his role as an agent of a cosmic despair. Ironically, entertainment becomes positive at precisely the moment when Mark Twain becomes most negative about the value of human existence.

In *The Mysterious Stranger* this conjunction is even more clearly articulated. *The Mysterious Stranger* is more pessimistic than *Pudd'nhead Wilson*, yet the vision of entertainment is the most positive since *Tom Sawyer*. Satan's appearance in the role of entertainer reasserts that centrality of entertainment which organized *Tom Sawyer* but it validates it as Tom Sawyer could never do. The thirst for entertainment still springs from and indicates the limitations of human existence, but in *The Mysterious Stranger* Satan's entertainments do not simply reiterate or intensify those limitations. Rather they suggest the possibility, however dim, of transcending them. In contrast to the connection established in *A Connecticut Yankee*, the villagers' responsiveness to Satan's entertainments manifests their link with divinity. Indeed, Eseldorf's preference for Satan's performances over the pale human shadows of it provides one of the few good things that can be said about the human race.

Satan is a major assuagement of Mark Twain's anxieties about entertainment. It is highly significant that Satan, who is Mark Twain's dream self, so consistently presents himself as an entertainer: musician, poet, storyteller, joker, creator of fantastic theater, supreme performer of vanishing acts, and provider of creative games. When Satan assumes the identities of others, dull village folk become instantly transformed into superior performers. Satan's entertainments cannot fail and he cannot bore. His very presence, even when invisible, enlivens his audience, and they are invariably worshipful. In addition, his entertainments are substantial; he is a feeder and the food he gives is both pleasure and knowledge. And finally, the fear that entertainment is a secret act of aggression and the relation between entertainer and audience one of hostility is cancelled out by the simple fact that aggression and hostility are meaningless in relation to Satan. Satan feels no hostility toward his audience because they are utterly unlike him, the distance between being cosmic. He needs nothing from his audience—*he* never eats and nothing they do affects him. On the other hand, their hostility toward him is obviated by the realization that the aggression apparent in his entertainments is only the product of their limited human vision. When Satan eliminates without a qualm one of his first entertainments, the boys are horrified by his lack of feeling for the little world he has created. Later they learn, through the example of Nikolaus, that, given the nature of human existence, death is in fact a gift and Satan's "cruelty" is revealed to be kindness.

God has revealed himself as an entertainer, but in the last analysis entertainment becomes a cosmic weapon. Satan exhorts the human race to laugh and by so doing to blow the world to bits. The supreme entertainment of the ultimate entertainer accomplishes that goal by dissolving the world into nothing. Mark Twain's anxieties emerge from the assuasive fantasy: in the final show, the audience realizes that the entertainer is a bad dream; nevertheless, his performance leaves them appalled.

CYNTHIA GRIFFIN WOLFF

The Adventures of Tom Sawyer:
A Nightmare Vision of American Boyhood

Twain's second book of boyhood has more or less cornered one segment of the American Dream. Read with admiration (read during the long years when *Moby-Dick* was relegated to obscurity), it captured both our lofty goals and our tragic weaknesses; and if it is not "the" American epic, it has epic dimensions. By comparison, its predecessor seems unworthy of serious attention (a "comic idyll of boyhood," says Leo Marx dismissively, on his way to a lengthy analysis of *The Adventures of Huckleberry Finn)*—no more than idealized reminiscences, pulp fantasies of an "Everyboy." Yet Huck himself is more particular about his antecedents: "You don't know about me," he says at the beginning of his story, "without you have read a book by the name of *The Adventures of Tom Sawyer*, but that ain't no matter. That book was made by Mr. Mark Twain, and he told the truth, mainly." In the first instance, *this* is where he has "been before"—the world of this other fiction— and one explanation for the questing need that fills Huck's own tale must be found here, in the fabricated town of St. Petersburg on the Mississippi.

We are certainly correct to see Huck as heroic—an American Odysseus (or Hamlet); but if, for the sake of contrast, we diminish the complexity of Tom Sawyer's world—relegating it to the simplistic category of "All-American Boyhood"—we will find ourselves led seriously astray.

It is no easy thing for an adult American reader to get at the "real" world of this novel. Our culture has provided us with too many colorful, fleshed-out reproductions of it: a bicentennial stamp depicting Tom and the

From *The Massachusetts Review* 21, no. 4 (Winter 1980). © 1980 by The Massachusetts Review, Inc.

whitewashed fence; commemorative plates and pictures; and countless stage and film productions—each one full of life and merriment, each exuding the security of childhood-as-it-ought-to-be in smalltown America. And every one of these sentimental evocations is false to the original.

In fact, Tom's world would be difficult to capture faithfully on film—impossible, perhaps, on stage: it is a phantom town inhabited largely by ghostly presences. Consider, for example, the buildings that actually appear in the novel; consider *all* of them. To begin with, there are private dwellings: Aunt Polly's house, Jeff Thatcher's house (where Becky visits), the Douglas mansion, the Welshman's farm, and the "haunted" house where Tom and Huck so nearly lose their lives. Then there are institutional buildings designed specifically to bedevil an active boy: the church and the schoolhouse. However, all of these—houses, church, school—are places from which an average, energetic male youth is expected to flee: "his" world, the world to be explored and conquered, lies beyond—in lush Edenic woods, a river, and (presumably) a healthy, industrious town of tolerable size. And here the shadow world begins. There is a river; there are woods. But of the town, only menacing fragments await. Two taverns (one housing criminals), a courthouse, a jail, and a deserted slaughterhouse. Nothing more.

Let us be more specific. No stores are mentioned in the novel. No blacksmiths. No livery stable. No bank. Mark Twain, who renders the steamboat's arrival so vibrantly in *Life on the Mississippi*, put no busy wharf in the world of this fiction—no commercial steamboat traffic at all. Every bit of the bustling business that an impressionable reader might impute to Tom Sawyer's world is, in fact, notably absent from the novel; the only downtown buildings that actually do appear in the St. Petersburg of Twain's creation are those few grisly emblems of crime and punishment. Two taverns, a courthouse, a jail, and a deserted slaughterhouse.

Placed against this somber background is a complex society of children, so tightly knit and so emotionally engaging that it tends to dominate the reader's attention. Ben Rogers and Billy Fisher and Joe Harper and Amy Lawrence and Jeff Thatcher: such names in this novel attach to people with specific histories and relationships, friendships and enmities, all of the subtle qualities that make them seem distinctive and "real." The slow accretion of this children's world renders Tom's and Huck's activities with a kind of palpable, three-dimensional plausibility.

> "Say—what is dead cats good for, Huck?"
> "Good for? Cure warts with."

"No! Is that so? I know something that's better."

"I bet you don't. What is it?"

"Why spunk-water."

"Spunk-water! I wouldn't give a dern for spunk-water."

"You wouldn't, wouldn't you? D'you ever try it?"

"No, I hain't. But Bob Tanner did."

"Who told you so?"

"Why he told Jeff Thatcher, and Jeff told Johnny Baker, and Johnny told Jim Hollis, and Jim told Ben Rogers and Ben told a nigger, and the nigger told me. There now!"

The very vividness of these children, then, makes all the more remarkable the peculiar air of vagueness, of faceless generality, that permeates Twain's evocations of most adult gatherings.

Consider these paragraphs describing Muff Potter's capture:

Close upon the hour of noon the whole village was suddenly electrified with the ghastly news. No need of the as yet un-dreamed-of telegraph; the tale flew from man to man, from group to group, from house to house, with little less than telegraphic speed.... Horsemen had departed down all the roads in every direction and the Sheriff "was confident" that he would be captured before night.

All the town was drifting toward the graveyard. Tom's heart-break vanished and he joined the procession.... Arrived at the dreadful place, he wormed his small body through the crowd and saw the dismal spectacle.... He turned, and his eyes met Huckleberry's. Then both looked elsewhere at once, and wondered if anybody had noticed anything in their mutual glance. But everybody was talking....

"Poor fellow!"... "Muff Potter'll hang for this if they catch him!" This was the drift of the remark; and the minister said, "It was a judgment; His hand is here."

Now Tom shivered from head to heel; for his eye fell upon the stolid face of Injun Joe. At this moment the crowd began to sway and struggle, and voices shouted, "It's him! it's him! he's coming himself!"

"Who? Who?" from twenty voices.

"Muff Potter!"...

People in the branches of the trees over Tom's head said he

wasn't trying to get away—he only looked doubtful and
perplexed.

"Infernal impudence!" said a bystander.

Here we have a convocation of most of the townsfolk. Yet not one is given
a name (only the "outsiders"—Muff Potter and Injun Joe). Instead, there is
a torrent of collective nouns: whole village, man to man, group to group,
horsemen, all the town, the crowd, anybody, everybody, the crowd, voices,
people, a bystander. Even the dignitaries remain nameless; they are merely
"the Sheriff" and "the minister." When it is compared with the density of
the scenes depicting children, this collection of citizens becomes vaporous:
as "people" within the novel, they can scarcely be said to exist. No more
than anonymous shadows—appropriate, indeed, to the illusory town of
which they are citizens. Small wonder, then, that films and pictures falsify.
Of necessity they give substance to entities—buildings and businesses and
hurrying, excited people—that either do not exist at all within this fictional
world or are, at best, only partially realized.

Since this is a boy's story, it is only fair to ask what a boy in such a
world might make of himself. Given the character of the town Twain has
created, given the social possibilities of St. Petersburg as we know it through
this novel, what will Tom Sawyer become when he is a man? The question
cannot be answered.

Initially Twain had intended the novel to be a kind of *bildungsroman*: as
Justin Kaplan reports, it was to have had four parts—" '1, Boyhood & youth;
2 y & early manh; 3 the Battle of Life in many lands; 4 (age 37 to [40?].' "
Yet the finished novel shows no sign of this early intention. In fact, Twain
writes his "conclusion" with a kind of defensive bravado: "So endeth this
chronicle. It being strictly a history of a *boy*, it must stop here; the story
could not go much further without becoming the history of a *man*." At least
one reason for the author's decision may be found in the very nature of the
world he was moved to create. There are no available men in it—no men
whom Tom can fancy himself imitating—no newspaper office with a gar-
rulous editor, no general store owner to purvey gossip and candy, no lawyer
lounging in an office buzzing with flies and heavy with the odor of musty
books. Of course there *is* Judge Thatcher, "a fine, portly, middle-aged gentleman with iron-gray hair." But Judge Thatcher presides in the county seat,
twelve miles away; he enters the novel only very briefly in chapter 4 (to
witness Tom's triumph-turned-humiliation in Bible class) and thereafter dis-
appears entirely until chapter 32, when he is summoned to rejoice in the
safe return of the children from the cave. Many adults who have not read

Tom Sawyer since the days of their youth are apt to recall Judge Thatcher as a rather more vivid personage than he truly is in the novel. Perhaps we are recollecting cinematic images, or perhaps our own imaginations supply his presence because we feel compelled to remedy the novel's deficiencies and "normalize" the town. But the stubborn fact remains. The town is not normal, certainly not congenial to a boy's coming of age.

It is, of course, a matriarchy (and in this respect, contrasts markedly with the various patriarchal systems that Huck encounters in his journey down the river), a world that holds small boys in bondage. The town that we are shown in this book is saturated with gentility, that is, with women's notions. A man may dispense Bible tickets or conduct the ceremony on Sundays; but the church service, the Sunday School exercises, the daily ritual of family prayers—these are all clearly defined as fundamental components of something that Aunt Polly (and other women like her) have defined as "duty" or "morality." Similarly, the mayor himself may judge the elocution contest; but this masculine salute to "culture" merely reinforces already established female allegiances to the melancholy and banally "eloquent" in literature. The very opening word of the novel establishes the situation. " 'Tom!' " The boy's name called by his impatient aunt. " 'Tom!' " The demanding tone permeates the novel, no other voice so penetrating or intrusive. What is a male child to do against this diminutive drill master? Surrender is out of the question: the dismal results of capitulation greet him in mournful, not quite masculine figures. Mr. Walters, the superintendent of the Sunday School, "a slim creature of thirty-five, with a sandy goatee and short sandy hair; he wore a stiff standing-collar . . . a fence that compelled a straight lookout ahead, and a turning of the whole body when a side view was required." And, more contemptible, "the Model Boy, Willie Mufferson [who took] as heedful care of his mother as if she were cut glass. He always brought his mother to church, and was the pride of all the matrons. The boys all hated him, he was so good."

Rebellion, however, is no easy thing to manage. Tom cannot bring himself to dislike Aunt Polly. Occasionally, he admits to loving her; and when he genuinely saddens her (as during his disappearance to the island), he discovers that "his heart [is] full of pity for her." Pity and its cousin guilt: these are Aunt Polly's most formidable weapons (no less so for being used without guile). " 'She never licks anybody,' " Tom complains as he sets about beginning to whitewash the fence. " 'She talks awful, but talk don't hurt— anyways it don't if she don't cry.' " Tom might be able to contend with open anger, but he receives only reproaches that insinuate themselves into that budding thing called "conscience." Discovered after a stealthy trip abroad at night, "Tom almost brightened in the hope that he was going to be flogged; but it was not so. His aunt wept over him and asked him how he could go and break her old heart so; and finally told him to go on, and ruin himself and bring her gray hairs with sorrow to the grave, for it was no use for her to try any more. This was worse than a thousand whippings, and Tom's heart was sorer now than his body. He cried, he pleaded for forgiveness, promised to reform over and over again." In Tom's world, female children are no easier to deal with than their adult models. Becky Thatcher rules him by alternating tears with lofty reproaches; and although Tom's angry feelings toward her are a good deal more available to him than any genuinely hostile feelings he might have toward the generation of mothers, he nonetheless continues to wish for a more direct and "manly" emotional code. "He was in a fine rage. . . . He moped into the schoolyard wishing she were a boy, and imagining how he would trounce her if she were."

With no acceptable model of "free" adult masculinity available, Tom does his best to cope with the prevailing feminine system without being irretrievably contaminated by it. His principal recourse is an entire repertoire of games and pranks and superstitions, the unifying motif of which is a struggle for control. Control over his relationship with Aunt Polly is a major area of warfare. Thus the first scene in the book is but one type of behavior that is repeated in ritual form throughout the book. Tom, caught with his hands in the jam jar—about to be switched. " 'My! Look behind you, aunt!' The old lady whirled round, and snatched her skirts out of danger. The lad fled, on the instant, scrambled up the high board fence, and disappeared over it. His Aunt Polly stood surprised a moment, and then broke into a gentle laugh. 'Hang the boy, can't I never learn anything? Ain't he played me tricks enough like that for me to be looking out for him by this time?' " Crawling out his bedroom window at night is another type of such behavior, not important because it permits this or that specific act, but significant as a general assertion of the right to govern his own comings and goings. Bartering is still another type of this behavior. Trading for blue Bible coupons or tricking his playmates into painting the fence—these are superb inventions to win the prizes of a genteel society without ever genuinely submitting to it.

The logical continuation of such stratagems would be actual defiance: the rebellion of authentic adolescence to be followed by a manhood in which Tom and his peers might define the rules by which society is to be governed. But manhood never comes to Tom; anger and defiance remain disguised in the games of childhood.

Twain offers these pranks to us as if they were no more than humorous anecdotes; Aunt Polly is always more disposed to smile at them than to take them seriously. However, an acquiescence to the merely comic in this fiction will blind us to its darker side. A boy who seeks to control himself and his world so thoroughly is a boy deeply and constantly aware of danger—justifiably so, it would seem, for an ominous air of violence hangs over the entire tale. It erupts even into the apparently safe domestic sphere.

When the children depart from their schoolmaster in chapter 21 to begin the lazy summer recess, they leave him disgraced—his gilded, bald pate blazing as the ultimate spectacle in the school's pageant. "The boys were avenged. Vacation had come." Mr. Dobbin (even his name invites laughter) is hilariously humiliated, and he is apt to linger in our memories primarily as the butt of a good joke. Yet for most of the children most of the time, he is a source of genuine terror.

The one "respectable" man whom Tom sees regularly, Mr. Dobbin, is a sadist. Having reached maturity with the unsatisfied ambition to be a doctor, he spends his free time perusing a book of "anatomy" (that is, a book with pictures of naked people in it). His principal active pleasure is lashing the children, and the preparations for the approaching commencement exercises merely provide an excuse to be "severer and more exacting than ever. . . . His rod and his ferule were seldom idle now—at least among the smaller pupils. . . . Mr. Dobbin's lashings were very vigorous ones, too; for although he carried, under his wig, a perfectly bald and shiny head, he had only reached middle age and there was no sign of feebleness in his muscle. As the great day approached, all the tyranny that was in him came to the surface; he seemed to take a vindictive pleasure in punishing the least shortcomings." If the village itself (with taverns, courthouse, jail, and deserted slaughterhouse) is composed of the elements of crime and punishment, then Mr. Dobbin might be construed as one of the executioners—disarmed at only the final moment by the boys' "revenge" and exiting to catcalls and laughter. The joke is a fine exercise in imaginative power, but it does not fully succeed in countering the potency of the masculine "muscle" that is used with such consistent vindictiveness and violence.

Violence is everywhere in Tom's world. Escape to the island does not answer: random, pitiless destruction can find a frightened boy just as lightning, by chance, can blast a great sycamore to fall on the children's camp and signify that catastrophe is never far away.

Clearly, Tom is a major figure in the play of violence, yet his part is not clear. Is he victim or perpetrator? Is the violence outside of him, or is it a cosmic reflection of something that is fundamental to his own nature?

His games, for example, have a most idiosyncratic quality; the rebellion and rage that never fully surface in his dealings with Aunt Polly and the other figures of authority in this matriarchal world find splendid ventilation in fantasy. Richly invigorated by his imagination, Tom can blend the elements of violence and control exactly to suit his fancy. Acquiescent to society's tenets in real life, in daydreams Tom is always a rebel.

> The idea of being a clown recurred to him now, only to fill him with disgust. For frivolity and jokes and spotted tights were an offense, when they intruded themselves upon a spirit that was exalted into the vague and august realm of the romantic. No, he would be a soldier. . . . No—better still, he would join the Indians, and hunt buffaloes and go on the warpath in the mountain ranges and the trackless great plains of the Far West, and away in the future come back a great chief, bristling with feathers, hideous with paint, and prance into Sunday-school, some drowsy summer morning, with a blood-curdling war-whoop, and sear the eyeballs of all his companions with unappeasable envy.

Safe in his own fictional world, Tom participates in carefully constructed rituals of devastation. He and his cohorts may be outlaws of any kind; however, whatever roles they choose, there are always careful sets of regulations to be followed. In games, control reigns supreme: " 'Guy of Guisborne wants no man's pass. Who art thou that—that—' 'Dares to hold such language,' said Tom prompting—for they talked 'by the book,' from memory."

The real import of these rules—this rigid regimentation of boyish fantasy—becomes clear several times in the novel as the children play. "Huck said: 'What does pirates have to do?' Tom said: 'Oh, they have just a bully time—take ships and burn them, and get the money and bury it in awful places in their island. . . .' 'And they carry the women to the island,' said Joe; 'they don't kill the women.' 'No,' assented Tom, 'they don't kill the women—they're too noble.' " And at the conclusion:

> "Tom Sawyer's Gang—it sounds splendid, don't it Huck?"
>
> "Well, it just does, Tom. And who'll we rob?"
>
> "Oh, most anybody. Waylay people—that's mostly the way."
>
> "And kill them?"
>
> "No, not always. Hide them in the cave till they raise a ransom."
>
> "What's a ransom?"
>
> "Money. You make them raise all they can. . . . That's the gen-

eral way. Only you don't kill the women. You shut up the women,
but you don't kill them. . . . It's so in all the books."

Pirates and robbers and Indians. Such are the figures of Tom's creation; and
so long as they remain merely imaginary, governed by the "code" of play,
they are clearly harmless. "You don't kill women. . . . It's so in all the books."

Given the precarious balancing of control and violence in Tom's fantasies, we can easily comprehend his terrified fascination with Injun Joe's
incursions into the "safety" of St. Petersburg. Accidentally witness to Injun
Joe's murderous attack, Tom's first response is characteristic: he writes an
oath in blood, pledging secrecy. "Huck Finn and Tom Sawyer swears they
will keep mum about this and they wish they may Drop down dead in Their
tracks if they ever tell and Rot." It is an essentially "literary" maneuver, and
Tom's superstitious faith in its efficacy is of a piece with the "rules" he has
conned from books about outlaws. However, Injun Joe cannot easily be
relegated to the realm of such villains. It is as if one element in Tom's fantasy
world has torn loose and broken away from him, roaming restlessly—a ruthless predator—genuinely and mortally dangerous.

He has murdered a man, but perversely, he does not flee. Instead, he
loiters about the town in disguise, waiting for the moment to arrive when
he can take "revenge." Humiliated once by the Widow Douglas's husband
(no longer available to the Indian's rage), Joe plans to work his will upon the
surviving mate. " 'Oh, don't kill her! Don't do that!' " his nameless companion
implores.

> "Kill? Who said anything about killing? I would kill *him* if he was
> here; but not her. When you want to get revenge on a woman
> you don't kill her—bosh! you go for her looks. You slit her nos-
> trils—you notch her ears like a sow! . . . I'll tie her to the bed. If
> she bleeds to death, is that my fault? I'll not cry, if she does."

It is almost a parody of Tom's concocted "rules" for outlaws; even Injun Joe
flinches from killing a woman. Sadistic torture (of a clearly sexual nature) is
sufficient.

His grievance is twofold: against the absence of the man who would be
his natural antagonist; and then against the woman who has inherited the
man's property and authority. Seen in this light, his condition is not unlike
the hero's. Tom, denied the example of mature men whom he might emulate,
left with no model to define an adult nature of his own. Tom, adrift in a
matriarchal world—paying the continuous "punishment" of guilt for the
"crime" of his resentment at genteel restraints, conceiving carefully measured

fantasies within which to voice (and mute) his feelings. Injun Joe is Tom's shadow self, a potential for retrogression and destructiveness that cannot be permitted abroad.

Yet genuine vanquishment is no easy task. No other adult male plays so dominant a role in the novel as Injun Joe. Indeed, no other male's name save Huck's and Tom's is uttered so often. The only contender for adult masculine prominence is that other angry man, Mr. Dobbin. But the schoolmaster's vicious instincts are, in the end, susceptible to control through humor: he can be humiliated and disarmed by means of a practical joke. After all is said and done, he is an "acceptable" male, that is, a domesticated creature. The Indian, an outcast and a savage, is unpredictable; he may turn fury upon the villagers or act as ultimate executioner for Tom. When Tom's tentative literary gestures prove insufficient, desperate remedies are necessary. Twain invokes the ultimate adventure. Death.

Death has several meanings for Tom. On the one hand, it is the final loss of self—a relinquishment of control that is both attractive and frightening. Confronted with reverses, Tom sometimes longs for the blissful passivity of death, deterred primarily by the sneaking fear that "guilt" might be "punishable" even in the unknown land to which he would travel. "It seemed to him that life was but a trouble, at best, and he more than half envied Jimmy Hodges, so lately released, it must be very peaceful, he thought, to lie and slumber and dream forever and ever, with the wind whispering through the tree and caressing the grass and the flowers over the grave, and nothing to bother and grieve about, ever any more. If he only had a clean Sunday-school record he could be willing to go, and be done with it all."

On the other hand, properly managed, "death" might be the ultimate assertion of control, the means a boy might use in this puzzling female world to win a satisfactory "self" after all. "Ah," Tom's fantasy runs, "if he could only die *temporarily!*"

The triumph of "temporary death" and the fulfillment of that universal fantasy—to attend one's own funeral and hear the tearful eulogies and then to parade boldly down the aisle (patently and impudently alive)— is the central event in the novel. The escapade is not without its trials: a terrible lonesomeness during the self-imposed banishment and a general sense of emptiness whenever Tom falls to "gazing longingly across the wide river to where the village lay drowsing in the sun." Yet the victory is more than worth the pain. Temporarily, at least, Tom's fondest ambitions for himself have come true. "What a hero Tom was become, now! He did not go skipping and prancing, but moved with a dignified swagger as became a pirate who felt that the public eye was on him." He has definitely become "somebody" for a while—and he has achieved the identity entirely upon his own terms.

Yet this central miracle of resurrection is merely a rehearsal. Its results are not permanent, and Tom must once again submit to death and rebirth in order to dispatch the specter of Injun Joe forever.

The escapade begins lightheartedly enough: a party and a picnic up river into the countryside. Yet this moderated excursion into wilderness turns nightmare in the depths of the cave. "It was said that one might wander days and nights together through its intricate tangle of rifts and chasms, and never find the end of the cave. . . . No man 'knew' the cave. That was an impossible thing." Existing out of time, the cave is a remnant of man's prehistory—a dark and savage place, both fascinating and deadly. Once lost in the cave, Tom and Becky must face their elemental needs—hunger, thirst, and the horror, now quite real, of extinction. For Tom alone, an additional confrontation awaits: he stumbles upon Injun Joe, who has taken refuge in this uttermost region. The temptation to despair is very great; however, "hunger and wretchedness rise superior to fears in the long run. . . . [Tom] felt willing to risk Injun Joe and all other terrors." Thus he begins his long struggle out. Holding a length of a string lest he be separated from Becky, he tries one dark pathway, then another, then "a third to the fullest stretch of the kite-line, and was about to turn back when he glimpsed a far-off speck that looked like daylight; dropped the line and groped toward it, pushed his head and shoulders through a small hole and saw the broad Mississippi rolling by!" Born again upon his beloved river, Tom has earned his reward.

Afterwards, as Tom recounts his adventures to an admiring audience, he becomes a "hero" once again—now the hero of his own adventure story. Even more, he has become rich from finding buried treasure; Judge Thatcher conceives a great opinion of his future and says that he hopes "to see Tom a great lawyer or a great soldier some day." Endowed with an excess of acceptable identities which have been conferred upon him as the result of his exploits (no clearer, certainly, about the particulars of the adult male roles identified by them, but nonetheless christened, as it were, into the "rightful" inheritance of them), Tom seems to have surmounted the deficiencies of his world.

Yet it is a hollow victory after all. Just as Tom must take on faith the pronouncement of his future as a "great lawyer" or a "great soldier" (having no first-hand information about these occupations), so we must accept the validity of his "triumph." The necessary condition for Tom's final peace of mind (and for his acquisition of the fortune) is the elimination of Injun Joe. And this event occurs quite accidentally. Taking the children's peril as a warning, the villagers have shut the big door to the cave and triple-bolted it, trapping Injun Joe inside. When the full consequences of the act are discovered, it is too late; the outcast has died. "Injun Joe lay stretched upon the ground, dead, with his face close to the crack of the door. . . . Tom was touched, for he knew by his own experience how this wretch had suffered. . . . Nevertheless he felt an abounding sense of relief and security, now."

Tom's final identification with the savage, valid as it certainly is, gives the lie to the conclusion of this tale. What do they share? Something irrational and atavistic, something ineradicable in human nature. Anger, perhaps; violence, perhaps. Some unnamed, timeless element.

> The poor unfortunate had starved to death. In one place near at hand, a stalagmite had been slowly growing up from the ground for ages, builded by the water-drip from a stalactite overhead. The captive had broken off the stalagmite, and upon the stump had placed a stone, wherein he had scooped a shallow hollow to catch the precious drop that fell once in every three minutes with the dreary regularity of a clock-tick—a dessert-spoonful once in four-and-twenty hours. That drop was falling when the Pyramids were new; when Troy fell; when the foundations of Rome were laid; when Christ was crucified; when the Conqueror created the British empire; when Columbus sailed; when the massacre at Lexington was "news." It is falling now; it will still be falling when all these things shall have sunk down the afternoon of history and the twilight of tradition and been swallowed up in the thick night of oblivion. . . . It is many and many a year since the hapless half-breed scooped out the stone to catch the priceless drops, but to this day the tourist stares longest at that pathetic stone and that slow-dropping water when he comes to see the wonders of McDougal's Cave. Injun Joe's cup stands first in the list of the cavern's marvels; even "Aladin's Palace" cannot rival it.

Whatever Injun Joe represents in this fiction—whatever his complex relationship may be to Tom—he cannot be dealt with by summary banishment. Shut up by fiat; locked away. It is an ending with no resolution at all.

Taken seriously as a psychological recommendation, the ultimate disposition of the problem of Injun Joe offers no solution but that of denial. Lock away the small boy's anger; lock away his anti-social impulses; shut up his resentments at this totally feminine world; stifle rebellion; ignore adult male hostility: they are all too dangerous to traffic with.

Thus Tom's final "self" as we see it in this novel is a tragic capitulation: he has accommodated himself to the oddities of his environment and given over resistance. A resolution to the story is established not by changing the bizarre quality of the fictional world (not even by confronting it), but by contorting the small hero into compliance. He becomes that worst of all possible things—a "Model Boy"—the voice of conformity in a genteel society. Huck complains. " 'The widder eats by a bell. . . . Everybody's so awful reg'lar a body can't stand it.' " And Tom responds. " 'Well, everybody does that way, Huck. . . . If you'll try this thing just awhile longer you'll come to like it. . . . Huck, we can't let you into the gang if you ain't respectable you know.' "

He has even lost his sense of humor.

The fault is Twain's, of course. Tom has earned the right to "be somebody"; but his creator's vision has faltered. Twain averts his attention from the struggle that should be central and shrinks from uncivilized inclinations. In the end, his hero must settle for security in a world that will always be run by its women.

However, Huck continues doubtful. And in his own book, he pursues the quest for fathers. Fully to understand his needs, we must know—exactly—where he has been before. Here, in *The Adventures of Tom Sawyer*.

BRUCE MICHELSON

Deus Ludens: The Shaping
of Mark Twain's Mysterious Stranger

"What is His Allness?"
"I pass."
"You which?"
"Pass. Theological expression."
—"No.44, The Mysterious Stranger"

Knowing more than ever now about the gloom of Mark Twain's final
years, we can imagine his miseries driving him into an artistic senility, a
senility in which he spent year after year, ream after ream of manuscript
"proving" to nobody that nothing and nobody are of any consequence, that
life is meaningless, reality a lie. We cannot pretend that the last fables, chief
among them the three variations on the Mysterious Stranger tale, reveal any
reconciliation with life, or that the theology in these stories will hold water,
or that as stories they are without serious flaw. But what the Stranger tales
do attempt, what kind of struggle they represent, needs considerable clari-
fication. Mark Twain's motives and his experiment are commonly misunderstood, and consequently our idea of how the tales complete his life in
literature remains off balance. Much has been said recently about the three
stages the story passed through; but still we lack solid explanations why
Twain began, in succession, three different tales, why he suddenly abandoned Philip Traum after going so far with him, brought a very different
emissary from Hell to the world of Tom and Huck, and finally completed
the story he did—about a strange adolescent named "Forty-Four" and an

From *Novel: A Forum on Fiction* 14, no. 1 (Fall 1980). © 1980 by Novel Corp.

anachronistic print shop in medieval Austria. Just what was it, especially in that last, meandering rendition, that Mark Twain was trying to work out? By way of an answer, I shall try to clarify here some of the technical problems Mark Twain was struggling with in each phase the story passed through— problems that grew out of a collision of his theme with the most basic requirements of his fiction—and then outline the complex solution he was moving towards in the tale he completed. For while the Stranger stories conceal no ingenious resolutions, no comforting last-minute transcendences, they do achieve a marvelous accommodation among style, storytelling, and an all-but-intractable theme. We need to understand this achievement better, for it has no match in the other works of Mark Twain's final decade. And though we must limit what we can infer from his breakthrough, it strongly suggests that for a time, however brief, there came back to Mark Twain a skill, an insight, and a spirit which we might otherwise assume was long gone.

Throughout the *Letters from the Earth, What is Man?*, and the numerous short pieces that Twain worked on after 1895, the same paradoxical truths assert themselves again and again: first, that even in his most agnostic moments, Mark Twain usually managed to keep his pen "warmed up" for the only God he could sensibly vilify: the finite conception of God that man develops out of his own stupidity; and second, that whenever God and the human condition are Twain's targets, he runs into both structural and stylistic trouble. Those most admirable qualities in his storytelling and his prose, his economy, his grace, his playfulness, drift out of his reach, and his late writings all too frequently deteriorate into mechanical fables or mere rant. Most readers of these works seem to agree that before the Mysterious Stranger experiment, Twain the storyteller and Twain the accuser of mankind's God have not mixed well at all. This is the common way now of explaining the challenge which all three versions of the Stranger tale try to face: to tell a good story somehow, a Mark-Twain story with vitality, wit, and grace, and still speak Twain's piece on God, fate, and mankind's muddled theistic imagination. But we can get a good deal farther in understanding the method of these tales if we can describe this general challenge in a somewhat different way.

Critics have commonly noticed that Mark Twain's masterworks are filled with people who go on holidays and play games: happy tourists, romantic greenhorns, pre-adolescent pranksters, giddy young recruits, Connecticut tinkers—the list is a long one. Play, games, make-believe, these are constant themes in the major fiction and constant obsessions in the man. Twain was himself a notorious game-player and practical joker, the greatest of our writers, perhaps, in recreating the make-believe of children and childlike adults; and very early on he had comprehended that any God who would bother with the petty affairs of mankind must do so as a cosmic Tom Sawyer, an all-powerful Player who amuses Himself recklessly at the world's expense. Such an idea can be traced back, in Twain's writings, earlier than *The Innocents Abroad*. In the *Alta California* letters from which Twain's first real book developed, there is a sketch for an "Apocryphal New Testament," in which Jesus returns to the earth as a playful boy:

> Jesus and other boys play together and make clay figures of animals. Jesus causes them to walk; also makes clay birds which he causes to fly, and eat and drink. The children's parents are alarmed and take Jesus for a sorcerer, and order them to seek better company. He goes on to the dyer's shop and throws all the clothes into the fire and works a miracle therewith. Whereupon the bystanders praise God.

This sketch was apparently as far as the idea was developed in writing, until Philip Traum comes to Eseldorf nearly forty years later, in Twain's first extended experiment with building stories around a playful, childlike God. In the intervening decades he offers up human gamesters in quantity, but never a divine Player, a Jesus or a Satan cavorting through the human amusement park. If this suggests some failure of the imagination, it should also suggest what an enormous obstacle the idea poses to viable fiction. An effective story about the play of children, divine or otherwise, must necessarily work at least to some extent as a vicarious play experience. A reader must be able to believe in the play *as* play, to sense its momentary rapture, its power to remove the absorbed player to a world apart from the everyday and the "real," to create special bonds among the players as enthralled participants in a shared illusion. As most authorities on the subject insist, the player must be sufficiently playful, making us feel his intensity as we watch him. No one in American literature knew better how to create such vicarious play-experiences than Mark Twain. No one seems to doubt Tom Sawyer's total involvement in his make-believe, thoughtless and ill-timed as it often is; and when Twain as the young tourist or the cub pilot sets out to have "ever such a fine time," to turn his fictive imagination loose on some dusty, unenchanted reality and make magic out of it, the spell he casts on himself is cast over the reader at the same time. But what a different matter it is to enchant with the play of gods. So much seems to stand in the way: the deadening solemnity that commonly surrounds the Divine, the damage that omnipotence necessarily wreaks on the tension and challenge of any make-believe, the mortal threat that such an unavoidably didactic arrangement poses to the life of fiction. And finally, there is this about play: that by nature it is an affirmative act when it is true, an act of celebration which, according to Huizinga, brings joy, promotes mystery, stirs wonder. The true player is happy in his play, not detached and cool; the player charms us much more than he instructs. And so we can come upon a central problem of the Stranger story from another angle: how are these essential attributes of true play, which reveal themselves to such advantage in the works of Mark Twain's major phase, to be reconciled with Mark Twain's case against life?

Bearing in mind the problems that play and cosmic fables can cause each other, one needs to go a step further, to recollect the special influence that play has upon the shape and tone of Mark Twain's earlier works, and what play commonly signifies when it turns up there. Not simply play and mood, but play and structure have had much to do with each other. When Twain sets a character loose to amuse himself in the world, the festivity has a way of reverberating in the narrative stance. The energy, the exuberant looseness of Twain's best writings have been accounted for variously; but most readers seem to agree that there is some sort of connection between this freewheeling, improvisatory storytelling and the play and games in the story told. Twain's own fun on tour, or Tom Sawyer's as master of local revels, or Hank Morgan's as master of a nation, finds its way into the language and structure of the novel. Narrative voices may come and go, scenes, anecdotes and whole plotlines may drift in and out of the pages, jokes and sideline issues pop up unexpectedly, sometimes to get out of hand—all reinforcing *our* sense of the pleasure someone has in simply telling the story. How often it is that loose plot structures, false leads, and altered purposes show us Mark Twain in full genius and high spirits—his genius and his high spirits being perhaps inseparable. In contrast, the controlled, linear, single-minded Mark Twain is the Twain of "Tom Sawyer Abroad" and *Personal Recollections of Joan of Arc*, the tidier mind-set of decidedly minor works. The point is not that flawed books are better than tidy ones, but rather that Twain's major fiction shows a kind of faith *in* fiction, a willingness to give himself over to the story the way a child gives all to a game of make-believe. And signs of that strange faith, when they show themselves in these final writings, should be taken seriously by anyone trying to understand Mark Twain's meaning and mind.

Among the work notes to the "Eseldorf" manuscript, the first version of the Stranger story, and the one Paine drew on most heavily to make the Philip Traum tale everyone knows, we find these lines, copied from Mary

Baker Eddy's *Science and Health*, a book Twain had led the country in laughing
at:

> Finite belief can never do justice to truth in any direction. It limits
> all things and would compress Mind, which is infinite, into a
> skullbone.

Finite, banal belief: this is the central theme of every version of *The
Mysterious Stranger*, and it is never clearer than here in the first manuscript
(without, we must recall, the ending Paine borrowed from the final one).
This is Twain's first attempt to build a story around the notion of Deus as
Deus Ludens, around God as a divine, omnipotent, playful Tom Sawyer.
The story's failure, apparently, provided him with a late education in re-
conciling games, gods, and literary necessities.

The stage is set promisingly enough. Passing into the tale through a
landscape of superstitions, we arrive convinced that Mark Twain's Austria,
1702, is a place where the idea of a personal God, the god of the Miss Watsons
and backcountry ministers of the world, has been carried to its inevitable,
laughable, frightening limits. Father Adolf and Frau Marx provide a prologue
as puppets in a kind of theological Punch-and-Judy show of absurd resti-
tutions and "miracles": the world of Eseldorf believes in a meddlesome Deity,
"personal" to the point of triviality. A god with a human face is what the
people insist on; and a human God is what they get. Philip Traum, angel,
alias Satan, nephew to the Prince of Darkness, is one of the Heavenly Host;
the name is meant to do what the name of Satan is always meant for in
Twain's stories, letters and humorous speeches: to thumb a nose at tidy
theistic arrangements of the universe, the clean division of the world into
Miss Watson's Heaven and everyone else's hell. There is really no question
whom Philip is meant to represent here. Seeking playmates and amusements
in Eseldorf, leading the others and deciding the game, Satan is a caricature
of a personal God; he is an omnipotent Tom Sawyer on a permanent holiday,
and those who have prayed for God's intervention in their small mortal lives
now get much more than they bargained for. The world is of course Philip's
playground; nothing to him is "for keeps," or of any consequence at all. And
just as obvious and familiar are the themes of Eseldorf: the utter inconse-
quence of humanity in the divine perspective, and the trivial game that human
life must seem to any infinite Being who might bother with it.

But this is precisely the paradox which spoils the story: Satan comes to
mankind as a playful child, spreading "rapture" among his mortal playmates;
yet there is no rapture at all in Philip himself. His tranquil indifference is
ruinously out of keeping with the spirit of true play. He does what the boys

want him to, improvises spectacular musical entertainments, wins chess games in a flash, performs miracles, impersonations, tightrope acts; but always there is that cool detachment about him, and his play strikes us, consciously or otherwise, as only gesture, gesture without substance, involvement, or delight. True play must catch and transform the player—on this issue Huizinga, Caillois, and most other authorities are in full agreement; and without this intensity, this enthrallment, play is hollow and false. Twain may mean to give us God the Player, but what we end up with is God the Lecturer, the teacher of ontological "truth"; and as such Satan makes an inept playmate for Theodor, Nikolaus, and Seppi. Never does Philip surrender himself to play's illusions; never does he lose himself in a fiction. He has been in town only a moment when he begins explaining himself, the nature of Reality, and the place of man in the universe:

> "Why, naturally I look like a boy, for that is what I am. With us, what you call time is a spacious thing; it takes a long stretch of it to grow an angel to full age." There was a question in my mind, and he turned to me and answered it: "I am sixteen thousand years old—counting as you count." Then he turned to Nikolaus and said, "No, the Fall did not affect me nor the rest of the relationship. It was only he that I was named for who ate of the fruit of the tree and then beguiled the man and the woman with it. We others are still ignorant of sin; we are not able to commit it; we are without blemish, and shall abide in that estate always. We—" Two of the little workmen were quarreling, and in buzzing little bumble-bee voices they were cursing and swearing at each other; now came blows and blood, then they locked themselves together in a life-and-death struggle. Satan reached out his hand and crushed the life out of them with his fingers, threw them away, wiped the red from his fingers on his handkerchief and went on talking where he had left off: "We cannot do wrong; neither have we any disposition to do it, for we do not know what it is."

And a moment later:

> "The *difference* between man and *me*? The *difference* between a mortal and an immortal? between a clod and a spirit?" He picked up a wood-louse that was creeping along a piece of bark: "What is the difference between Homer and this? between Caesar and this?"

I said—

"One cannot compare things which by their nature and by the interval between them are not comparable."

"You have answered your own question," he said. "I will expand it. Man is made of dirt—I *saw* him made. I am not made of dirt. Man is a museum of disgusting diseases, a home of impurities; he comes to-day and is gone to-morrow, he begins as dirt and departs as a stench; I am of the aristocracy of the Imperishables. And man has the Moral Sense. You understand? he has the Moral Sense. That would seem to be difference enough between us, all by itself."

If all this is true, why has Satan come? In chapter 6, thinking over the cavalcade of woes since young Satan's arrival, Theodor decides that the Stranger is "the only person concerned that got any rapture out of it." But even that rapture is nearly impossible for us to believe. When in that same chapter Philip reappears and sweeps Theodor off to China, ostensibly for a lark, there is, as usual, no indication that Satan delights in his holiday. In the midst of the excursion, as he delivers his "red spider and the elephant" sermon, he seems to deny again that he could take any pleasure, find even satisfactory challenge, in the trivialities of this world:

Man is to me as the red spider is to the elephant. The elephant has nothing against the spider, he cannot get down to that remote level—I have nothing against man. The elephant is indifferent, I am indifferent. The elephant would not take the trouble to do the spider an ill turn; if he took the notion he might do him a good turn, if it came in his way and cost him nothing. I have done men good service, but no ill turns.

Philip Traum is a mysterious stranger indeed, offering no excuse for his presence other than this joyless teaching of inconsequential life-forms, something they cannot understand. This, then, is the hollow ring one hears in the first version of *The Mysterious Stranger*; and this gives us some idea why Mark Twain abandoned Philip Traum, whose spoil-sport coolness and spiritless, lesson-teaching mock play is paralleled by a spiritlessness in Mark Twain's telling of the tale. While the specific connections of play with literary creativity are finally unresolvable, the vitality of Twain's fiction apparently has much to do with his own involvement in his characters and in the very act of storytelling, a self-loss in the make-believe of the story—a self-loss much like that of fictive, improvisatory play. In contrast to the works of

Twain's major phase, "Eseldorf" is oddly linear, monochromatic in tone. Satan never escapes from Mark Twain's didactic nets the way Huck does, the way Hank Morgan does, the way Mark Twain the narrator does in the earliest of his book-length triumphs. Or rather, when Satan does show signs of getting away, Twain drops the story. He abandons it not because Satan's escape into India, royal palaces, and diamonds hidden in magic balls has brought the tale to ruin, for much foolery of this sort turns up again in "Number 44." Rather, Mark Twain here finds himself at a crossroads: he might develop this genuinely playful stranger who begins to emerge at the last, and give that play impulse its own head in transforming the story; or he might drop the game-playing altogether and transform his Stranger into an earnest messiah of hopelessness. Either option suggests a way out of the trap of "Eseldorf"; but to pursue those options new stories were called for. Twain broke off here to follow his playful-serious Stranger first down one path, then down the other. Choosing the path of the serious Stranger first, briefly, he finally followed the story of the truly playful Stranger to a far better fruition.

> "The fundamental change wrought in man's nature by my father's conduct must remain—it is permanent; but a part of its burden of evil consequences can be lifted from your race, and I will undertake it. Will you help?"

Thus the young Stranger (calling himself Forty-Four now) of the "Schoolhouse Hill" manuscript, a fragment too brief to make its intentions nearly as clear as either "Eseldorf" or "Number 44, the Mysterious Stranger." Forty-Four is straight from Hell, now, not Heaven; he is a son to Satan, no longer one of the nephews, and the divine visitor's portentous names have been dropped for this puzzling, ludicrous number. Forty-Four is a paragon of seriousness and purpose; but "Schoolhouse Hill" is not simply a false step in that direction. In spite of the great difference between the deadpan boy who turns up here and the "44" who brings bedlam to a print shop in the last version, Mark Twain is beginning to find his grip on the essential story,— or rather, in the manner of his best writings, he is beginning to let the story take hold of itself. First, the boy visitor, for all his supernatural brains and power, is now something more like a *true* stranger and a true boy. Instead of Philip Traum's jaded awareness of the ways of mankind, we have instead a Forty-Four who, at the outset, cannot speak the language, cannot understand bullies or schoolyard fights, or death or pipe smoking, cannot imagine why anyone would trouble themselves over saving total strangers caught in a blizzard. Forty-Four knows the ways of a thousand planets, yet mankind has mysteries to teach him. This naiveté is not just a charming adornment, it signals a fundamental shift in Mark Twain's relationship to the Stranger idea. Fable is transforming into a story, and the Stranger into a character with weaknesses to match his power. Further, Mark Twain is beginning to sense the comic possibilities of the coming of the Stranger; he is beginning to improvise, to play with the idea. We begin to get interludes which enrich the story and suggest a pleasure in the mere telling of it, rather than a sober advancement of a sober theme. Aunt Rachel—and Mark Twain—on the candles Forty-Four has conjured up for the Hotchkiss House:

> "Dat new cannel's *wax!*"
> "Oh, come!"
> "Fo Gawd she is. White as Miss Guthrie's store-teeth."
> A delicate flattery-shot, neatly put. The widow Guthrie, 56 and dressed for 25, was pleased, and exhibited a girlish embarrassment that was very pretty. She was excusably vain of her false teeth, the only ones in the town; a costly luxury, and a fine and showy contrast with the prevailing mouth equipment of both old and young—the kind of sharp contrast which white-washed palings make with a charred stump-fence.

Moreover, the satire on conventional theism is extended further in the direction it should sensibly take. Philip Traum comes from a realm of strangeness and beauty; there is a grand, solemn enchantment to those moments when he offers a glimpse of his better home. But Forty-Four's Hell is itself a spoof on the preposterous tenets of conventional belief. Witness the sudden appearance of his attendant devils, "real little devils," in the Hotchkiss parlor:

> The servants became visible; all the room was crowded with them. Trim and shapely little fellows they were, velvety little red fellows, with short horns on their heads and spiked tails at the other end; and those that stood, stood in metal plates, and those that sat—on chairs, in a row upon settees, and on top of the bookcase with their legs dangling—had metal plates under them—"to keep from scorching the furniture," the boy quietly explained, "these have come but this moment, and of course are hot, yet."

In short, there is more whim, more improvisation in "Schoolhouse Hill," even though the piece is doomed by a rigidity that Twain still has not shaken off. There is real progress here: the lecturing unsatisfactory boy-sage of "Eseldorf" has dropped away, yet in his place now is a simple, unsatisfactory mechanical reversal of Christian convention. The son of Satan, straight from Hell, is kind, helpful, respectful; his red demons are models of politeness and efficiency; he is on a Christlike quest to set the world right, and so on. Conventional theism stood neatly on its head—a fine source of true comedy at least, but what hope is there yet for a full, rich story? Mark Twain's own play impulse has broken out of its confinement. It is clashing now with the fixedness of the tale's basic arrangements. For good or ill, a more festive mood is making itself felt in his storytelling, and the Stranger tale had to change again to accommodate it, if the story was to make a genuine escape from tract.

But there may be one more recognition, more important than any structural or aesthetic discovery behind the last and best of the Stranger stories— an ontological recognition, growing straight out of both his own despair and his unextinguishable play-impulse: if man's God, as man has conceived him, is truly a gamester and practical joker, then a story about the antics of this Tom Sawyer-God, a story meant to dispel banal imaginings and confront man with the mystery *behind* the Gamester, should *itself* be an act of celebration of that mystery. To put in another way, a story about a playful God must serve two ends: the play must reveal the essential foolishness of the God we imagine, and it must celebrate the God we cannot imagine—the Unknown, the "God beyond God" to borrow the famous phrase from Paul Tillich. True play and the sacred always have much to do with each other, and so the potential in the story was enormous for solving its own greatest problem. The divine Improvisor, and Twain's own talent and love for improvisation, may have offered him more than the intense, momentary pleasures of yarn-spinning. A truly playful Stranger would be truly mysterious, as well as more effectively satiric. And there is reason to think that it *was* mystery that Mark Twain sought for in his last version of the tale—not mere nihilism and misanthropy. Only that last manuscript was titled "The Mysterious Stranger," suggesting that Mark Twain had fully recognized that without mystery the teleological farce made no sense at all. The problem he faced now was this: how to balance his rejection of theological theism with an affirmation, however dim, of the possibility of something greater than the limited, man-conceived, theistic God? There is no pretending that "No. 44, The Mysterious Stranger" is a perfect answer. But in understanding how this tale works in comparison to its predecessors, we can marvel at how close Mark Twain finally came.

The Stranger who comes in now is younger, psychologically, as well as more mysterious. His bloodlines are perfectly obscure, and without even a shirttail connection to God or Satan, he arrives in Stein's print shop as a vulnerable innocent, more capricious and more needful of companionship than any of his surrogates. He seems fully a boy now—immature for his seventeen years—and certainly neither the teacher nor the messiah of Truth. Befriended first only by the house watchdog, the Stranger endures chapter after chapter of abuse, working his miracles only to aid those few who secretly befriend him. He comes to the world as a kind of supernatural Oliver Twist; for all his power to stop bullies, summon invisible help for emergencies, and bring hot bedtime drinks out of thin air, there is a pathos about Forty-Four now. Not only does he look like a "singed cat," he apparently feels his isolation acutely, and rejoices like a true child in August's stealthy attempts to relieve it. There are no practical jokes, no games from him—yet. He is the first magic-working Stranger were are cajoled into both liking and pitying.

All this, of course, turns out to be the set-up for one long practical joke. That, finally, is the structure the tale follows: that of one great practical joke. In chapter 15, the rug is pulled out from beneath us. Forty-Four seems to be under a sentence of death from the magician Balthasar Hoffman—we have as yet no reason to suspect that Forty-Four is the real worker of the magic— and August resolves to give himself to the "rescuing of this endangered soul." A little serious theology is all it takes to spring the trap: mention God and the Divine order of things, and suddenly our meek and suffering servant is capering on the ceiling:

> "*You* pray if you like—never mind me, I will amuse myself with a curious toy if it won't disturb you."
>
> He got a little steel thing out of his pocket and set it between his teeth, remarking "it's a jew's harp—the niggers use it" and began to buffet out of it a most urgent and strenuous and vibrant and exceedingly gay and inspiriting kind of music, and at the same time he went violently springing and capering and swooping and swirling all up and down the room in a way to banish prayer and make a person dizzy to look at him; and now and then he would utter the excess of his joy in a wild whoop, and at other times he would leap into the air and spin there head over heels for as much as a minute like a wheel, and so frightfully fast that he was all webbed together and you could hear him buzz. And he kept perfect time to his music all the while. It was a most extravagant and stirring and heathen performance.

From this point on the circus is in town, the Feast of Fools is declared, and prayer and pity are banished. The suffering little Christ-figure has been swept away by the Supreme joker, Show-off, Thrillseeker—and the play of this new Stranger is both convincing and infectious. Forty-Four can truly lose himself in his fun; August, by the sheer rambling run of his narration

in the above paragraph, is certainly caught up too. And what of Mark Twain?
The exuberance that sweeps into the prose at this point, the variety of jests
and sports and whatnot that heap into the story hereafter, and most importantly the sheer affection Mark Twain shows for the fun-loving, childlike
Forty-Four, all demonstrate that Twain has begun to delight in this playful
Stranger rather than merely to use him. One way or another, theologically,
emotionally or otherwise, Twain's last long story is moving towards some
kind of celebration. How else can we explain moments like this, as Forty-
Four, our all-wise but marvelously undidactic and unjaded divinity, introduces eighteenth-century Austria to the joys of downhome eating:

> "Hot corn-pone from Arkansas—split it, butter it, close your eyes
> and enjoy! Fried spring chicken—milk and flour gravy—from
> Alabama. Try it, and grieve for the angels, for they have it not!
> Cream smothered strawberries, with the priarie dew still on
> them—let them melt in your mouth, and don't try to say what
> you feel! Coffee from Vienna—fluffed cream—two pellets of sac-
> charin—drink and have compassion for Olympian gods that know
> only nectar!"
>   I ate, I drank, I reveled in those alien wonders; truly I was in
> Paradise!
>   "It is intoxication," I said, "it is delirium!"
>   "It's a jag!" he responded.

Indeed it is, and the rest of the story is also a jag. For the first time in
the Stranger experiments, for the first time in ten years, Twain is trusting
his tale to a child who ingeniously plays, plays more wildly and capriciously
and truly, in fact, than Tom Sawyer ever did. There is the constant succession of disguises: Forty-Four's taste for masquerade serves no purpose. His
poses as the magician, as the old man, as Mr. Bones from the minstrel show
are for fun—his fun, and Twain's as well.

Still more important is the fact that Forty-Four, as a true player, respects
the fragility of make-believe, puts himself wholeheartedly into play's illusions, and takes enormous delight in doing the trick right, in showing off,
in promoting the festivities. As a true player, he puts himself on the line.
He carries off his games and jests with innocent self-satisfaction. If he is
unsuccessful or unappreciated, he is crushed. After the wild performance
with the Jew's harp:

> He came and sat down by me and rested his hand on my knee
> in his winning way, and smiled his beautiful smile, and asked me

how I liked it. It was so evident that he was expecting a compliment, that I was obliged to furnish it. I had not the heart to
hurt him, and he so innocently proud of his insane exhibition. I
could not expose to him how undignified it was, and how degrading, and how difficult it had been for me to stand it through;
I forced myself to say it was "ideal—*more* than ideal;" which was
of course a perfectly meaningless phrase, but he was just hungry
enough for a compliment to make him think this was one, and
also make him overlook what was going on in my mind; so his
face was fairly radiant with thanks and happiness, and he im-
pulsively hugged me and said—

"It's lovely of you to like it so. I'll do it again!"

And as he begins his wonderfully incongruous performance as Mr. Bones:

Then out of nowhere he got that thing that he called a banjo, and
sat down and propped his left ancle on his right knee, and canted
his bucket-hat a little further and more gallusly over his ear, and
rested the banjo in his lap, and set the grip of his left fingers on
the neck of it high up, and fetched a brisk and most thrilling rake
across the strings low down, giving his head a toss of satisfaction,
as much to say "I reckon *that* gets in to where you live, oh I guess
not!"

This is the true child, a spirited, vulnerable, thoroughly likable child
who can be thoughtless, asinine, argumentative, even "leather-headed" in
his self-consuming play. Sarcasm is lost on his divine but naive ear, and
when August must talk this friend out of harebrained ideas, he must play
the teacher as much as the disciple. At times the helpless human seems to
play the stern parent of the playful god:

"Now then, after we've got them killed—"

"Damnation, we are not *going* to kill them!—now don't say
another word about it; it's a perfectly atrocious idea; I should
think you would be ashamed of it; and ashamed to hang to it and
stick to it the way you do, and be so reluctant to give it up. Why,
you act as if it was a child, and the first one you ever had."

He was crushed, and looked it. It hurt me to see him look
cowed, that way; it made me feel mean, and as if I had struck a
dumb animal that had been doing the best it knew how, and not
meaning any harm; and at bottom I was vexed at myself for being
so rough with him at such a time; for *I* know at a glance when

he has a leather-headed mood on, and that he is not responsible
when his brains have gone mushy; but I just couldn't pull myself
together right off and say the gentle word and pet away the hurt
I had given.

Once the joke has been sprung on us, the series of jags that follows
hardly makes for a tidy narrative. There is much about transforming a servant
girl into a housecat, including some poetry recitations in "catapult, or ca-
taplasm, or whatever one might call that tongue." There are Dream-Selves
and Waking-Selves and a slapstick comedy of errors and love; there are
rambling, funny, gratuitous variations on Mary Baker Eddy and "Christian
Silence," in which theology is explained as a kind of poker. There are "effects"
to top Hank Morgan's—not only an eclipse, but a reversal of time as well.
And finally a grand Assembly of the Dead, not as procession to teach August
and the reader some moral lesson, but a parade for the sheer spectacle of it.

What difference does all this make, that on the third try, the divine
Player becomes a real player and the play real play, wild and exuberant
enough to tie the story itself in knots? Indeed it makes a great difference.
We have seen already that a certain boisterousness, an air of celebration, has
come back to Twain's prose after long absence, back into the tone and fabric
of his fiction; but there is something further, and still more important to
notice. To recognize what Twain has achieved with his playful stranger is
to have a vital clue—perhaps the only textual clue—to making any sense of
the ending of the tale, the ending that has been worried over since Paine
attached it to the wrong story sixty years ago.

Many of the interpretators—and they are not scarce—of the famous
"dream conclusion" overlook one or another important contradiction in those
last hundred-odd lines, some ontological short-circuit which damages any
attempt at a solipsistic, or nihilistic or cautiously theistic reading. We shall
never understand that conclusion any better unless we recognize how it grows
out of and completes the particular story it ends—and what Forty-Four's
previous antics have to do with it. Forty-Four's genuine, convincing, playful
rampage has disrupted everything else, wrecking the sentimental melodrama
that the first dozen chapters set up, boggling all our expectations and logical
plot developments, confounding our sense of individual characters, our sense
of place and time, and upsetting any effort by anybody in the story to be
logical and serious. The world of logic, the tidy imagination confined by the
skull-bone, the very human faculties which create the banal theistic God, all
these are put to rout—and it is Forty-Four's play that does the job. As readers,
we are left, even before the concluding chapter, in a kind of vertigo, with

every structural and thematic rug pulled out from under us. Vertigo is precisely one of the conditions sought for in true play. With our sense of reality thrown off balance, the player is left open to new perceptions, new possibilities. The end of the story is the confirmation of the story: the disruptive player's final blow at anyone's complacent notion of the real and of man's place in it. It is very possible that Forty-Four's object remains, to the very end, quite the same—not to instruct, but to astound us, to dizzy us, as countless readers have been astounded before drawing back from the story and rationalizing its irrational last pages. What is August left with, what are we left with but a kind of thematic empty space through which to reach out to better dreams? Through play, the world we have trusted has been set reeling; through play, the absurdities of the theistic God have been driven home. But the marvelous paradox in that sustained negation is this: that through play, a vital, enduring hopeful festivity and life have been restored to Mark Twain's fiction. Through play the world we cannot understand is celebrated in and by the very act of overthrowing the world we thought we knew. At the last, Mark Twain has dreamed a better dream out of the Stranger idea. The argument may go on forever about just how nihilistic Twain really was in his final years, but as it does so, one needs to bear in mind that in the last and best version of the Stranger tale, Twain's fiction does recover that mysterious power of great fiction to celebrate even as it denies, to say even as Forty-Four says to August very near the story's end: "Sit down. Keep your head. There's no hurry. Things are working; I think we can have a good time."

ALFRED KAZIN

Creatures of Circumstance:
Mark Twain

He was a redhead five feet, eight inches tall, liked to make it five feet, eight and a half, and he talked constantly. He had a professional drawl and a resonant twang even in private that struck William James as perverse, his brother Henry as wistful. But from the "lecture" platform on which he performed for a lifetime he was the delight of audiences from Western mining camps in the 1860s to Freud's Vienna in the 1890s. He would shuffle out on the stage in slippers, hands in his pockets, stare impassively at the eagerly waiting faces until the first giggles told him that he had them thoroughly at his mercy. "His carefully studied effects," Howells wrote in *My Mark Twain*, "would reach the first rows in the orchestra first, and ripple in laughter back to the standees against the wall, and then with a fine resurgence come again

From *An American Procession*. © 1984 by Alfred Kazin. Alfred A. Knopf, 1984.

to the rear orchestra seats, and so rise from gallery to gallery till it fell back, a cataract of applause from the topmost rows of seats."

He had only to make some pleasantly derisive sounds to leave them "howling" with delight. "Howling," along with "astonishment," were among Samuel Langhorne Clemens's favorite words. They stood for the raw, total, unlimited gush of pleasure he expected to arouse by just talking. He was the champion funnyman, the smartest voice out of the West. When he was in his late sixties and lived on lower Fifth Avenue, people went into raptures at the sight of Mark Twain talking to a friend and followed him up the avenue for miles. "Howling" also stood for his scale of feeling; his scorn was equally extreme. The loud clarity and positiveness of his feelings explain the brightness of his style. Anything he said, because of the confidence with which he said it, sounded right. And all this arose not just from his love of talk, from his perfected and professional skill in writing as if he were still talking, but from his enjoyment of himself, which he exuded like the smoke from his ever-present cigar. There was a tradition in the South and on the frontier of "selling" oneself by talk. His father, a transplant from Virginia to Missouri who failed to make anything out of the "Tennessee land" he had once bought, talked his family into the dream that the land would yet make them rich. Talk would become the son's favorite show of power.

Long before he "astonished" all those drifters, prospectors, gamblers, and other stray journalists in Nevada, young Sam Clemens in Hannibal must have sounded like his Tom Sawyer—amazing the home folks by his inventiveness and spiel. His style was formed on his lifelong relish of himself as a performer. And forever pushing the performer into action was this perennial boy's awareness of being a favorite, a star. He expected people to hang on his words, and he always meant to "astonish" them, to take them over. The glow of his style would obscure the raw dread he got into *Huckleberry Finn*, the violence of *A Connecticut Yankee in King Arthur's Court*.

He was the favorite, the winner, the Jim Dandy all-American boy (and man: in old age his entourage spoke of him as "King"). Like many another "real live nephew of my Uncle Sam," he was always on stage; his delivery was sardonic and his message the wisecrack. All in the "American" style. And what was that style, now, but "irreligion," skepticism in all things, dissolution in any direction of the eternal verities? No one before the Civil War, no one not from the West, would ever have mustered the poker face to get away with "the calm confidence of a Christian with four aces." In Mark Twain everything went to express suspicion and to conceal hostility by laughing at something or someone established. He was a Southern Presbyterian scornful of sky-blue transcendental Yankee idealism, a poor boy from a family that still believed itself to be "quality," and he was kept hysterical by expecting wealth from the "Tennessee land." An overpowering egotist as well as an always vulnerable one, he had acquired in mining camps, saloons, and newspaper offices a bumptiousness, a special swagger. He was everlastingly the verbal winner, the fastest mouth in Virginia City, San Francisco, and Hawaii.

What formed Mark Twain's perennial "act" was the underplayed but unmistakable attack on belief and believers. No matter how friendly he remained to the end of his life with the Reverend Joe Twichell, no matter how often he assured "Livy" that he might yet be as content with churchgoing as others in their prosperous Hartford set, a preeminent object of his many dislikes was the church, churchgoers, prayer meetings, and the complacent banalities of established clerics. A profoundly middle-class soul himself for all his mischievousness, the very type of the boastful, loud, frantically unsure promoter, he used his "low" experiences to needle the "quality" without for a moment sacrificing the aggressiveness of the one and his respect for the other. His striking doubleness in so many American activities, his histrionic expressions of guilt at being a divided soul, were the predicament that he turned into his greatest feat. Mark Twain never ceased to be Mr. Clemens.

What rankled most (in a nature that luxuriated in irritations) was Christianity's assumption of unity, of a creation overseen by Providence. The truth was not in any organized body or systematic belief, for there was no single truth. It was certainly not in the mind alone, as Emerson had preached. There was nothing but the mixed-up pieces of our raw human nature. This realism was crucial to Mark Twain's enduring popularity; after Cooper, he was the first significant American writer to whom people turned just for pleasure, without thought of improving themselves. Just as his one great book is an example of what the French call *le roman fleuve*, the novel which carries life along like a river and is as wayward as the great river that flows through *Huckleberry Finn*, so his genius was always in some sense for the circumstantial, never the abstract formula. After Mark Twain, many an early American classic would seem too ardent. His large, ever-larger audience, in Europe as well as in America, made him the most loved and the best rewarded of American writers. His humor—always on the attack—was certainly not "ardent" about anything. He lacked the intellectual will to give life one dominating shape. His work required none of the training needed to meet Captain Ahab when the great man ranted, "Who's over me? Truth hath no confines!"

Mark Twain's famous "naturalness," his ability beyond anything else to give an episodic quality to life, spoke to a generation not altogether alarmed by the recognition that there was no necessary connection between man and the universe. His genius for improvisation was as important as his instinct for ridicule. Nothing he ever wrote—not even the determinism of *What Is Man?* and his other outcries in old age against the old American confidence and self-approval—was deliberated for a pilgrim race to make use of. His worst books were written as spontaneously as his best, and many of his projects resembled promoters' schemes in Western lands that came to nothing. He thought *Joan of Arc* his best book. *Huckleberry Finn* was dropped for six years on the principle that "as long as a book would write itself, I was a faithful and interested amanuensis and my industry did not flag, but the minute that the book tried to shift to *my* head the labor of contriving its situations and conducting its conversations, I put it away and dropped it out of my mind." When he picked it up again, he did not understand how much this novel-as-river had been moving in some deep channel of its own. Before he turned the last ten chapters over to Tom Sawyer, he established in the book's harshest scene, the murder of Boggs and the simplicity of the people in this "little one-horse town in a big bend," the hateful yet comic truth written entirely from inside Southern society.

Emerson dreamed that the earth revolving in space was an apple and that he ate it. By contrast with the Romantic will to absorb the world into oneself, Mark Twain made the world laugh as he exposed the rawness and deceitfulness of human nature. He softened the awful truth by enjoying his own performance so much. There was nothing to fear—not yet. Mark Twain darkened only as the century did. The performer kept a certain lordly air, like Colonel Sherburn in *Huckleberry Finn* deriding the mob come to lynch him, even as he paraded the new Western frontiersman. He flourished in all possible American worlds and was free to comment on anything in his own way. He was a dissolvent of the old ways while unmistakably keeping some privileged independence and, like a good Southerner, his ancestral place.

II

Henry James is supposed to have said that only primitive people could enjoy Mark Twain. Mark Twain was always more popular in England than James, who was not popular there at all. He was a favorite on the Continent, where James would never have an audience. Of course "delicious poor dear old M.T.," as James condescended after their one meeting, was no more "primitive" than James himself. He was intensely respectful—for himself—of all Victorian amenities. But growing up with the country, as James never did, absorbing its unrest, its extremes of poverty and wealth, its crudest lust for power and position, he naturally identified himself with the many Americans who were forever fighting it out, just barely keeping their heads above water. James gave primacy to his own impressions; this made Europe sacred as the favorite source of his impressions. Mark Twain's first book, *The Innocents Abroad* (1869), typically took him to Europe and other holy places as a destroyer, the "American vandal."

These two major storytelling talents, of a time and place when realistic fiction began to dominate our literature, did not feel that *they* were living in the same time or place. They could not read each other. Mark Twain said he would rather be "damned to John Bunyan's heaven" than have to read *The Bostonians*, conceivably the one James novel he might have attempted for its satire on respectable New England. But as he confessed to Kipling, he did not read fiction at all; he preferred biography and history, *fact* books. The genius of fiction and the waywardness of nineteenth-century America permitted James and Mark Twain to make contraries of storytelling, of form, of literature itself, while retaining their parity as individualists.

In the end both came to what James called "the imagination of disaster"— James because his conservative "tradition," sacred Europe, was as corrupt as anything else; Mark Twain because nothing failed him like success. But disasters were only the outer shell of capitalism, the great God of chance, the Balzac novel of grandeur and decline that every ambitious nineteenth-century soul lived through. James, who was to say that the starting point of all his work was "loneliness," tried to find in society imaginatively considered what he despaired of finding in lasting affection. Mark Twain came to say that "the greater the love, the greater the tragedy." Even the women in his family were too frail to support his demand for constant assurance; wife and daughters sickened, then died on him.

But James and Mark Twain were certainly Americans of their time and place. Both began life under the rule of overwhelmingly religious fathers: James became indifferent to organized religion, Mark Twain hostile. Both were wanderers from earliest age; both were significantly without the conventionalizing university stamp that our bravest speculative minds—Whitman, Melville, Dickinson—were also free of. Both became preeminent literary figures very early, always with *some* audience for James, an eager one for Mark Twain, and were indefatigable producers into their seventies. Both were star writers for the new magazines that made fiction a going concern in their time. Yet both were increasingly idiosyncratic and uneasy in relation to the mainstream of fiction in English; both felt in old age that their audiences had not kept up with their originality and independent force.

Both, despite their great success in society, their attraction (Mark Twain's was magnetic) for the great and powerful, ended up American isolates like Hawthorne, Melville, Dickinson, Whitman.

Mark Twain's harshly Calvinist father died broke when his younger son was twelve, leaving with him a searing memory of having to look at his father's corpse—no doubt because it exposed the ultimate humiliation of the human body. He was a wandering printer in his teens, a newspaperman, a silver miner, an editor, a correspondent, a professional humorist, and finally, after a practical and respectable Victorian marriage, a newspaper owner, property owner, and best seller on the subscription system. This fabulous American career, representing America to itself, made Mark Twain the legendary example of what his friend William Dean Howells called the post-Civil War type—"the man who has risen." Unlike the general type, Mark Twain became the man who saw through the pretenses of society. The frontier, Howells said, made Mark Twain more "the creature of circumstances than the Anglo-American type." It broke up all cultural traditions even when it wanted to respect them; it was derisive of the consolations of religion even when it retained the church as an institution and a social control; it *lived* the survival of the fittest; it naturally venerated the profit motive, the predatory character, the rich strike, and the eventual domination by monopoly. It took violence as the proof of manhood, made a cult of woman, the "good" woman, at a time—as you never learn from Mark Twain—when whoring as well as boozing and gambling were the chief distractions from prospecting. The frontier, having no tradition, worked on images of the past like acid.

It also created the picturesque figure of the liar, the deceiving teller of tales, the professional hoodwinker of the innocents back East. The West became an idyll even when—sometimes because—its inescapable savagery could not be concealed. It became a fundamental article of romance for some new realists. His assiduously pleasing friend Howells, from the old Western Reserve (Ohio) but long since merged into Boston, adored "Clemens" (the two were always "Clemens" and "Howells" to each other) because the Western environment seemed to stick to him. Howells said he never tired, even when he wished to sleep, watching his friend lounge through hotel rooms in the long nightgown he preferred and telling the story of his life, "the inexhaustible, the fairy, the Arabian nights story, which I could never tire of even when it began to be told again."

As Howells told it in *My Mark Twain* after his friend's death in 1910, the man melted into the career, the career into the country, the country into a legend of endless advancement, freshness, gusto. Somehow the legend always came back to the idea of Mark Twain as the perfect American type, a Westerner, "more dramatically the creature of circumstances than the old Anglo-American type."

> He found himself placed in them and under them, so near to a world in which the natural and the primitive were obsolete, that while he could not escape them, neither could he help challenging them. The inventions, the appliances, the improvements of the modern world invaded the hoary eld of his rivers and forests and prairies, and, while he was still a pioneer, a hunter, a trapper, he found himself confronted with the financier, the scholar, the gentleman. They seemed to him, with the world they represented, at first very droll, and he laughed. They set him to thinking, and, as he was never afraid of anything, he thought over the whole field and demanded explanations of all his prepossessions— of equality, of humanity, of representative government and revealed religion. When they had not their answers ready, without accepting the conventions of the modern world as solutions or in any manner final, he laughed again, not mockingly, but patiently, compassionately. Such, or something like this, was the genesis and evolution of Mark Twain.

Howells, like Mark Twain a self-educated printer and reporter, had learned very early how to play up to Boston's good opinion when Boston was still authority. Charles Eliot Norton must have been thinking of the smoothly dutiful Howells when he described the writers *he* knew as "the best that the world has seen . . . the pleasantest to live with, the best-intentioned and honestest." Howells knew how to please—and to be pleased. Mark Twain was an endless surprise and delight to him, he was so "free." Howells constantly praised Mark Twain's freedom to Mark Twain even when, reading proof on *Tom Sawyer*, he sighed over Huck Finn's saying "they comb me all to hell" and had it changed to "they comb me all to thunder": "I'd have that swearing out in an instant. I suppose I didn't notice it because the locution was so familiar to my Western sense, and so exactly a thing that Huck would say. But it wont [sic] do for the children." Mark Twain's endless spoofs and explosive temper were prime contrasts to the fat little man who in one photograph of the two eminent authors is wearing spats while his famously temperamental friend looks as if he is about to tear into the photographer.

In *My Mark Twain* Howells purred over Mark Twain dead as he had purred over Mark Twain alive. Mark Twain was not really a pioneer and he was never a hunter or a trapper. At the end of his life he felt betrayed by many a financier, but he adored the Standard Oil Company's Henry Huddleston Rogers. "Hellcat Rogers," as he was known on Wall Street, helped rescue him from bankruptcy when the rich and successful Mark Twain lost almost everything trying to get still richer on the ill-fated Paige type-setting machine. While Mark Twain was a satirist of get-rich-quick schemes as early as *The Gilded Age* (1873), "the genesis and evolution of Mark Twain" can hardly be credited to his demanding "explanations of all his prepossessions—of equality, of humanity, of representative government and revealed religion." He ended up an angry and rebellious critic of many American beliefs, but only after he had come to feel that they had betrayed *him*.

Howells ended *My Mark Twain:* "Emerson, Longfellow, Lowell, Holmes—I knew them all and all the rest of our sages, poets, seers, critics, humorists; they were like one another and like other literary men; but Clemens was sole, incomparable, the Lincoln of our literature." The highest tribute from Howells is "Western sense." And it is true that Mark Twain, like Lincoln, was a Westerner, a type which, as late as 1925, F. Scott Fitzgerald could hymn at the end of *The Great Gatsby* as the soul of honesty fated to be corrupted by the East.

Like Lincoln, Mark Twain was restless and ambitious for the main chance before he knew what it was. Growing up in America's border country, a drifter in a generation of drifters, Mark Twain could have said, as Lincoln did during the Civil War, that he was never really in command of events. And if he seemed to have sprung out of the American ground, as Lincoln did, he also knew a hidden America of emptiness and secret terror. The celebrated funnyman was "often crazy in the night" and, like Lincoln, suffered the melancholy and unrest that deprecated self and told jokes. Unlike Lincoln, Mark Twain was a booster, believed for the longest time that success was his destiny, and was enraged by the slightest failure. Until he was old and it was almost too late, he did not know what it was like to stand apart from the circumstances of his life. He could describe them dynamically, picturesquely, but until life took him by the throat and amazed him by frightening him, he saw no alternative to the American epic of progress. His genius, his special luck, was to offer himself up as a new environment.

Turning his friend into "the Lincoln of our literature," Howells slighted an important aspect of Lincoln: his rationalism, objectivity, fixity of purpose. Lincoln never had a personal God; as he admitted in his greatest public utterance, the Second Inaugural, "the Almighty has His own purposes." This represented to Lincoln not chance but a divinity which he humbly recognized as beyond personal desire; it filled him with awe and made him feel that it was worthwhile living in a universe in which could be detected some mysterious tendency toward justice.

Mark Twain's world was all personal, disjointed, accidental. He was indeed, as Howells said, the "creature of circumstances." And so were his characters, which made them creatures of chance in a world more skeptical than had been seen before in the literature of "God's own country." "Circumstances" made Mark Twain, and the shock and fascination of them in succession gave the airy tone to his work. His genius lay in accumulating episodes; he turned life into a stream of facts and pictures—comic, unpredictable, exaggerated, wild—without overall meaning, without ideology, without religion.

From the beginning, Mark Twain's real subject—against a landscape of unlimited expectations and constant humbling—was the human being as animal nature, human cussedness taken raw, single traits magnified as fun, pretense, burlesque, spectacle, and violence. He took from the blatant demonstrativeness of frontier humor its central image of man undomesticated, removed from his traditional surroundings—a stranger wandering into a thin and shifting settlement of other strangers, then plunging into a dizzying succession of experiences always "new."

Mark Twain is the ancestor of all that twentieth-century fiction of Southern poverty, meanness, and estrangement that was out of step with American moralism and pious abstractionism. The characters are generally low, and there is no attempt to make them less so. Southern characters just *lived*, without ostensible purpose, sometimes in mud everlasting, as do the "Arkansaw" characters in that "little one-horse town in a big bend"—chapter 21 of *Huckleberry Finn*—where Colonel Sherburn will shoot down poor, miserable Boggs. This is the poor white's South before (and after) the Civil War, not the plantation house from which Colonel Sherburn scorned the mob.

All the streets and lanes was just mud; they warn't nothing else *but* mud—mud as black as tar, and nigh about a foot deep in some places; and two or three inches deep in *all* the places. The hogs loafed and grunted around, everywheres. You'd see a muddy sow and a litter of pigs come lazying along the street and whollop herself down in the way, where folks had to walk around her, and she'd stretch out, and shut her eyes, and wave her ears, whilst the pigs was milking her, and look as happy as if she was on salary. And pretty soon you'd hear a loafer sing out, "hi! *so* boy! sick him, Tige!" and away the sow would go, squealing most horrible, with a dog or two swinging to each ear, and three or

four dozen more a-coming; and then you would see all the loafers
get up and watch the thing out of sight, and laugh at the fun and
look grateful for the noise. Then they'd settle back again till there
was a dog-fight. There couldn't anything wake them up all over,
and make them happy all over, like a dog-fight—unless it might
be putting turpentine on a stray dog and setting fire to him, or
tying a tin pan to his tail and see him run himself to death.

Mark Twain, as he could have said, "sort of specialized" in characters
who "just lived"—who perhaps lived to talk. They talked all the time, per-
forming for each other in a world relieved from emptiness only by the comic
imagination in talk. What other writers always noticed about Mark Twain
was how professional he was with them, tailoring himself to a particular
audience. He talked as he wrote, wrote as he talked, to the point of developing
the most "lifelike" "right " rhythm in sentence after sentence of just the right
length, with always the telling emphasis in just the right place. He talked
and talked so inexhaustibly at any audience that in his regular changes of
mood he felt sheepish and even guilty for making such demands on everyone
within earshot. But talk was the way he lived and in a sense what he lived
for. As he said in his account of his brief and inglorious time as a Confederate
volunteer, "The Private History of a Campaign That Failed," he was "an
experienced, industrious, ambitious, and often quite picturesque liar." Everything came out of the "perversest twang and drawl," that endless flow of
words, sweet and right in its rhythm for all occasions.

His always appreciative friend Howells, who was never picturesque but
became a dainty and unerring Victorian stylist, had also learned the right
use of words at the type fount and the newspaper desk. Those once self-
educated, literature-mad American writers and speechifiers! Howells knew
that his friend's extraordinary power to write as cleverly as he talked represented a tapping of the half-conscious mind in its most relaxed rhythm. It
seemed to Howells that no other writer had ever captured the elusive spontaneity of the human mind.

Near the end of his life Mark Twain dictated from bed the fragmentary,
supposedly daring passel of unrelated reminiscences and anecdotes he called
his *Autobiography*. There he spoke of his instinctive method.

With the pen in one's hand, narrative is a difficult art; narrative
should flow *as* flows the brook down through the hills and the
leafy woodlands, its course changed by every boulder it comes
across and by every grass-clad gravelly spur that projects into its

path; . . . a book that never goes straight for a minute, but *goes*, and goes briskly, sometimes ungrammatically, and sometimes fetching a horseshoe three-quarter of a mile around . . . but always going, and always following at least one law, always loyal to that law, the law of *narrative*, which *has no law*. Nothing to do but make the trip, the how of it is not important, so that the trip is made.

III

Where did Mark Twain learn to write like that? To catch on paper, as he did in speech, the exact cadence of words as they fall within the mind? Of course the South produced great talkers, and like so many of its vehement personalities up to and including Lyndon Johnson, they knew how to apply pressure on people. Mark Twain must have learned very early that the mouth must always be ready. The celebrated funnyman began as a bookish, sensitive, undersized, violently moody youngster who learned how to defend himself, then—like Tom Sawyer—to command a situation by throwing in occult references, interspersing a string of words between himself and every bit of trouble at hand.

The special "trick," the infallible trigger-quick snap and emphasis on the right word, was something more distinct, and purer, than the traditional gift of gab. Mark Twain's instinct is for the sentence, the thunderclap of surprise essential to the monologist—an effect usually more suited to the short poem, which must be all style, than to prose fiction. He knew, as Robert Frost was boastfully to put it, that "a sentence is a sound on which other sounds called words may be strung." A sentence in Mark Twain, as in Frost, is above all a right sound. Hemingway, for all his homage to *Huckleberry Finn* as the initiator of modern American writing, was a rhetorician who brought an ironic and brutal simplicity to a style not "natural" like Mark Twain's but ostentatiously reduced. Hemingway (like Thoreau) does not try to capture the spoken sound of a sentence. You can sense him checking his own spontaneity as he writes. He is a painter, a whittler, not a listener. Henry James, carrying his wholly mental English to the farthest periphery of consciousness, somehow managed not to stumble even when he composed in rhythms that were not only removed from ordinary speech but were inconceivable from anyone but Henry James. Frost could have been speaking for Mark Twain when he wrote in a letter, "The vital thing, then, to consider in all composition is the ACTION of the voice,—sound—posturing, gesture. . . . Why was a friend so much more effective than a piece of paper in drawing the living sentences out of me? . . . I can't keep up any interest in sentences that don't SHAPE *on some speaking tone* of voice."

Some speaking tone of voice became the everyday voice of Mark Twain as he wrote. And what he heard in himself was often mimicry. The *edge* in people's voices, their littlest emphases and explosions, was something he could never resist putting down. They were the little "snags," in the mouth as on the river, the clots natural to speech before it floods on. Of course he knew from steamboat days, having had to memorize everything on the Mississippi, how to make words reproduce the river—"and by and by you could see a streak on the water which you know by the look of the streak that there's a snag there in a swift current which breaks on it and makes that streak look that way." But much of the line in a character's mouth is mimicry of every quantity of sound Mark Twain got down from someone's speech. "The streets was full, and everybody was excited." "The place to buy canoes is off of rafts laying up at shore. But we didn't see no rafts laying up so we went along during three hours and more." Mark Twain's often shrewish voice can be heard in Colonel Sherburn's scorn of the mob flocking up to his gate to lynch him after he has contemptuously murdered Boggs. The all-assertive inflections, the complacent self-reference, the unsparing *absoluteness* of every ad-hominem shot, is straight from the repertoire of Southern vocal duelling, public insult: "The idea of *you* lynching anybody! It's amusing. The idea of you thinking you had pluck enough to lynch a *man*! . . . Do I know you? I know you clear through. I was born and raised in the South, and I've lived in the North; so I know the average all around. The average man's a coward."

The pleasure we share in all this assertiveness is the pleasure of command—to command attention, to command the crowd. Mark Twain was sometimes "radical" when things went against him; he was no egalitarian. It is the eternal ego power of Tom Sawyer, that nonstop performer, that the old Mark Twain came to recognize in another show-off, Theodore Roosevelt, and heartily detested. No doubt with something of a twinge, for in old age, when he resembled King Lear more than he did Tom Sawyer, he called himself "an old derelict" and "God's fool." But the everlasting type, the genius of the ever-ready verbal topping, is Tom Sawyer. Tom, so prompt to trick and direct others, is clearly one version of what saved his alter ego, Mark Twain; the boy makes his way and always has his way by words alone. What pleasured Mark Twain most about youth—and this is the genius of Huck Finn, who is also no mean talker and a ready deceiver—is its capacity for first impressions, the aspect of discovery. Mark Twain's fellow Missourian T. S. Eliot, reading *Huckleberry Finn* in late middle age for the first time, noticed that the adult in Mark Twain was boyish, "and only the boyish side adult." The boy seems to have learned very early in life how to "handle" adults as well as the boy gang with words. His "angelic," decidedly mature, easily suffering wife sighingly called him "Youth."

IV

"It is a pity we cannot escape from life when we are young," Mark Twain wrote when he was seventy-one. His two most famous creations, Tom Sawyer and Huckleberry Finn, never had to grow up. They remain eternally boys—*the* American boys of legend. More than any other characters in our literature, they convey a fabled freedom. Now virtually enshrined in time and place, the "old" Southwest frontier on the edge of the Mississippi, they seem to represent forever the newness of a new country.

Although no other writing in America has made boyhood seem so idyllic, a state sufficient unto itself, Mark Twain's own boyhood in Hannibal was secretly contradictory in feeling, often touched with dread. *The Adventures of Tom Sawyer* (the ingratiatingly offhand title) is for the most part, but not entirely, an equally chummy portrait of boyhood against a setting almost mythic in its selective use of the past. Mark Twain said that the book was "simply a hymn, put into prose to give it a worldly air." But when Howells, who counselled that the book be directed to children, allowed himself to wonder "why we hate the past so," his friend responded from the depths, "It's so humiliating."

The forty-year-old who composed *Tom Sawyer* in 1875–76 was far from his boyhood poverty and the old Southwest but not from the vehement uncertainties that were as much a mark of his character as his aggressive humor. The author of that "hymn" had become perhaps the most commercially successful author in America; his books were sold by a network of subscription agents who were hard to turn away from the door. He was one of the most public characters in America; somehow everyone knew how happy and prosperous Mark Twain was as he doted on his wife and four children and "humorously" complained of what it cost him to keep up in Hartford the large, overdecorated, ornately stuffed Victorian mansion. The house was another one of Mark Twain's many fantasies come to life. It had everything that the genteel tradition required of a successful man, but like Mark Twain himself for all his heartburnings, it was also defiantly up-to-date. It was the first house in Hartford with a telephone; Mark Twain was the first eminent American writer to possess a typewriter. There was a large staff; their flamboyant employer alternately boasted and cringed at what his servants cost him when he compared his laundry woman's wages with what his family in Hannibal had lived on. The Hartford enclave, Nook Farm, was literary, prosperous, clerical—"the quality" to the life. For a poor and once "shiftless" boy who at thirteen had been apprenticed to the local newspapers, and at eighteen had started his wandering career as a printer in St. Louis, New York, Philadelphia, Muscatine, Keokuk, and Cincinnati, Mark Twain at forty was certainly that post–Civil War type, "the man who has risen."

And he had done it all through *words*—which at times made him feel that everything he had gained by quicksilver cleverness, the stage drawl and the platform manner, was unreal. His life resembled a work of fiction made by works of fiction. He already had a disposition to think of his life as a "dream"—the American dream, of course, but one that also revealed a writer's tendency to wonder whether the thoughts and projects that occupied him day and night had any existence outside himself. At the end of his "wonderful century" whose many wonders he personified to his countrymen, he was to write in *The Mysterious Stranger* that the universe itself was a dream, thus rounding out a century of American solipsism.

In Nook Farm, Hannibal itself became a dream. The proud, opulent, but endlessly reminiscent Mark Twain was writing *Tom Sawyer* in the smug atmosphere of postwar Republicanism; the ragged Confederate volunteer was now a favorite orator at reunions of the Grand Army of the Republic. He could not help touching up the past, to the point where it would all come back less humiliating. But he now invented the past more than he renovated it. After all, *Tom Sawyer* was his first real novel.

Postwar America was already looking to the "old West" for a golden age. Our now-celebrated author had revisited Hannibal on a sentimental journey; he had gone up and down the great river to write his utterly sunshot pieces for the *Atlantic Monthly* on learning to be a steamboat pilot, "Old Times on the Mississippi." The undestroyed vividness of his old associations amazed him. Had he ever left Hannibal?

> The things about me and before me made me feel like a boy again—convinced me that I was a boy again, and that I had been simply dreaming an unusually long dream.... During my three days' stay in the town, I woke up every morning with the impression that I was a boy—for in my dreams the faces were all young again, and looked as they had looked in the old times.

He recognized the melancholy limitations of his old life—how remote and isolated a village like "St. Petersburg" in *Tom Sawyer* could be, and how it forced "good" people together. (The "good" people furnish the authority figures in the town, and Tom Sawyer knows how to overcome them from time to time without displacing their authority, which he needs more than anything else to keep him perpetually in adventures.) The sunny togetherness of the town is really everyone's similarity; it excludes people different in "blood," like Injun Joe, the villain of *Tom Sawyer*, who is only half Indian but like a good citizen knows "the Injun blood ain't in me for nothing." Hannibal was bounded by the always mysterious and changeable river, by creepy stretches of forest and uninhabited river islands. Although the whole town seems to have spent Sunday going to church and getting recalcitrant boys and girls to Sunday school, anxiety and superstition came down to children from their elders, along with the rituals and superstitious oaths (Nature was still the Great Adversary) passed on by one generation of children to another.

V

Mark Twain had great trouble deciding whether *Tom Sawyer* was for children or for adults. In 1876, when he finally decided that it was a "children's book," the contrast between the respectable life he led and the untiring devotion of his hero to fun and games made it necessary for him to be arch— to keep a proper distance from his brat. Archness is all over *Tom Sawyer*. He may have had to return to the past in "Old Times on the Mississippi" and *Tom Sawyer* in order to make Nook Farm real. There may have been some obscure guilt as he hobnobbed with the genially prosperous literati, preachers, and businessmen. With *Tom Sawyer*—the first of his books to show him entirely as objective storyteller—he capitalized on his early life. Before *Huckleberry Finn*, he had no greater story to tell than one about an irrepressibly imaginative boy who could make other boys submit to his (book-learned) fantasies.

It was a story to be told at a comfortable remove. The archness fitted the benevolence of middle-aged successes toward their younger selves, of urban leaders toward the old farm and the rustic village. Heavily Victorian Americans could feel that America was still young. Now that the dire Calvinist suspicions that children were as damnable as everyone else were done away with, boys and girls emerged sweet and cute, lovable and cherishable— as nice and as good, in short, as grownup Americans.

The growing comfort and self-satisfaction of middle-class life made happy families dote on their children as never before. There was little religious consolation when they died—Mark Twain was to lose three, and the death of one particularly beloved daughter at twenty-four was a shock he never got over. Anxiety in prosperity made the now-lovable American child as significant a type as the "shrewd" self-respecting Yankee. The child in popular American literature becomes a dear little fellow, the lovable urchin and "scamp," the professional "bad boy." These were milksops turned inside out, future leaders of American enterprise, from Thomas Bailey Aldrich's Tom Bailey to Booth Tarkington's Penrod.

One began to miss the clairvoyant Pearl in *The Scarlet Letter*. That child of sin had a cool and deadly Puritan eye for concealment. What simpleminded "rascals" barefoot American boys become in the illustrations to children's books, as they skip off to the ole fishing hole in a frayed straw hat and with one gallus trailing down their torn pants. What little darlings girls become in their yellow curls and starched ruffles—what "spirit" they show in the face of adversity!

Henry James in the last, unfinished volume of his autobiography, *The Middle Years*, described the passing of youth as a raid on "the enemy country, the country of the general lost freshness." Perhaps nowhere as in New England, with its race pride making up for its loss of moral authority, were so many children's books manufactured for magazines like *Youth's Companion, St. Nicholas, Riverside Magazine for Young People, Wide Awake, Our Young Folks*. No wonder that Mark Twain, at ease in Hartford, got into the game. Nowhere else did comfortableness with one's racial, social, religious, and financial well-being get itself complacently expressed in so many images of the *manly, sturdy, bright,* and *cheery* Protestant boy. Thomas Bailey Aldrich in *The Story of a Bad Boy:* "an amiable, impulsive lad, blessed with fine digestive powers, and no hypocrite . . . in short, I was a real human boy, such as you may meet anywhere in New England, and no more like the impossible boy in a storybook than a sound orange is like one that has been sucked dry."

No wonder that Mark Twain in Connecticut remembered the raw Missouri of the 1850s so fondly in *Tom Sawyer* as a place where children had no life but play. Of course he could not decide until the last moment whether this idyl, this hymn put into prose to give it a worldly air, was for children or adults. Howells, who knew the middle road in all things (until in the darkening nineties he grew weary of the Establishment and moved to New York), persuaded his friend to call *Tom Sawyer* a children's book. And it was Howells who had him remove innocent bits of real life from the novel (Becky sneaking a look at a naked body in teacher's anatomy text) as "awful good but too dirty." Howells always knew what the public would take, and he wrote straight *to* this public, whose inquiring photographer in fiction he was for so long that he felt he had been created by the reading public.

Nowhere as in America after the Civil War were there so many books for adults about children having fun. If the prosperous middle class in the United States already impressed European visitors as a society somehow geared to children, that was because it showed how prosperous, easy, and self-indulgent, how happy, prodigal, and *young*, adults could remain in America. The young had become the real Americans. This was a society that children could love without question. A child's high expectation of life, his high spirits and his general air of having a surplus vitality that, like surplus cash, had to be spent, proved the extraordinary good fortune that so many Americans were experiencing. The splendor of children in American literature of the time! Obviously some Americans felt as protected as only children ever do.

In *Tom Sawyer* Mark Twain was not yet ready to disclose the deep as well as the bright side of a Mississippi River boyhood. He celebrated boyhood as a state sufficient unto itself, almost entirely removed from the contingencies of the adult world. It is removed even from the looming sexuality of childhood and adolescence.

VI

When he revisited Hannibal and climbed Holiday's Hill to get a comprehensive view, Mark Twain felt himself back "in the midst of a time when the happenings of life were not the natural and logical results of great general laws, but of special orders, and were freighted with very precise and distinct purposes—partly punitive in intent, partly admonitory, and usually local in application." (Mark Twain could become self-consciously elevated when he was among the "quality" and writing *down*.) The world of *Tom Sawyer* is indeed under "special orders"—not only from adult to boy but from boy to boy. In imagination it is limited so generously to the wishes of boyhood that from one point of view it is unreal, which explains why Tom Sawyer himself, as well as his adventures, has become legendary. This boyhood will seem forever special to itself, privileged, a sport. There is no real family life in the book—Tom's mother is dead, he is being raised by his Aunt Polly; the father is never mentioned; nor do we ever find out why Sid is only Tom's half-brother or why cousin Mary seems to live in the same household. Joe Harper and other boys in the gang do have families—at least they have mothers, and thus God-fearing homes.

Huck Finn is the exception to all this. His father is the town drunk, and Huck has no home at all.

Huckleberry came and went, at his own free will. He slept on doorsteps in fine weather and in empty hogsheads in wet; he did not have to go to school or to church, or call any being master or obey anybody; he could go fishing or swimming when and where he chose, and stay as long as it suited him; nobody forbade him to fight; he could sit up as late as he pleased; he was always the first boy that went barefoot in the spring and the last to resume leather in the fall; he never had to wash, nor put on clean clothes; he could swear wonderfully. In a word, everything that goes to make life precious, that boy had. So thought every harassed, hampered, respectable boy in St. Petersburg.

But Huck as exception to the respectable world of St. Petersburg is of only slight importance in *Tom Sawyer*. Tom is the driving force of the gang. Tom the "bad" boy—the supposedly bad boy, the predictably good boy— is not so much "bad" as he is impossibly romantic and even visionary. He is what he is because he reads "pirate" books and such, then tries to make his pranks (and those of the gang) live up to them.

Mark Twain as a famous author confessed that he did not care to read fiction. The young Sam Clemens in Hannibal must have read himself sick on stories of pirates, Robin Hood, medieval knights and ladies. (He was always romantic about the Middle Ages.) Tom Sawyer represents the future author's greatest fantasy: to turn life into a book. Of course there is a good deal of routine, boys-will-be-boys mischief. "And when she closed with a happy Scriptural flourish, he 'hooked' a doughnut." Tom must get the best of every encounter, confrontation, negotiation. Skeptics may see a future corporation type in Tom's ability to swap his inferior store of boy's goods— "twelve marbles, part of a jew's harp, a piece of blue bottle-glass to look through . . . a dog-collar but no dog"—for stuff slightly less inferior. His chief trait, which leads to his many (sometimes unbearable) intrigues, is his un- questioned sense of himself as guide and leader to every other boy in town. He is a born dominator, for he is totally—as young Sam Clemens must have been—at the mercy of his imagination. Whatever he has read of that world beyond the village, in which pirates and Robin Hood and medieval knights act out some "gorgeous" code, Tom himself must act out. Other boys follow him because they can no more resist Tom's wild fancy than we can resist Mark Twain's.

The most famous episode in *Tom Sawyer*—Tom's persuading his friends to pay him for the "privilege" of whitewashing Aunt Polly's fence—can be believed only if you recognize what a power of fantasy drives this mighty spieler. Tom can talk people into anything because no one else really shares, much less understands, his determination to live by the book. This gives him a power over them that reminds us of an author's power.

From his guardian, Aunt Polly, on down, the adults in St. Petersburg must also participate in the book Tom is acting out; they are the chorus, plaintive but unavailing, as Tom goes through his adventures. Near the opening of the book Aunt Polly laments the fact that Tom has just (again) escaped her control. "He's full of the Old Scratch, but laws-at-me! he's my own dead sister's boy, poor thing, and I ain't got the heart to lash him, somehow. I've *got* to do some of my duty by him, or I'll be the ruination of the child." So Tom can persuade even "hard-eyed" Joe Harper into sailing off with him as pirates to Jackson's Island. (Huck Finn "joined them promptly, for all careers were one to him; he was indifferent.") Tom can cajole the other boys into staying on the island when they are homesick; a great storm seems to bring the end of the world. In the book's most astonishing scene, a cold-blooded Tom can secretly revisit his home and stay mum while Aunt Polly and Mrs. Harper are lamenting the boys' death. Tom manages the shattering appearance of the boys at their own "funeral." As everyone says, you never did see a boy like him.

This writer has never found Tom "lovable." Tom is so bent on having life live up to his favorite stories that he takes over people's lives. But like the townspeople of St. Petersburg, one is impressed and even abashed by Tom's power. That is the fascination of the book: Tom believes himself irresistible. A main consequence of *Tom Sawyer*'s being told in the third person is that Tom becomes a direct creation of Mark Twain's own arbitrary power to make this boy seem forever "special." Mark Twain keeps him a professional boy, incessantly a boy, nothing but a boy.

Tom is so special a boy that even though there are contradictions in his makeup, we can hardly bear to notice them—so compelling is the overpowering role he has to play throughout as the young prince behind all mischief. When asked in Sunday school for the names of the first two disciples, he at last comes up with "David and Goliath!" This gets its laugh. But how is it possible for a boy who reads so much, and is forever hearing the New Testament being read at him in school, in church, at home, not to know better? It is possible because Tom (like everyone else in the book, even Huckleberry Finn) is all of one piece, limited to a few traits. As in all true comedy, these traits are trotted out over and again; the fun depends on the power of repetition.

Tom does "grow" in the story from a bad boy into a hero. When Muff Potter is put on trial for murdering Dr. Robinson in the cemetery at night,

Tom overcomes his fear and gets himself to court to nail the real murderer, the villainous half-breed Injun Joe. When his adored Becky Thatcher cannot keep away from the anatomy book that the schoolmaster secretly keeps in the closet and then accidentally tears the page showing a "human figure, stark naked," our Tom takes the blame, bears the punishment—and wins Becky's "love." At the end Tom nobly safeguards Becky when they stray away from their friends and cannot easily find their way out of the cave. The stolen treasure bestowed on Tom and Huck is their reward for behaving well in a crisis. To conclude the book, Tom even accommodates himself to the adult values he has hitherto defied; Huck must go back to the Widow Douglas if he wants to be accepted into the gang. (This proves conclusively that the activity of the gang is really playacting by respectable people. It is necessarily where *The Adventures of Huckleberry Finn* will begin, for Huck is not middle-class and respectable, so he must escape the "Widder.")

In *Tom Sawyer* all the shenanigans at the end denote the happy ending and spirit of reconciliation natural to comedy. By writing Tom's adventures in the third person, Mark Twain could "handle" Tom any way he liked. He admitted that there was no real plot to the book.

In his original preface to *Tom Sawyer*, from Hartford in 1876, when he was living in such grand style, he wrote: "part of my plan has been to try to pleasantly remind adults of what they once were themselves, and of how they felt and thought and talked, and what queer enterprises they sometimes engaged in."

This was not and could not have been all that the floodgates of memory opened up. Tom and his friends are superstitious about many things in a way that shows their dread of the unknown powers behind nature as well as their childish ignorance. Why do they visit a tumbledown cemetery *at night* just in time to see a grave robbery and murder? Why does Huck carry a dead cat with him? Why is a recurrent image in the book that of the moon dropping behind a cloud? All these people are alone with natural forces that, as in the scene of the terrible thunderstorm, seem to sport with the tiny settlement on the mysterious great river. Tom and Huck, being boys, think they can control the occult forces of darkness, dread, and violence by laying spells on them. But evil in the background is necessary to comedy, for evil is defeated. Wickedness in the person of Injun Joe dies of starvation in the cave; the fears of the cave are overcome by Tom and Becky; our prankster is a hero. He has really been a hero all along—a hero disguised as a mischievous and disobedient boy. This adds folklore to comedy. Everything works out for the best in this best of all possible Americas. Successful, benevolent Mark Twain is looking back on his own boyhood so sweetly, so archly! The prose in which Tom is put through his paces could not be more heavily facetious: "he uncovered an ambuscade, in the person of his aunt; and when she saw the state his clothes were in, her resolution to turn his Saturday holiday into captivity at hard labor became adamantine in its firmness."

This is far from being the easy, "natural" first-person style of *Huckleberry Finn*. Mark Twain had to put a certain distance between himself and his famous boys before he could enter more deeply and *recklessly* into a boy's life with *Huckleberry Finn*. There is a lot of carefulness and anxious propriety behind the writing of *Tom Sawyer*. It now seems absurd for a near-adolescent like Tom to ask Becky for a kiss only because it is the ritual he has read about in books when people get "engaged." "Now, Becky, it's all done—all over but the kiss. Don't you be afraid of that—it ain't anything at all. Please, Becky." In the closing pages Huck bitterly complains how unbearable he finds life with the Widow Douglas: "She makes me git up just at the same time every morning; she makes me wash . . . them ways comb me all to thunder." Since Mark Twain had persuaded himself (prodded by his wife and Howells) that the book was really "a boy's and a girl's book," he was glad enough to change "hell" to "thunder." The naked human figure Becky Thatcher steals a glance at in the schoolmaster's anatomy book apparently belongs to neither sex and contains no sexual interest for Becky.

All this marks the gentility from which Mark Twain looked down on his boyhood. So much propriety and prudent respectability were perhaps necessary to describe boyhood under "special orders." Adulthood and boyhood are absolutely divided here between authority figures and escapees from authority. Tom is the immortal boy because there is no chance of his growing up—of ever becoming anything more than a boy. Tom is everlastingly the type and legend of the American boy because his youthful sense of freedom still represents the youthfulness of the United States—before Mark Twain settled down. Tom is legendary because he is an adult's fantasy of defying the many adults we cannot defy so lightly when we become adults. Above all, Tom is "immortal" because he always wins.

Huckleberry Finn is not middle-class like Tom, and he will never be rewarded for his propriety by the proper people in town. Huck says at one point, "You see, I'm kind of a hard lot—least everybody says so, and I don't see nothing against it." Tom has the whole town to defy, for he is securely a part of it. Huck does not even have a home. Everyone disapproves of him in this book, even Tom Sawyer. He is "low company," the kind of character that stretched Mark Twain's imagination to the uttermost and became his genius. Still, it had been genius for Mark Twain to put Huck into the company of Tom. Each is so necessary to the other that it was perfect instinct for Mark Twain, once he came to the end of *The Adventures of Tom Sawyer*, to write *The Adventures of Huckleberry Finn*. Huck says at the beginning of the new book, "You don't know about me, without you have read a book by the name of *The Adventures of Tom Sawyer*."

VII

When Mark Twain turned to *The Adventures of Huckleberry Finn* after finishing *The Adventures of Tom Sawyer* in 1876, he clearly meant to write another "boy's book" in the light comic tone that for the most part had carried Tom and his friends in St. Petersburg from one escapade to another. Despite the dread, the fear-soaked superstitions, and the violent deaths described in *Tom Sawyer*, the book is a comedy and in tone benign and more than a shade condescending to boys who, when all is said and done, are merely boys. Mark Twain had become a wealthy and ultrarespectable member of the best society in Hartford by the time he sat down to recreate his own boyhood in *Tom Sawyer*—minus his own religious fear and loneliness.

His benevolence toward childhood and boyhood is a little smug. Mark Twain undertook more than he anticipated when he turned to *Huckleberry Finn*. By an instinct that opened the book to greatness, he wrote Huck's story in the first person and so at many crucial places in the book *became* Huck. Yet the facetious "Notice" facing the opening page is only one of many indications that *Huckleberry Finn* was intended to be just a sequel to *Tom Sawyer*:

> Persons attempting to find a motive in this narrative will be pros-
> ecuted; persons attempting to find a moral in it will be banished;
> persons attempting to find a plot in it will be shot.

From the moment Mark Twain began to describe things as Huck would see them, and to make of Huck's vernacular a language resource of the most captivating shrewdness, realism, and stoical humor, Mark Twain was almost against his will forced to go deeper into his own imaginative sense than he had ever gone before. Odd as it may seem, he was compelled—in this one book—to become a master novelist.

He had not been a novelist at all before writing *Tom Sawyer*; obviously everything having to do with his early life in Hannibal recharged him and opened not only the gates of memory and imagination but also his unexpected ability to write close, sustained narrative. Writing in the first person became the deliverance of Mark Twain. Still, given his training in one vernacular style after another during his days as a frontier humorist, it was not in itself exceptional for him to impersonate a fourteen-year-old vagabond, the son of the town drunk, who hates being "adopted": "The Widow Douglas, she took me for her son, and allowed she would sivilize me; but it was rough living in the house all the time, considering how dismal regular and decent the widow was in all her ways."

What made the difference between this and just another humorous "oral delivery" was that Mark Twain had fallen completely into Huck's style and Huck's soul. (There were to be passages in which Huck became Mark Twain.) Smart-alecky and sometimes mechanically facetious as Mark Twain was when he first assumed Huck's voice, winking at the reader as he presented Huck's ignorance of religion, of polite language, of "sivilized" ways, Mark Twain would soon be committed to a great subject—Huck the runaway from his father and Jim the slave running away from Miss Watson, going down the river, hoping to enter the Ohio River and freedom. Freedom from respectable ways for Huck, freedom from slavery for Jim: the quest is eternal even though they miss the Ohio River in the dark and keep going South. In the last third of the book they return to the purely boyish world of *Tom Sawyer*, with Tom the everlasting kid, prankster, brat, forcing a Jim who was really free all the time (as only Tom knows) to be a "prisoner" on the Phelps farm.

The quest for freedom is eternal because Huck and Jim have nothing in this world but that quest. Mark Twain the ultrasuccess in Hartford had returned to what he once knew, most feared, and what always excited his imagination most—the Mississippi Valley world at its human bottom, the world of the totally powerless and unsettled. He, too, remained something of a vagrant, a drifter; in old age he called himself a "derelict." He would never, despite appearances, be content with his celebrated position in life; like Huck at the end of this book, he wanted "to light out for the Territory ahead of the rest."

Huckleberry Finn is above all a novel of low company—of people who are so far down in the social scale that they can get along only by their wits. In 1885 the Concord Public Library excluded *Huckleberry Finn*. It was not altogether mistaken when it complained that the humor was "coarse" and that the substance was "rough, coarse and inelegant, dealing with a series of experiences not elevating, the whole book being more suited to the slums than to intelligent, respectable people." The wonderful satire in chapter 17 on the genteel way of life in the Grangerford family would not be possible without Huck's unpreparedness for such a way of life; the hilarious Victorian sentimentality is put into true perspective by Huck, the anguished observer of the murderous feud between the Grangerfords and the Shepherdsons.

Huck has *nothing* but his wits. As he says about himself, "I go a good deal by instinct." The society along the river is class-conscious, but the classes cannot help knowing each other and entering into each other's lives. In chapters 24–29 the awful Duke and Dauphin enter into the family of the dead Peter Wilks, pretending to be its English branch, and the fact that they do not talk "educated," but make the most ridiculous mistakes, does not alert the family until it is almost too late. From time to time Huck temporarily attaches himself to plain middle-class folks like Mrs. Judith Loftus; in chapter 11, when he disguises himself as a girl, it is his sex rather than his low speech that gives him away.

Huck certainly gets around. He can be pals with Tom Sawyer and be taken in hand by Judge Thatcher, the Widow Douglas, and Miss Watson; he convinces Mrs. Judith Loftus that he *did* grow up in the country; in chapter 13, he steals the canoe attached to the foundering *Walter Scott* and so helps to send the robbers caught on the boat to their deaths; he can play the servant to professional con men like the Duke and Dauphin, who at successive times masquerade as actors, medicine men, and Englishmen.

In a great novel of society—which *Huckleberry Finn* so acidly turns out to be whenever Huck and Jim go ashore—what counts is the reality behind the appearance. That reality, though sometimes naively misinterpreted by Huck (but only for a self-deluded moment), depends always on Huck's inexperience. Nothing could be more devastating as social satire than the Victorian gingerbread and sentimental mourning described absolutely "straight" by the homeless and admiring Huck. All this turns into a hideous bloodbath as a consequence of Huck's ingenuous help to the lovelorn couple from feuding families. To go from the Grangerford parlor to the riverbank where Huck covers the heads of the Grangerford boys slain in the insane feud is to travel a social epic. Only the classic "poor white," Huck, goes the whole route—as the onlooker that Mark Twain remained in his heart.

The riverbank scene ends on one of those recurrent escapes that make up the story line of *Huckleberry Finn*—"I tramped off in a hurry for the crick, and crowded through the willows, red-hot to jump aboard and get out of that awful country." Huck *has* to keep running from "quality" folks like the Grangerfords, the Wilkses, the murdering "awful proud" Colonel Sherburn. He "weren't particular"; he just wants to go "somewheres." He chooses to *stay* low company, as his father does. Vagrancy is his first freedom. He does not even choose to go traipsing down the Mississippi with Jim, who just happens to be on Jackson's Island when Huck gets there. The novel is one happening after another; Huck *happens* to fall in with a runaway slave instead of living by the book with Tom Sawyer. As Pap Finn chooses the mud, so Huck chooses the river. Or did the river in fact choose him?

Thanks to the everlasting river, the "monstrous big river," the always unpredictable river, Huck and Jim on their raft float into a tough American world. It is full of hard characters, crooks, confidence men, kindly widows and starchy spinsters who in good Mark Twain fashion never seem to be sexually involved with anyone; slaveowners and slave hunters who can never be expected to regard Jim as anything but a piece of property; pretty young girls for whom Huck's highest accolade is that they have "the most sand"— grit and courage, the power to disbelieve and defy the lying elders around them. The church is fundamental to these people, but their religion emphasizes duty to God rather than brotherhood for the outcast and the slave. They are hard without knowing it, for they are hysterically self-protective. They are a human island in the midst of a great emptiness.

So Huck, not yet fourteen, has to struggle for a knowledge of adult society without which he will not survive. In *Tom Sawyer* children and adults lived in parallel worlds without menacing each other; in *Huckleberry Finn*, as in real life, children and their elders are in conflict. A middle-class boy like Tom Sawyer has to "win" a game in order to triumph over his inevitable defeats in later life. Huck has to survive now. He has to win over Pap Finn's meanness and the Widow Douglas's strictness; over Tom Sawyer's boyish silliness and Jim's constant terror that he may be caught; over the murderous robbers on the *Walter Scott* and even the protectiveness of Mrs. Judith Loftus; over the horrible arrogance of Colonel Sherburn and the lynch mob foolishly crowding Colonel Sherburn's door; over the greediness of the "King" and the cool cynicism of the Duke.

Huck on the river, becoming a part of the river, making the river one of the principal characters, reminds us of the genesis of *Tom Sawyer* and *Huckleberry Finn*. Mark Twain recalled in "Old Times on the Mississippi" that he had had to learn the *whole* river in order to become a pilot. Huck has to be the unresting pilot of his life and Jim's; he must become the American Ulysses in order to survive. This is why from time to time he can lie back and take in the beauty and wonder of the scene, as in the glorious description of sunrise on the Mississippi that opens chapter 19. This chapter significantly has the book's meanest characters, the Duke and Dauphin, coming aboard. Think of a boy Huck's age struggling against a father who wants to keep him down, who tries to rob him, and who beats him and keeps him locked up. Whereupon *our* Ulysses contrives his own "death" and gets away with it after making as many preparations for his deception and escape as a spy going into enemy country. No wonder he is always on "thin ice," or as he says in one of his best descriptions of flight, "I was kind of a hub of a wheel."

There, in the struggle of a boy to establish himself over hostile powers, in the discovery of menace when confronting life on one's own terms—there is the true meaning of a "boy's book"; it explains why boys can read *The Adventures of Huckleberry Finn* as boys and then grow up to read it as an epic of life that adults can identify with. The great epic, the tale of the wandering hero triumphing over circumstances—this is the stuff of literature that a boy is nearest to, since every initiation into the manhood he seeks must take the form of triumphing over an obstacle. Whether he is planning to deceive his father into thinking he is dead, scaring off slave hunters with stories of smallpox on their raft, or (in the last ten chapters) submitting to Tom Sawyer's games and thus subjecting poor Jim to real imprisonment, the hero of this book is still only a boy. This proximity to both real danger and made-up danger is how life appears to a boy, who must steal from the adult world the power, but also the fun, that he needs in order to keep feeling like a boy. Even though he must trick this world, lie to it, outwit it, he is a boy in his conventional attitudes. The Wilks girl had "the most sand" you ever did see in a girl, and the Grangerford house was the splendidest.

Huck does not have the easy out of pretending to despise a middle-class world whose love comes his way without his seeking it. Nor does love from people he has just met mean as much to him as his own measure of people. He is attachable, but not for long; adoptable, but he will not admit liking this. You remember his boyish inexperience when you see how much he values, in the sunrise along the river and in the circus into which he has sneaked, the beauty and "splendidness" the world has kept in store for him. The nature of the life experience, as the story of a boy always brings out, is that we just pass through and are soon different from what we thought we were; are soon gone. Life is a series of incommensurable moments, and it is wise to enjoy them; one minute the Grangerford boys are bloody dead along the river, and the next morning or so, "two or three days and nights went by; I reckon I might say they swum by, they slid along so quiet and smooth and lovely."

Pap Finn in delirium tremens cries out to the Angel of Death, "Oh, let a poor devil alone!" This expresses the real struggle, against underlying despair, that Mark Twain admitted for the first time in *Huckleberry Finn*, before he savagely settled into the despair of his old age. The river that "holds" the book in its grasp is full of menace as well as an unreal floating peace. For the most part travelling the river is a struggle, a wariness, even when Huck is temporarily on land. In the marvellous and somehow central scene in which Huck methodically arranges his "death" and then, worn out, prepares to catch a few "winks," he is still a river rat who feels himself pursued at every turn.

From the very beginning of their flight, Huck and Jim are in ecstasies whenever they are safe for a while. Early in the book, when Huck watches the townspeople shooting off a cannon to raise his "body" from the bottom, he says with an audible easing of his breath, "I knowed I was all right now. Nobody else would come a-hunting after me." Just treading on a stick and breaking it "made me feel like a person had cut one of my breaths in two and I only got half, and the short half, too." A boy is up against forces bigger than himself, the greatest of which can be his inexperience. So he has to play "smart." But the smarter the boy, the more fatalistic he is; he knows who runs things. Wary of people, Huck weaves his way in and out of so many hazards and dangers that we love him for the dangers he has passed. He *is* our Ulysses, he *has* come through. Yet coming up from the bottom, he has none of Tom Sawyer's foolish pride; the "going" for this boy has become life itself, and eventually there is no place for him to go except back to Tom Sawyer's fun and games.

The sense of danger is the living context of the book's famous style, the matchless ease and directness of Huck's language. Huck and Jim are forever warding off trouble, escaping from trouble, resting from trouble—then, by words, putting a "spell" on trouble. Jim is always getting lost and always being found; Huck is always inventing stories and playing imaginary people in order to get out of scrapes before they occur. As Jim in his ignorance is made to play the fool, so Huck in the full power of his cleverness is made to play the con man. They need all the parts they can get. They live at the edge of a society that is not prepared to accept either one of them; they are constantly in trouble, and it is real trouble, not "prejudice," that menaces Jim. Although Mark Twain often plays to the gallery when he mocks the iniquity of slavery from the complacent perspective of Connecticut in the 1880s, the feeling that Huck and Jim attain for each other is now deservedly the most famous side of the book. For once, black and white actually love each other because they are in the same fix. "Dah you goes, de ole true Huck; de on'y white gentleman dat ever kep' his promise to old Jim."

But we never forget what the hard American world around them is like and why they are both in flight. For people who are penniless, harried, in real danger of death, vigilance alone gives a kind of magical power to a life over which "mudsills" and slaves have no power. The superstitions Huck and Jim share are all they have to call on against the alien forces of nature.

Equally effective, a kind of superstition as well, is the spell they put on things by arranging them in strict order. Although Huck sometimes becomes Mark Twain when Mark wants to satirize old-time property "rights" in slaves, Mark sinks into Huck when, in the crucial scene preparing his getaway, Huck doggedly lists everything he has, everything he is taking with him, everything he *knows*—in order to shore himself against danger.

It must have been this scene in chapter 7 of *Huckleberry Finn* that so deeply drew Ernest Hemingway to the book. All modern American writing, he said in *Green Hills of Africa*, comes out of *Huckleberry Finn*. He called the much-disputed end of the book "cheating," but he recognized his affinity with the book as a whole. Hemingway surely came to his famous "plain" style through his compulsion to say about certain objects, *only this is real; this is real; and my emotion connects them.* In Hemingway's great and perhaps most revealing story, "Big Two-Hearted River," the suffering mind of the war veteran Nick Adams seeks an accustomed sense of familiarity from the stream he fished before the war. He then puts his catch away between ferns, layer by layer, with a frantic deliberateness. So Huck preparing his getaway in chapter 7 tells us:

> I took the sack of corn meal and took it to where the canoe was hid, and shoved the vines and branches apart and put it in; then I done the same with the side of bacon; then the whisky jug; I took all the coffee and sugar there was, and all the ammunition; I took the wadding; I took the bucket and gourd, I took a dipper and a tin cup, and my own saw and two blankets, and the skillet and the coffee-pot. I took fish-lines and matches and other things—everything that was worth a cent. I cleaned out the place. I wanted an axe, but there wasn't any, only the one out at the wood pile, and I knowed why I was going to leave that. I fetched out the gun, and now I was done.

The boy without anything to his name finally has something to carry away. Taking the full inventory of his possessions is a ritual that Huck goes through whenever he is in danger and about to hunt up a new place to "hide." This element of necessity can be the most moving side of the book. It "explains" the unique freshness of the style as much as anything can. A writer finds his needed style, his true style, in the discovery of a book's hidden subject, its "figure in the carpet." Here is a book which is an absolute marvel of style, but in which, by a greater marvel, life is not reduced to style and is certainly not confused with style. Huck Finn's voice has many sides, but fundamentally it is the voice of a boy-man up to his ears in life, tumbling from danger to danger, negotiating with people, and fighting back at things as necessity commands. The sense of necessity that only bottom dogs know is what gives such unmediated, unintellectualized beauty to the style. Mark Twain, fully for the first time, knew how to let life carry out its own rhythm.

The interesting thing is that he did not particularly intend to do this. When he took the book up again several years after he had written chapter 16, planning to describe the comedy and horror of the Grangerfords' existence, he was tougher on the society along the river than he had ever expected to be. For starting with chapter 17 he had to describe the folly of "quality" folk like the Grangerfords, the inhuman arrogance of Colonel Sherburn, and the stupidity and loutishness of "ordinary" plain people.

Mark Twain's fascinated loathing extends to the whiskey-sodden towns-people who egg on poor old Boggs as he stumbles about, foolishly threatening Colonel Sherburn. Because that imperious man murders Boggs, Mark Twain can disgorge himself of his own exasperation with "ordinary" Americans by describing the crowd around the dying man.

> There was considerable jawing back, so I slid out, thinking maybe there was going to be trouble. The streets was full, and everybody was excited. Everybody that seen the shooting was telling how it happened, and there was a big crowd packed around each one of these fellows, stretching their necks and listening. One long lanky man, with long hair and a big white fur stove-pipe hat on the back of his head, and a crooked-handled cane, marked out the places on the ground where Boggs stood, and where Sherburn stood, and the people following him around from one place t'other and watching everything he done, and bobbing their heads to show they understood, and stooping a little and resting their hands on their thighs to watch him mark the places on the ground with his cane; and then he stood up straight and stiff where Sherburn had stood, frowning and having his hat-brim down over his eyes, and sung out, "Boggs!" and then fetched his cane down slow to a level, and says "Bang!" staggered backwards, says "Bang!" again, and fell down flat on his back. The people that had seen the thing said he done it perfect; said it was just exactly the way it all happened. Then as much as a dozen people got out their bottles and treated him.

The famous speech by Colonel Sherburn after the murder ridicules the crowd that has come to lynch him. The speech is wonderful in its lordly contempt for the townspeople, but of course it is not Sherburn but Mark Twain who is telling the crowd off. The crowd admiringly watching the man in the "big white fur stove-pipe hat" act out the killing is Mark Twain at his best. In this pitiless scene, one of the most powerful blows ever directed at the complacency of democracy in America, life becomes farce without ceasing to be horror. The grotesqueness of the human animal has put life to the final test of our acceptance. And we accept it. The absurdity and savagery that Mark Twain captured in this scene proved more difficult to accept when, no longer young and now humiliated by near-bankruptcy, he found himself face to face with a driving, imperial America that was harsher than anything he had known on the frontier.

JAMES M. COX

Life on the Mississippi *Revisited*

I should first explain my title. It has been more than fifteen years since I wrote about *Life on the Mississippi*. I then sought the formal connections in the book that would betray a coherence beneath the drifting and disparate current of narration. Failing to find enough of them to satisfy my craving for literary unity, I tended to conclude that the book, though remarkable in parts, could not really stand by itself. And so, in dealing with it in my book on Mark Twain, I treated "Old Times on the Mississippi" as a separate entity precisely because it offered sufficient focus and form to represent a complete moment in Mark Twain's progression toward and away from what I, along with most other critics, determined was his masterpiece: *Adventures of Huckleberry Finn*. My determination determined me to use Mark Twain's long account of his return to the river in *Life on the Mississippi* as little more than a preview of Huck Finn's adventures. This time I want to see the book as a book in the life of Mark Twain.

Given its title, it ought to be a book about life on the Mississippi River, yet anyone who has read it realizes that, though it is about the great river running out of and through the heart of the nation, it is just as much a book about the life of Mark Twain. No, that is not quite right. It is rather a book in which the life of Samuel Clemens is both converted and enlarged into the myth of Mark Twain. But there is more. We cannot read this book—or any of Mark Twain's books—without helplessly participating in and even contributing to this myth, for all his works, rather than being ends in themselves, seem means toward the end of mythologizing their author. Thus I

From *The Mythologizing of Mark Twain*. © 1984 by The University of Alabama Press.

shall begin by suggesting how both we and he have collaborated in creating the myth.

No one would deny that we have mythologized Mark Twain as a native literary genius—and that "we" is not merely the popular audience but the academic or literary audience as well. The very fact that two audiences always come to mind in our thinking about Mark Twain indicates how profoundly Mark Twain (as the name implies) divided and still divides his audience. He was, after all, a popular writer and at the same time a great writer. He was recognized as such in his own time and remains so recognized to this day. And as such he represents a division—almost a contradiction—for there is more than a little doubt on both sides of the equation whether the two identities are not mutually exclusive. We on the academic side are even more prone to see the mutual exclusiveness, it seems to me, than those who love Mark Twain as a popular writer.

This initial or "master" division is but an index to a host of divisions Mark Twain has both represented and excited. There are the embattled arguments about whether he is Western or Eastern, vernacular or genteel in identity; whether he is a journalist or an artist, a writer or performer, a confident voice of the people or an embittered misanthrope; and finally whether he is an author or a businessman. Far from being of recent vintage, these arguments, or some of them, took shape in Mark Twain's lifetime; and in the work of Paine, Mencken, Brooks, De Voto, and Henry Nash Smith they were developed, intensified, and refined. Their persistence until this day reminds us of how deep the divisions have always been.

Equal to the divisions, and even controlling them, is a unity of a very special kind. The reason the persistent divisions have attracted adherents is that Mark Twain always seems to occupy both sides of each division. If there was some underground rift, there was nonetheless the single public personality operating under an exposed pen name—a personality which seemed in his own time, and seems in our time too, to be larger than his writing, or at least seemed and seems not confinable to what we are pleased to call literature. It was just this larger figure that spent itself in lecturing, investing, philosophizing, advertising, and tycooning in the expansive age of finance capitalism in which he had his being. We see, and Mark Twain's contemporary audience saw, the divisions because Mark Twain in both his lecturing and writing railed at his own involvement in such "extra-literary" activity. At the same time, there was a single Mark Twain who never even tried to conceal Samuel Clemens (though Samuel Clemens on occasion recklessly tried to conceal Mark Twain) because the pen name, even as it exposed the divisions, nonetheless contained them. The containment was managed through a humor and a clarity that perpetually disarmed the anger and the contradictory complexity the divisions somehow generated.

To face Samuel Clemens's pen name is not only to see the divisions Mark Twain's audience saw but also to see the figure of the author who projected them. Much as we might wish to see this author in the businessman's or lecturer's role of betraying his "literary" career, making the writer in him subordinate to the businessman or speculator or inventor also in him, there remains a Mark Twain who emerges before us as nothing but writing. To read his notebooks is to see him turning everything at hand into writing. If he is traveling, it is never to take a vacation to get away from his "profession" but to turn every trip and every observation into a book.

Of course it is possible to say that the books aren't literature so much as padded filler to meet the subscription contracts he had entered into, as if writing were a business instead of a profession. There is no gainsaying such an evaluation; not even Mark Twain could gainsay it as he struggled to complete the books on time (and "completion" for him often meant filling out or up a number of pages even as he angrily knew his inspiration tank was dry) for the best market moment. Yet if he could not gainsay the evaluation, he nonetheless had a deeper knowledge that something about the whole realm of what had come to be called literature in the nineteenth century was confining, even suffocating, for the figure he all but helplessly knew himself to be. The literary world was a world that, in its refinements, became filled with grown-up one-horse men, whereas the world toward which he journeyed was to be occupied by boys he would imagine in a mythic form much larger than the race of men that descended from them. Moreover, this author of boyhood knew that he would always be freer and larger than the books he wrote. In other words, the books, rather than effacing him and thereby becoming representations of his authorship, or dramatizing him and thereby reducing him to a character, were made to *enlarge* him precisely because they could not contain him.

By way of touching upon this enlargement, I want to stress just how the East–West division, though it has constituted a continual critical debate about Mark Twain's identity, is actually a very reduced image of the geographical space Mark Twain mythically occupied. Such an axis—accentuated by the criticism and contention of Brooks and De Voto—fails to take into account the North–South axis that Mark Twain also occupied. For Mark Twain touches all four points of this country's compass. Small wonder that he would finally wish to girdle the world in *Following the Equator* even as he was beginning to imagine fantasies of polar seas.

If we look at Hannibal, Missouri, where Samuel Clemens grew up, we see that it is on the Mississippi River, which was then flowing south into slavery. At the same time, it is just far enough north to be where West was South and East was North—since the Missouri Compromise of 1820 had polarized the country on a North–South axis along the line that surveyors Mason and Dixon had driven west in the eighteenth century. That political axis came to dominate the identity of his home state and village. And if the drift of the river of his youth was directly north to south, dividing east from west (as the Appalachian Mountains, running south-southwest, had previously divided them), the stretch of river he piloted was from St. Louis due south (albeit meanderingly so) to New Orleans.

If we sketched his life out of this historical and geographical configuration, we could say that Samuel Clemens fled (or deserted or escaped) the political North–South axis, once it completely volatilized, to go West where he would find a pseudonym with its origins inescapably in the river world he had left behind him, and then came into an East (which had been North) as a Westerner, there to begin reconstructing, in the age of Reconstruction, a South of Boyhood which had never existed but which he made the most real dream in our literature. That is why the language of *Huckleberry Finn*, predicated on the profound Northern sentiment of freedom, is nonetheless Southern much more than Western in its identity—which is why, by virtue of its one fatal word, it is under threat of ban to this day.

Seeing ourselves at the edge of the ban, we might be able to understand that the Concord Public Library was trying to tell us something when it banned the book upon its appearance. How wonderful that it was the Concord Library that did it, confirming just how literary the home of Emerson, Thoreau, and Hawthorne had become by 1885. I find it extremely comforting when touring Concord to remember the fact. It would never do to assault the guides with the knowledge; it is so much better to keep it in genteel restraint, at the threshold of consciousness, as one gapes at the impressive Emerson collection in the library.

But I digress. Back to the Mark Twain who at once designates the four points on the American compass and spans the time in which those four points had been confused by politics, morality, law, and finally war. If the war was the violence which clarified the morality and politics by rewriting the law, it was also the moment when Samuel Clemens found the pseudonym by means of which he reentered the Union, to which he had been a traitor, and evaded the Confederacy from which he had deserted.

He was indeed a Western outlaw in the deepest sense of the term. Of all our major writers, only Ezra Pound is a match for him in this regard. Unlike Pound, who was completing his long revolutionary poetic life when he became a traitor, Mark Twain's treason preceded his long career in prose, and, when the Civil War ended, he needed all of the humor afforded by his pseudonymous identity to disarm the moral sense of the Northeastern society he determined to enter—a society ready to judge, and even to sentence, the historic identity of Samuel Clemens.

When, after fifteen years of humorously reconstructing himself in New England society, he returned to the Mississippi in 1882 for the express purpose of writing the travel book that was to be *Life on the Mississippi*, he was at last returning in the person of Mark Twain to the river where the very term of his pen name had its origin. By the time of his return, he had made what he rightly called his *nom de guerre*, if not a household word, at least sufficiently famous that he met a steamboat of that name on the river of his youth.

He had, as we know, already returned to the river in his writing, having written seven sketches which William Dean Howells had published in the *Atlantic* (from January to August 1875) under the title "Old Times on the Mississippi," and when he came to the actual business of writing his travel book, he inserted those sketches wholesale. They constitute chapters 4 to 18 of *Life on the Mississippi* and are often referred to as the "first half" of the book, though they constitute only one-fourth of its contents. These are inevitably the chapters critics cite as the "strong part" of the book, whereas the remaining three-fourths are often dismissed as one more example of Mark Twain's unfortunate hauling and filling and padding for the subscription trade. Rarely are they incorporated into a critical vision of the book's esthetic; they are instead used by biographers to fill out the life of Samuel Clemens.

It is not my purpose in revisiting this book to show the marvelous unity that is perceptible beneath the discontinuous multiplicity of these chapters. When I wrote my book fifteen years ago, I think that was my purpose, and when I could not really see the unity, I found ways of devaluing this portion of the book. I was proceeding chronologically through the work of Mark Twain, and having devoted a chapter to "Old Times on the Mississippi," I merely used *Life on the Mississippi* as a means of beginning a discussion of *Huckleberry Finn*. Unable to reduce this travel book to the closed form literary criticism can comfortably deal with, I tended to see the book as material with which to reinforce a critical construct of Mark Twain's progress toward *Huckleberry Finn*. Lest I fall into the easy indulgence of self-criticism, I should emphasize that Mark Twain pursued exactly the same strategy in using "Old Times on the Mississippi" to build up the very book I am revisiting.

Even so, that earlier writing, "Old Times on the Mississippi," seems to have more so-called unity than the travel portion of the completed book.

Being a work of memory rather than a book worked up from travel notes, and being devoted to the more univocal subject of Mark Twain's apprenticeship as a pilot, it has a more continuous narrative line than the discursive chapters that recount the actual return to the river. Yet anyone who truly detaches all seven sketches and looks at them will see that there was much discontinuity in "Old Times," particularly in the last two sketches, in which Mark Twain, departing from the Bixby-Cub vaudeville structure to detail the nature of the pilot's power and independence, thrusts in statistics of racing times and records to accompany a string of anecdotes and historical incidents connected with the great days of steamboating. And anyone who looks at the critical literature on Mark Twain will see that what has been most emphasized about "Old Times" is the humorous vision of Mark Twain learning to be a pilot who could "read" the river. Indeed, the famous passage that invariably is trotted out of that book (as if it might be a "trot" for all future students) is the one in which Mark Twain sees the river as a text the pilot literally has to read in order to see the snags and reefs which, while dimpling the surface and adding beauty to the current, pose the threats and potential disasters that the experienced pilot's eye recognizes on the face of the water.

Such a passage, in addition to standing out as a wonderfully easy landmark for literary readers whose stock in trade is seeing the world in the figure of a text, has the summarizing clarity that is the very trademark of Mark Twain's prose. I certainly don't want to negate it, but it shouldn't be allowed to characterize either the book or the river.

At the same time, if we see why it is such a dominating passage we can by inference begin to see why "Old Times" is equally dominating in the later structure of *Life on the Mississippi*. The passage, in projecting the river as a text, shows the relation of piloting to writing. Similarly, in the career of Mark Twain "Old Times" represented (and here I am seeing it *as* the *Atlantic* sketches, not as part of *Life on the Mississippi*) that moment when Samuel Clemens, reconstructing his life under his pen name, had, in reaching the river of his youth, reached the place in his life where the name "Mark Twain" is sounded. And of course it is sounded in those sketches—once when Bixby runs the Hat Island Crossing, to the applause of an audience of experienced pilots who, having gathered to watch, have stayed to admire the feat. The call "Mark Twain" is in this instance a crisis call, not a safe-water sign. But Bixby, calm and deadpan, guides the boat through with such ease and grace that one of the onlookers says: "It was done beautiful." The second time the term is sounded, the perennially confident and complacent cub is at the wheel. By way of administering a lesson to Pride, Bixby has arranged for the leadsman to make false calls in safe water, and has also arranged for an audience to watch the fun. Hearing "Mark Twain" in what he has hitherto been confident is a bottomless crossing, the cub loses his confidence and desperately shouts to the engine room, "Oh Ben, if you love me, *back* her! . . . back the immortal *soul* out of her," only to be met with a gale of humiliating laughter from the assembled onlookers. Thus, as Samuel Clemens reconstructs his life under his pen name, he sounds the name not once but *twice* (which takes us right back to the divisions with which we began): once as a mark of the crisis so close beneath the deadpan mastery of Bixby's art, and once as a false call arranged by the master to humiliate the cub. And always this sound rings out for an audience's admiration or ridicule.

From these two moments which define the art of the master and the humiliation of the apprentice, who themselves constitute the division contained in the unified humorous reconstruction of the past (written in the waning years of national reconstruction), we can, I think, begin to see the dimensions of the world Samuel Clemens was inventing under the signature of Mark Twain. It was a world where art was a guild of master and apprentice come into the industrial age of steam; it involved both experience and memory (the master artist and pilot, Bixby, had both to know the river and to remember it); and it was art as a performance before an audience—in other words, public art, or at least art performed in public.

The signature of the author, who had once been the humiliated cub and now humorously reconstructs the past, was actually a call—a *sound*—and thus was a *sounding* in the full meaning of the word. In its original meaning it designated shallow water that could be safe or precarious, depending on whether a steamboat was approaching shallows or leaving them. The art of piloting lay precisely in negotiating depths so slight that the dangerous bottom could all but be perceived on the surface. Moreover, the greatest demands of the art were required in going downstream. In such a situation, the pilot had force behind him in the form of the natural, powerful, treacherous, and wandering drift of a mighty current he had to cross and recross as he pursued the unmarked channel forever changing on each trip he made. The art of piloting, though it all but enslaved the pilot to the current on which he rode, paradoxically conferred upon him a privilege and power that made him independent of all social and political pressures. Majestically isolate in the pilothouse, he looked with lordly freedom upon the beauty and danger of the moving river bearing him upon its current.

The pilot and his art were, as every critic of Mark Twain sooner or later comes to realize, not only the embodiment of Mark Twain's experience on the river; they were metaphors for the figure of Mark Twain the writer.

The remembered independence of the pilot was thus an expression of the writer's dream of autonomy and his determination to be free of conventional form. And the pilot's necessarily skeptical eye, surveying the deceptions of current and surface, was but a promise of the very identity of the writer and his pen name. For even in discussing Mark Twain's art we cannot quite tell whether we are discussing the art of Samuel Clemens. What we know, and all we know, is that there is a difference between them, a difference exposed in the text of every title page. Yet, for the life of us, we can't quite tell what the difference is. Neither Mark Twain nor Samuel Clemens could, I think, quite tell the difference—other than that a division was being signified even as a reconstructed unity was being discovered.

We can perhaps tell this much. The past life of Samuel Clemens was being humorously invented by virtue of, and by vice under, the authority of Mark Twain. The virtue was no doubt the art; the vice was no doubt the lie. And in "Old Times" the reconstruction had reached back across the division of the Civil War (which, if it had once divided the country, now divided the history of the country between the Old Republic and the New Union) to the river where Samuel Clemens could remember his youth even as Mark Twain could at last be sounded. To see so much ought to allow us to see that the signified division between Mark Twain and Samuel Clemens comes to us as a doubt—a doubt as deep, we want to say, as that with which Nathaniel Hawthorne invested his creative enterprise. But I want to say that it was and is as shallow as the depth the sounding "Mark Twain" designates. It is not a deep doubt but is right on the surface where we always see it but never know how to read it precisely because it is so easy to see and is humorously and pleasurably and clearly and easily right in front of us.

So much for the "Old Times" of the *Atlantic* sketches; now for *Life on the Mississippi*. Here the first point to see is that it is not Mark Twain reconstructing the life of Samuel Clemens as his own life but the record of Samuel Clemens returning to the Mississippi in the person of Mark Twain whom he cannot hide. In "Old Times" the *I* of the narrative, effacing both Samuel Clemens and Mark Twain in the comic act of apprenticeship played out by Bixby and the Cub, showed Mark Twain approaching the edge of fiction. It is hardly accidental that, at the time of writing the *Atlantic* sketches, he had just finished collaborating with Charles Dudley Warner on the satiric novel *The Gilded Age* (the collaboration itself signifying Mark Twain's entry into fiction, as well as his—and Samuel Clemens's—inability to write a novel by himself/themselves). But *The Gilded Age* and "Old Times" put him at the threshold of full-length fiction. As a matter of fact, even before he completed the *Atlantic* sketches he was at work on *Tom Sawyer*—the book he was to call a hymn written in prose to give it a worldly air.

In the figure of Tom Sawyer, he had indeed reached the poetic origins of youth lying behind the past of both Mark Twain and Samuel Clemens. More important, through the figure of Tom Sawyer, Mark Twain had discovered Huck Finn, whom he would release to begin his own narrative. But Huck's voice, released in the first centennial of the Republic (and surely one of the best things invented in that first centennial), couldn't complete its own story in that first surge. Instead, Mark Twain's inspiration tank ran dry.

This early portion of *Huckleberry Finn*, Mark Twain's raft book, stands in relation to the completed novel much as "Old Times" stands in relation to *Life on the Mississippi*, his steamboat book—and I think it of no little consequence that Mark Twain was actually in the process of completing both books as he returned to the Mississippi. He had already begun the latter, publicly, in "Old Times" (though of course he had given no public inkling in the sketches that this was to be the beginning of a travel book, and there is no evidence that he thought of it at the time *as* a beginning). The other he had driven to the point where the raft is run over by a steamboat (a hiatus which shows, both precisely and symbolically, the two books running into each other). To begin to see such a possibility is to see that it would take a trip back to the great river itself to drive the books on their parallel courses.

When he actually came to compose *Life on the Mississippi*, Mark Twain set up a casual but nonetheless definite structure, dividing the history of the river into five stages. Here is the way he asserted his structure on the fourth page of the Author's National Edition:

> Let us drop the Mississippi's physical history, and say a word about its historical history—so to speak. We can glance briefly at its slumbrous first epoch in a couple of short chapters; at its second and wider-awake epoch in a couple more; at its flushest and widest-awake epoch in a good many succeeding chapters; and then talk about its comparatively tranquil present epoch in what shall be left of the book.

Using his declaration of structure as a means of finishing off the three-page first stage, the river's physical history, he proceeded to devote the slight remainder of chapter 1 and all of chapter 2 to the historical history, primarily concentrating on the river's great explorers. To the third stage, the wider-awake epoch, he devoted only one chapter, despite his promise of two, and that chapter is primarily made up of the raftsman passage from *Huck Finn*.

"Old Times" is converted from the seven sketches into fourteen chapters that make up the flush-times epoch. And the actual travel book, detailing the "tranquil present epoch," comprises chapters 18 to 60. His casual declaration of structure, accentuated by repeated references to writing as speaking ("say a word about," "so to speak," and "talk about"), points up the fact that the first two stages—the physical history and the historical history—take up all of 16 pages of the total 496 in the Author's National Edition. The other three stages, which Mark Twain inversely calls epochs, convert the history of the river into the life of Mark Twain.

But that is only the beginning. The two epochs that precede the travel-book account of the tranquil present epoch, constituted (as they are) of the manuscript episode of Huck Finn and the wholesale importation of "Old Times," show that even as Mark Twain was doubly capitalizing on his past published writing he was also looting his future masterpiece. Nor is that all. If we did not know that the raftsman episode had been taken out of *Huckleberry Finn*, we would never miss it; moreover, it can be inserted wholesale into that book without disturbing the narrative sequence. Of course, arguments can be and have been made as to whether the episode should be left out or put into *Huckleberry Finn*, but the fact that it can be either in or out tells us more about the nature of *Huckleberry Finn* than a host of critical elucidations about its place in or out of the narrative. And beyond that, if we did not know that the chapters constituting "Old Times" were previously published as a unit, I am not at all sure that we would or could so confidently say that these chapters are the exquisite sections of the book. Knowing so much keeps us, in a real sense, subtracting from the structure and art of the book in order to add to the figural myth of Mark Twain. The only comfort I can see in this nice problem is that if we participate in making Mark Twain somehow larger than his books, we are doing just what Mark Twain himself did.

So much for the declared structure and the enlarged Mark Twain. We are still left with the devalued travel book. By way of showing how we might look at the material of the book, I want to quote its opening paragraph. Unlike the famous river-as-text passage, previously alluded to, or the "When-I-was-a-boy" passage opening "Old Times," or the "You-don't-know-about-me" beginning of *Huckleberry Finn*, this passage has never, to my knowledge, been singled out for attention.

> The Mississippi is well worth reading about. It is not a commonplace river, but on the contrary is in all ways remarkable. Considering the Missouri its main branch, it is the longest river

in the world—four thousand three hundred miles. It seems safe to say that it is also the crookedest river in the world, since in one part of its journey it uses up one thousand three hundred miles to cover the same ground that the crow could fly over in six hundred and seventy-five. It discharges three times as much water as the St. Lawrence, twenty-five times as much as the Thames. No other river has so vast a drainage basin; it draws its water-supply from twenty-eight states and territories; from Delaware on the Atlantic seaboard, and from all that country between that and Idaho on the Pacific slope—a spread of forty-five degrees of longitude. The Mississippi receives and carries to the Gulf water from fifty-four subordinate rivers that are navigable by steamboats, and from some hundreds that are navigable by flats and keels. The area of its drainage basin is as great as the combined areas of England, Wales, Scotland, Ireland, France, Spain, Portugal, Germany, Austria, Italy, and Turkey; and almost all this wide region is fertile; the Mississippi valley proper, is exceptionally so.

The resonance of the passage—with its array of facts, its grandly marshaled parallelisms, and its imposing quantitative crescendo—obscures what seems a grand joke. For right at the center of this first paragraph, and as a culminating fact about the great river's size, Mark Twain climactically announces that the Mississippi drains Delaware. This "fact," set in the majestic current of an imposing list of seemingly scientific and geographic measurements, is difficult to see precisely because it is in such a *current* of prose. If we take the passage and juxtapose it against the celebrated passage on reading the river, I think we can see how, implicitly, we are challenged to read a text.

That joke in the center of the first paragraph is equivalent to a snag in the river big enough to tear the bottom right out of a steamboat. If we have missed the snag on our first or second or third reading, seeing it instantaneously exposes what has been mere absence of vision as humiliating stupidity, and at the same time converts the feeling of humiliation into an enormous gain of pleasure as we recognize ourselves in the act of becoming master pilots. The sudden glory of our pleasure in this new-found identity shouldn't blind us to the fact that we both have and need the ignorant and complacent cub in us.

But I want to make more of this initial joke in *Life on the Mississippi* in the return visit to the book. It shows that if the Mississippi is a mighty current, so is language. The reason we miss the joke or "stretcher" is that the effect of the parallel clauses extending the size of the Mississippi carries us right by the snag. To see this force of language working is to be at the heart of narrative deception; it is also to see the function of the snag, which is nothing less than Mark Twain's deliberate deviation from a sequence of "truths" to which we have too complacently become adjusted. Those who miss the snag won't be killed, as they might be if they were pilots on the other current. They will just be comfortable jackasses, of which the world of readers is already full. Those who "get it," while they won't be sold, had better remember that they didn't always get it, and so will have a humiliatingly complacent past they have to convert into the pleasure of looking at others miss what they have lately come to see. Then there will be those who always got it—some of whom will of course be lying, whereas others will too much lie in wait, always on the lookout for every lie and every joke. And of course there will be those who insist that it wasn't much of a joke anyway, some of whom never had, and never will have, a sense of humor, and others who will be inwardly miffed that they had to have it shown them. Finally, there will be those adamant few who contend there is no joke. After all, they could say, the passage *means* to say that the Mississippi draws its water from the twenty-eight states and territories *between* Delaware and Idaho.

Read with that determination, "from Delaware on the Atlantic seaboard" is what we might call Mark Twain's redundant stutter in preparing himself to assert the area of the river's drainage basin. Against such resistance, I can't claim with arrogant assurance that this *isn't* Mark Twain's intention; I merely want to retain a skeptical eye on the passage, keeping the possibility that it might be—just *might* be—a joke. It would not be a big joke, since Delaware is after all a small state; and considering the geographical centrality I have claimed for Mark Twain, there is a rich conclusiveness in seeing him have the Mississippi "suck in" an Eastern Seaboard state. But the more important point is to see all these enumerated responses to the passage, including this last contention, as constituting an expansive humorous consciousness in Mark Twain's audience.

Seen from such a perspective of expansion, the book becomes what it is: an accumulating of every kind of narrative—Mark Twain's past, masquerading as present narrative; his importation of what he calls the emotions of European travelers as they confront the Mississippi; the broadly humorous tall tales the pilots tell him in order not so much to deceive him as to draw him out of the incognito with which he futilely tries to conceal his identity; the bogus letter of a supposedly reformed criminal preying upon the charity of gullible do-gooders wishing to believe lies (the letter, actually written by a Harvard confidence man, dressed out in the form of sentimentally appealing illiteracy); the fake narratives of spiritualists claiming to have conversations with the dead; the self-advertising lies of salesmen hawking oleomargarine and cottonseed oil as manufactured replacements for traditional substances; the intruded yarns of gamblers conning other gamblers; the romantic guide-book legends of Indian maidens (and on and on). Yet all along the way there is penetrating information, exquisite criticism of other books on the Mississippi, pungent observations of the culture of the great valley, acute commentary on the society, literature, and art of both pre- and post-Civil War America. Information and history are so interlaced with tall tales, intruded jokes, and seemingly irrelevant "loitering and gab" that truth and exaggeration scarcely can be told apart. Finally there are the episodes that Mark Twain recounts of his boyhood as he reaches Hannibal—narratives which biographers have all too often taken as the traumatic, true experience of Mark Twain's childhood, although they have about them the aspect of indulgent (as well as invented) guilt fantasies.

A way of seeing it all, in a bit of nubbed down compression, would be to remember that the pilot whom Mark Twain meets on the *Gold Dust* is called Rob Styles (the actual name was Lem Gray, and he was killed in a steamboat explosion while Mark Twain was writing the book). How right a name to be waiting for Mark Twain as he hopelessly tries to hide his own identity! For Mark Twain does indeed *rob styles*, showing us, by implication, our outlaw writer operating as a literary highwayman, ready to raid even his own work to flesh out his book. How much of the King and the Duke he has in him! No wonder he comes back to that name of his in this part of the book, showing that it had first been used by Isaiah Sellers (and here what is presumably the true name is nonetheless perfect), a veritable Methuselah among riverboat pilots.

Samuel Clemens had thoughtlessly yet irreverently parodied the old man's river notes and the lampoon had, according to Mark Twain, silenced the old captain, leaving him to sit up nights to hate the impudent young parodist. And so Mark Twain says that when, on the Pacific Coast, he had set up as a writer, he *confiscated* the ancient captain's pen name. He concludes his account by saying that he has done his best to make the name a "sign and symbol and warrant that whatever is found in its company may be gambled on as being the petrified truth."

Never mind that Samuel Clemens didn't first use his *nom de guerre* on the Pacific Coast (we experts see *that* joke). The point is that, if in "Old Times" Mark Twain had shown the memory, skill, anxiety, courage, humiliation, and the joke attending the leadsman's call, he now shows the aggression, theft, parody, and comic guilt attending the act of *displacing* the ancient mariner of the river. Having confiscated the old man's pen name, he makes his own life and writing identical with the *epochs* of the river's emergence from the sleep of history.

The "petrified truth," which the name Mark Twain is said to signify, is itself the broadest of jokes. The actual truth is as elusive as the shape of the river that Horace Bixby had said the pilot must know with such absolute certainty that it lives in his head. Through all the shifts of perspective in this book, through all the changes of direction, the abrupt compression of space, and wayward digressions to kill time, there is yet a single writer whose shape seems somehow in *our* head, rather than in the shifting book before us. That figure is of course the myth of Mark Twain, growing out of and beyond the book that cannot contain him. We might devalue, and have devalued, this book, but in devaluing it we are already preparing to use it as a foil for *Huckleberry Finn*, the book that was waiting to be finished even as Mark Twain brought this one to an abrupt conclusion.

And this mythic figure, always materializing above his books, whose shape is in our heads, seems in his way as real as the great river—seems, indeed, to be that river's tutelary deity. He is the figure who, more than any of our writers, knows the great truth that Swift exposed in the fourth book of *Gulliver's Travels*: that if man cannot tell the truth, neither can language. Language can only lie.

In this connection, it is well to remember those Watergate days when Richard Nixon said that he would make every effort to find out "where the truth lies." Apparently, Nixon never saw the joke in his assertion, but Mark Twain would certainly have seen it since he knew that the truth lies everywhere, and nothing can really lie like it. Being our greatest liar, he knew how much he believed in and needed the beautiful and powerful and deceptive river at the center of his country. It was a muddy river—the river he knew—so that you couldn't see the bottom, which was always so near, and it ran south into slavery just as man's life runs down into the slavery of adulthood. It rolled from side to side, wallowing in its valley as it shifted landmarks and state boundaries. It could hardly be bridged, and to this day has few bridges on it between New Orleans and St. Louis. It was, and still is, a lonely river for anyone upon its current. Lonely as it is, and monotonous too, it remains a truly wild river. Even now it may burst its banks and head through the Atchafalaya Bayou, leaving New Orleans high and dry. For it is a living river, always changing, always giving the lie to anyone who counts on its stability.

If Mark Twain grows out of the lie that language can't help telling, the great river grows out of some force that language cannot name. To begin to study the current of Mark Twain's prose in this book is to begin to sense the power of that other current that his discontinuous narrative displaces more than it represents. How good it is that Mark Twain does not spend all his time—he actually spends quite little—in describing, analyzing, or celebrating the river. If his book is not a great book, as great books go, it is well worth revisiting.

Revisiting it makes me know that it is time for the present generation of critics to take up Mark Twain. With their problematics, their presences-become-absences, and their aporias, they will be able to see the river as the genius loci of Mark Twain's imagination. I very much believe that this newer criticism, dealing as it can and does with discontinuity and open-ended forms, should be able to give a better account of Mark Twain's structure and language than the generation of New Critics who relied on the closed structures of lyric, drama, and novel. In the gap—I had almost said aporia—between Samuel Clemens and Mark Twain, these critics may see, as if for the first time, the writer's two I's which yet make one in sight.

ROY HARVEY PEARCE

"Yours Truly, Huck Finn"

Huck Finn's closing words, as he is about to light out for the Territory, pose a dilemma not for him but for his reader. Huck has been throughout a liar aspiring to be a shape-shifter, or vice versa. And he has not been altogether successful in either role. Moreover, as if his failure weren't enough, he is burdened—so one interpretive line has it—with the failure of Mark Twain to invent for him in the final, the Evasion, chapters an action and a demeanor that will, from a reader's perspective, justify his special mode of credibility, his own way with the truth.

The problem centers on the ending of *Adventures of Huckleberry Finn*, to which in the end I shall come, in the hope of demonstrating that Huck has in fact, in the ironic rendering of his very factuality, wholly deserved that "Yours Truly," although at a great cost to us; and surely at a greater cost to Mark Twain. (Understanding this last would entail understanding the relationship between Samuel Clemens and Mark Twain—something beyond my competence.) For we must come to realize that rather than being possibly one of us—someone with whom, according to the canons of nineteenth-century realism, we might "identify"—Huck is exclusively a project of his own, Mark Twain-given possibility: in the end we must acknowledge the impossibility of his truth—all of it, and on its own terms—being ours. In the end we discover that we belong "realistically" at best with the Tom Sawyers of Huck's and our world, at worst with the Colonel Sherburns and

From *One Hundred Years of* Huckleberry Finn: *The Boy, His Book, and American Culture.* © 1985 by the Curators of the University of Missouri. University of Missouri Press, 1985.

the Dukes and the Dauphins—and, in a kind of merciful artistic transcendence, with the Mark Twains. But we also discover in the end that we are only possibly Tom Sawyers, Colonel Sherburns, Dukes and Dauphins, Mark Twains. Hope for something better, defined with high irony, does remain. But not for those interpreters among us who want guarantees beyond hope. The hope of *Huckleberry Finn* is the hope of utopianism, but necessarily (because ours is the way of the world of Tom Sawyer, of Colonel Sherburn and the Duke and the Dauphin, of Mark Twain) a failed utopianism. *Huckleberry Finn* teaches us (we should not flinch at the phrase) that whereas utopianism is possible, utopians are not.

Huckleberry Finn, then, is the sort of book that becomes absolutely central to the experience of a reader, American or otherwise, who would try to understand his sense of himself as against his sense of his culture. Its domain is Western America, but its purview, as in its art it universalizes Huck's experience, is the whole world. Through Huck's account of his world and those who inhabit it, Mark Twain renders Huck for us too—Huck at once in his world and apart from it. This of course is the abiding pattern of most of the masterworks of nineteenth-century American fiction, which project for our experience and understanding the central problem for the American in the nineteenth century, and also in the twentieth: How, in Emerson's words, satisfy the claims of the self as against those of the world? How, in Whitman's words, conceive of the person who must exist simply and separately and also as part of the mass? The mass protagonists of nineteenth-century fiction before Mark Twain are put through trials and tribulations whereby they are readied for a return to a society whose integrity they, in seeking too fiercely to discover their own private identities, have somehow violated. At the end Hawthorne's Hester, Melville's Ishmael, and many others of their kind are ready to accommodate themselves to their society, and in their newfound knowledge of the complexities of relations between self and society are perhaps capable of contributing to the "improvement" of both. The tales told of them are open-ended, finally ambiguous, and problematic. Under such terminal conditions, they have earned their right to try out the future. They have come to be endowed with a sense of their own history.

None of this is true of Huck. Return and accommodation—above all, the capacity to be an agent of "improvement"—are quite beyond him. His function, it turns out, is to demonstrate the absolute incompatibility of the sort of self he is and the sort of world in which he tries so hard to live. He gains no sense of his own history and has no future. Nor, as I shall show, need he have. Unlike Hester, Ishmael, and their kind, unlike the kind of committed person whom Emerson and Whitman envisaged, Huck neither could nor should be one of us. He exists not to judge his world but to furnish us the means of judging it—and also our world as it develops out of his.

The means to the judgment are the superb comedy and satire deriving from Huck's quite immediate and lyrical accounts of his own person and from his resolutely deadpan rendering of the doings of those among whom he has his adventures. The lyrical accounts abound and almost always establish his consonance with the natural world, as opposed to the civilized:

> Miss Watson she kept pecking at me, and it got tiresome and lonesome. By-and-by they fetched the niggers in and had prayers, and then everybody was off to bed. I went up to my room with a piece of candle and put it on the table. Then I set down in a chair by the window and tried to think of something cheerful, but it warn't no use. I felt so lonesome I most wished I was dead. The stars was shining, and the leaves rustled in the woods ever so mournful; and I heard an owl, away off, who-whooing about somebody that was dead, and a whippowill and a dog crying about somebody that was going to die; and the wind was trying to whisper something to me and I couldn't make out what it was, and so it made the cold shivers run over me.

Against this tone, there is that of the witness to civilized falseness, foolishness, and cruelty to others. Here, Huck and Jim have taken on the Duke and the Dauphin and Huck has listened patiently to their outrageous stories about themselves:

> It didn't take me long to make up my mind that these liars warn't no kings nor dukes, at all, but just low-down humbugs and frauds. But I never said nothing, never let on; kept it to myself; it's the best way; then you don't have no quarrels, and don't get into no trouble. If they wanted us to call them kings and dukes, I hadn't no objections, 'long as it would keep peace in the family; and it warn't no use to tell Jim, so I didn't tell him. If I never learnt nothing else out of pap, I learnt that the best way to get along with his kind of people is to let them have their own way.

The range in style—from lyrical to matter-of-fact—delineates Huck's character. In the latter style, he can make judgments, but no judgments that lead to significant action. Above all, he is not one to change the world. What is important is that he be allowed at critical moments to be himself, so as to combine in that self the directness, naiveté, and often helplessness of a boy with the practical wisdom of a man, clever in the ways of surviving in towns and woods and on the river. His authentic self as Mark Twain develops it makes him essentially a witness, even when he is a participant. His is a vital presence. In the long run, what he does is altogether secondary to what he is.

It was, as we now know, Mark Twain's original intention to involve Huck all the way in the practical—and in effect radical—action of helping Jim achieve his freedom. Hence the opening words of chapter 15 consolidate the action thus far: "We judged that three nights more would fetch us to Cairo, at the bottom of Illinois, where the Ohio River comes in, and that was what we was after. We would sell the raft and get on a steamboat and go way up the Ohio amongst the free States, and then be out of trouble." It is in this chapter, too, that Huck's instinctive sense of Jim as a person becomes clear; he can even bring himself to "humble [himself] to a nigger" and not be sorry for it. In the next chapter, although he is conscience-stricken at realizing what helping Jim means, still he protects him. And then they discover that they have gone by Cairo, are still on the Mississippi in slave territory. If Mark Twain had let Huck and Jim find Cairo and the Ohio River, he would have realized his original intention and made Huck into the moderately "activist" type he first conceived him to be. Likely the story would have ended there. In any case, Mark Twain knew little or nothing about the Ohio River and almost everything about the Mississippi and would have been hard put to find materials with which further to develop the story. In his plotting he seems to have come to an impasse. For he stopped writing at this point, in 1876, not finally to complete *Huckleberry Finn* until 1883. At the end of chapter 16, a steamboat smashes the raft, and Huck and Jim, diving for their lives, are separated.

In the context of the Evasion episode, the fact of Mark Twain's impasse is worth pointing out, because the Huck of the rest of the book, although continuous with the Huck of the first sixteen chapters, is not confined to his own small world and the river, not just dedicated (but in an agonized way) to helping Jim achieve his freedom, but also made witness to the full panoply of people and institutions that, as we see even if he does not, would deny freedom not only to Jim but to themselves.

Between October 1879 and June 1883, while he finished *A Tramp Abroad* and *The Prince and the Pauper*, Mark Twain was able to write only chapters 17–21 of *Huckleberry Finn*, for he still had not discovered the means of turning Huck's adventures with Jim into something of a wider compass. During the winter of 1882–83, he was writing *Life on the Mississippi*, developing it out of a series of magazine articles, "Old Times on the Mississippi," published in 1875. In preparation for that development he had revisited the Mississippi

River and was depressed to see how much of all that he had so lovingly recalled in the magazine articles was disappearing. Indeed, his life during the period 1876–83 had been difficult and too often personally disappointing. Traveling to Europe, he despaired of the development of those traditional free institutions that most of his contemporaries had persuaded themselves had been Europe's glorious gift to the world. Reading Dicken's *Tale of Two Cities*, Carlyle's *History of the French Revolution*, and Lecky's *History of European Morals*, he began to think of man's history as only confirming the view he (and his collaborator, Charles Dudley Warner) had taken of corruption in government and business in *The Gilded Age* (1873). Thinking about the Mississippi again, meditating the downward path from past to present, finding his increasingly desperate view of the human situation confirmed by his reading, he discovered his imagination empowered and vivified. It was as though he were compelled to finish *Huckleberry Finn*. He finished a draft of the book during the summer of 1883, spent seven months revising it, and saw it published in England in December 1884 and in the United States in February 1885.

Despair, then, is, as antecedent and consequence, a prime characteristic of *Huckleberry Finn*. But in the book itself it produces mainly comedy and satire of a superb order. For counterbalancing the despair that went into the writing of the book, there is the abounding joy of Huck when he is most fully himself. In all his cleverness and dexterity, he is—except for what he does for Jim—essentially passive. He lives in the midst of violence and death; yet his only violence, if it can be called that, is the mild, ritualistic sort whereby when necessary he feeds himself. He hunts and fishes only when he has to. His joy is virtually private—to be shared, because instinctively understood, only by Jim. He is of course given no comic or satiric sense. He is given only his own rich sense of himself—richest when he is alone with Jim, on the river.

Comedy and satire derive from Huck's conviction that he must report fully what he sees—and further from the fact that it is he, capable of such joy, who does the reporting. Irony, a product of a tightly controlled point of view, is everywhere enforced for us by the fact that Huck, all unknowing, is its agent. He does not understand much of what he sees. Mark Twain's irony, however, lets us understand. What Huck is witness to again and again are doings of people who have contrived a world that distorts the public and private institutions—ranging from forms of government to forms of play— that just might make his sort of joy possible for all. His relationship with Jim—gained through his acceptance of the private guilt entailed by refusing to accept the injunction called for by public tradition and law—stands as a kind of utopian pattern for all human relationships. And we judge those in the book accordingly. Still, it is an appropriately primitive, even precivilized relationship; for Huck sees Jim not as a man with the responsibilities of a man but as one essentially like himself. This is his fundamental limitation, and yet the source of his strength. So long as that strength exists, so long as he exists, he can participate in the world only as a role-player, willing to go along with all the pretensions and make-believe that he witnesses. He accepts other names, other identities almost casually. Living them, he seems to "belong" in his world. But not quite. For always there is a certain reserve. Always there is the joy of his simple, separate self, to which he returns again and again as though to renew himself. Set against that self, the world in which he has his adventures can be constituted only of grotesque, marvelously distorted beings who are the stuff of comedy and satire.

In 1895, planning to "get up an elaborate and formal lay sermon on morals and the conduct of life, and things of that stately sort," Mark Twain defined Huck's situation in his world:

> Next, I should exploit the proposition that in a crucial moral emergency a sound heart is a safer guide than an ill-trained conscience, I sh'd support this doctrine with a chapter from a book of mine where a sound heart and deformed conscience come into collision and conscience suffers defeat. Two persons figure in this chapter: Jim, a middle-aged slave, and Huck Finn, a boy of 14, . . . bosom friends, drawn together by a community of misfortune. . . .
>
> In those slave-holding days the whole community was agreed as to one thing—the awful sacredness of slave property. To help steal a horse or a cow was a low crime, but to help a hunted slave . . . or hesitate to promptly betray him to a slave-catcher when opportunity offered was a much baser crime, and carried with it a stain, a moral smirch which nothing could wipe away. That this sentiment should exist among slave-holders is comprehensible—there were good commercial reasons for it—but that it should exist and did exist among the paupers . . . and in a passionate and uncompromising form, is not in our remote day realizable. It seemed natural enough to me then; natural enough that Huck and his father the worthless loafer should feel and approve it, though it now seems absurd. It shows that that strange thing, the conscience— that unerring monitor—can be trained to

approve any wild thing you *want* it to approve if you begin its
education early and stick to it.

Not only the distinction between heart and conscience but also the quite
sophisticated notion of how culture, or society, or the world, forms conscience and so makes possible the death of the heart—these conceptions are
central to the very structure of *Huckleberry Finn* as Mark Twain finally developed it, as is the fact that he gives Huck a sense of his own heart which,
at however great a cost, persuades him that he can be in the great world
only a player of roles.

At the beginning Huck tells us that this time, unlike the occasion of
Tom Sawyer, he is going to speak out on his own and so correct Mr. Mark
Twain in a few matters. His truth, in a consummate irony, is to be set against
the conscience of even his creator. Huck now is letting himself be civilized
and reports mildly on how it is. Yet at the end of the first chapter (in the
first passage cited above), we know that he is in full possession of his truthful
self. Assured of that fact, we can rest easy while he goes along with Tom
Sawyer's complicated make-believe and even plays a trick on Jim. His sojourn
in the Widow Douglas's world, as in Tom's, is throughout marked by role-
playing and make-believe. And he can as easily adjust to his father's world,
play his role there and sustain the make-believe, as he can to Tom's and the
Widow Douglas's. Perhaps the patterns of make-believe in *their worlds* are
harmless; no one is hurt much; everyone can make himself out to be aspiring
to something better or nobler. But the pretenses and distortions of his father's
world are dangerous and frightening; and Huck suffers accordingly—still
managing, however, to record, in his frankness, his sense of his own truth.
The make-believe and role-playing of Tom's boy's world are Huck's way
into the make-believe and role-playing in the world of adults. The formal
design is surely carefully contrived, allowing us easily to move with Huck
from one world to the other, and demanding of Mark Twain that at the end
of the adventures he arrange things so that Huck attempts to come back to
his proper world, which, according to a proper pattern of conscience-
directing institutions, must be a boy's world.

Indeed, the episodes of *Huckleberry Finn* evolve one into the other on
Huck and Jim's trip downriver as so many exempla of the nineteenth-century
American "conscience—that unerring monitor"—as it "can be trained to
approve any wild thing you *want* it to approve if you begin its education
early and stick to it." The murder of Pap, Jim's running away, Huck's
information-seeking visit with Mrs. Loftus, their finding the wreck of the

Walter Scott, Huck's cruel joke on Jim and the beginning of his sense of
dedication and obligation to him, the separation, Huck amid the Grangerfords in all their distorted pride and nobility, his escape from the feud and
reunion with Jim—these opening episodes, as we recall them, regularly involve Huck as either role-player or witness, or both. At their conclusion (at
the end of chapter 18 and the beginning of chapter 19), Huck with Jim on
his own, is his truest self:

> We said there warn't no home like a raft, after all. Other places
> do seem so cramped up and smothery, but a raft don't. You feel
> mighty free and easy and comfortable on a raft.

> Two or three days and nights went by; I reckon I might say they
> swum by, they slid along so quiet and smooth and lovely.

So it goes for the time being; and we are reassured. But almost immediately Huck and Jim are with the Duke and the Dauphin, consummate
artists in those forms of make-believe that fool all of the people most of the
time, possessors of consciences distorted enough to make them (most of the
time) masters of all whom they survey—including Huck and Jim. Again (in
the second passage cited above), Huck is willing to go along. Or rather, he
has no option but to go along.

The point is that he knows what he is doing, and accordingly we are
reassured that his sense of his authentic truth will sustain him. He stands
by—what else can he do?—while the Dauphin bilks a Pokeville campmeeting
and the Duke takes over a print-shop and while they fleece the public with
their promised obscene "Royal Nonesuch" show. Too, he is witness to Colonel Sherburn's denunciation of a small-town mob and his shooting-down of
the town drunkard. There is no impulse to prevent any of this; this is beyond
his capacities; and, after all, like the rest of the townspeople he too is fooled
by the act of the comic drunk in the circus. Make-believe, all of it, and
constant role-playing. Only with the attempt to fleece the Wilks girls does
Huck's truth come to be powerful enough to bring him to act. Here, too,
he acts by role-playing, but this time his role is set according to his truth.
The failure of this attempt of the Duke and the Dauphin brings them to sell
Jim. And there comes Huck's great crisis, in which truth once and for all
triumphs over conscience, instinct over training, the self over society and all
the good and needed things it offers.

The famous passage (in chapter 31) begins:

> Once I said to myself it would be a thousand times better for Jim
> to be a slave at home where his family was, as long as he'd *got*

to be a slave, and so I'd better write a letter to Tom Sawyer and tell him to tell Miss Watson where he was. But I soon give up that notion, for two things: she'd be mad and disgusted at his rascality and ungratefulness for leaving her, and so she'd sell him straight down the river again; and if she didn't, everybody naturally despises an ungrateful nigger, and they'd make Jim feel it all the time, and so he'd feel ornery and disgraced. And then think of *me*! It would get all around, that Huck Finn helped a nigger to get his freedom; and if I was ever to see anybody from that town again, I'd be ready to get down and lick his boots for shame. That's just the way: a person does a low-down thing, and then he don't want to take no consequences of it. Thinks as long as he can hide it, it ain't no disgrace.

This is the voice of conscience, and it torments Huck. He tries to pray but realizes he "can't pray a lie." For he knows he will sin against his conscience by continuing to try to help Jim. He goes so far as to write a letter to Miss Watson, telling her where Jim is, and feels "all washed clean of sin." But then he recalls his relationship with Jim and makes the great decision—to "steal Jim out of slavery again." And so he says, "All right, then, I'll *go* to hell."

But stealing Jim out of slavery, it turns out, is yet a matter of role-playing. At the Phelpses, Huck is taken for Tom Sawyer and thereupon enters the last of his adventures—once more by assuming the name and, in part, the conscience of another. Tom comes, assumes his brother's name, and plunges them both into the work of the Evasion. Fittingly, necessarily, Huck must be brought back into that segment of the society that is, by the world's standards, appropriate to him—a boy's world.

The complications of the Evasion episode, and also its detail and length, tend to put off many readers of *Huckleberry Finn*. They see it as Mark Twain's evasion of the moral implications of his story, especially when they learn that Jim has been free all along. Huck, they say, should have seen Jim all the way to freedom. It might well be that the episode is in fact too complicated and too long, overbalancing the end of the story. Still, in the necessary scheme of the novel, in the necessary contrast between Huck's assumption of various forms of conscience and the truth he constantly has within him— in that scheme, it is imperative that the book begin as it ends: in effect, with a grotesque and sardonic comment on the nature of the forms of make-believe, pretense, and distortion that set the life-styles of those whose consciences they shape. It is all in the end very stupid. Men have given up the authentic

truth they might well have had as children for the falsifying forms of conscience that lead to the violence, destruction, and predation that transform
their society into the enemy of the very men it should sustain and preserve.
Tom Sawyer here as earlier patterns his play principally after the romances of
Sir Walter Scott. For boys it is moderately harmless play, although Tom is
slightly wounded in the final scuffle. Yet we recall the episode of the wrecked
steamboat, itself called *Walter Scott*, and are forced to realize what will necessarily ensue when boyish make-believe and role-playing become the mode of
life of mature men and women. Conscience will not let truth survive.

Indeed, in this world Huckleberry Finn cannot continue to exist. He
says at the end that he will not return to St. Petersburg: "I reckon I got to
light out for the Territory ahead of the rest, because Aunt Sally she's going
to adopt me and sivilize me and I can't stand it. I been there before." The
plan to go to the Territory is Tom's, of course, for whom it is another
opportunity for "howling adventures," this time "amongst the Injuns." Huck
will survive, that is to say, by playing yet another role in this make-believe,
conscience-stricken world. Here, however, he speaks only as witness.

II

In the last chapter of *Huckleberry Finn*, Huck in fact speaks twice of
going to "the Territory." The first time he is reporting Tom's plans, now
that the Evasion has been managed successfully, "to slide out of here, one
of these nights, and get an outfit, and go for howling adventures amongst
the Injuns, over in the Territory." The second time he is speaking of his
own plans: "I reckon I got to light out for the Territory ahead of the rest,
because Aunt Sally she's going to adopt me and sivilize me and I can't stand
it. I been there before."

I suppose that the obvious irony of the two passages has not been pointed
out precisely because it is so obvious. The Territory is, of course, the Indian
Territory, which was to become Oklahoma. From the 1820s on, it had been
organized and developed as a region to which Indians could be safely removed
away from civilized society, since their lands were needed for higher purposes
than those to which they could put them. The cruelty and deprivation of
removal were generally taken to be the inevitable price American society had
to pay as it passed through its God-ordained stages of development. One
part of this price was said to be the yielding of a certain amount of freedom
or, to put it as an article of faith in Manifest Destiny, the surrendering of a
"lower" for a "higher" freedom. It seems fairly evident that the man who
was to write "To the Person Sitting in Darkness" and other such pieces

would be fully aware of the removal episode, with its justifications and consequences, and that he intended his readers to be aware of it too. Read in this light, what for Tom is yet another willful adolescent fantasy becomes for Huck a compelling actuality. Tom's willfulness effects a parody that points up some of the grotesqueness of the historically authentic pioneering, civilizing spirit. Huck's compulsion effects a satire that simply denies that that spirit is authentic, despite its historical actuality. Huck will seek the freedom of the Territory just because it is an uncivilized freedom. (A better word, perhaps, is *noncivilized* freedom.) It is, indeed, the only true freedom for the authentic human being Huck eventually comes to be—in spite of himself.

Yet there is more to the passages, particularly the second, than this. Huck, we recall, speaks of lighting out for the Territory "ahead of the rest." Here, at the end, Mark Twain introduces his own point of view, which, of necessity, is more encompassing than Huck's; as a result Huck is given more to say than he could possibly know. From Huck's simple point of view, the allusion is to Tom's vague plans to go to the Territory; for Mark Twain, it is to the Boomer movement that was a prime factor in the taking over of Indian lands, "sivilizing" the Territory, and creating another American state. The effect is that Huck, all unknowing, is given a kind of prescience that his adventures at this point surely justify. No matter where he goes, he will be one step ahead not only of the Tom Sawyers of his world but also of the sort of people into whom the Tom Sawyers grow.

After the Civil War, there was constant agitation in Kansas and Missouri to open up the unsettled parts of the Indian Territory to whites. To this end, bills were repeatedly, if on the whole unsuccessfully, introduced in Congress. Pressures were put on the so-called Five Civilized Nations (Cherokees, Creeks, and Choctaws principally) to cede part of their lands in the Territory to be used as reservations for other Indians and, for due payment, to make them available for settlement by whites. In the late 1870s and into the 1880s, white incursions into the Territory were numerous enough to call for the use of troops to defend Indian rights. Moreover, in 1879 a court decision found that even those lands in the Territory that had been ceded to the government by Indians could not be settled by whites, since such lands had been ceded conditionally for future settlement by other Indians.

Inevitably, however, white incursions—by groups who came to be known as Boomers—increased in tempo and number. Invaders were not jailed but fined. When they could not pay the fines, they were simply escorted to the territorial border by soldiers. The economics of the situation were complex: railroads encouraged and propagandized Boomers; cattlemen, wanting to use the lands for grazing, opposed the Boomers, who were farmers, and defended Indian rights, which included the right to rent their lands for grazing. The story (one of confusion, broken promises, and violence—all in the name of "civilization") moved toward its resolution in 1889, when the government bought certain lands from Indians and opened them to settlement as the Territory of Oklahoma.

Boomerism, then, was the most recent expression of the westering American spirit. In the words of an 1885 petition to Congress, drawn up by B. L. Brush and John W. Marshall in Howard, Kansas, on behalf of Boomerism:

> Resolved, That we are opposed to the policy of the Government in using the army to drive out or interfere with actual settlers upon any of the public domain, as being foreign to the genius of our institutions. . . .
>
> Resolved, As this selfsame, bold spirit, that is now advancing to the front, has ever existed since the Pilgrim Fathers set their feet on Plymouth Rock, and will ever exist so long as we remain citizens of this grand Republic, that we, the citizens of Howard and vicinity, pledge ourselves to firmly support this grand element—the vanguard of civilization. . . .
>
> Resolved, That we are opposed to the settlement of any more bands of wild Indians on the Indian Territory.

Although I know of no direct allusion in Mark Twain's writings to the troubles in the Indian Territory, I think it likely that he was well aware of them, for they were widely publicized and debated and of great interest to Congress. A considerable amount of Boomer ferment developed in Mark Twain's—and Huck's—Missouri, although Kansas was a more important center. The summer of 1883, when Twain was writing the last part of *Huckleberry Finn*, David Payne and his Boomers were particularly active in promoting their cause. One historian of Oklahoma reports that the general whose responsibility it was to turn Boomers back declared that in 1883 "the whole affair had become simply a series of processions to and from the Kansas line."

Thus it would seem that in 1883, Mark Twain, now finally committed to a conception of Huck Finn whose fate it must always be to seek a freedom beyond the limits of any civilization, ended his novel by contrasting Tom's and Huck's sense of the Territory. Note that Huck is willing to go along with Tom, if he can get the money to outfit himself for those "howling adventures amongst the Injuns." Jim tells Huck that, now that his father is dead, he does have the money. However, he will have to claim it himself.

The matter of the money and the "howling adventures" is then dropped. Since Tom is "most well" now, Huck says, there "ain't nothing more to write about." He will "light out for the Territory ahead of the rest." In one sense, perhaps, he simply means ahead of Tom and Jim; in a larger sense (so I think we must conclude) he means ahead of all those people whose civilizing mission Boomerism actualized in fact. The realities of the case are, as ever, contrasted with Tom's fantasies.

The Huck who seems willing to go along with Tom is, of course, not the Huck who, against the dictates of his conscience, has helped Jim in his quest for freedom. It is altogether necessary that this latter Huck must, alone, "light out for the Territory ahead of the rest." With the curious prescience that Mark Twain gives him, he knows that in antebellum days (as Mark Twain surely knew that summer of 1883), even in the Territory, he will be only one step ahead of the rest: Boomers, Dukes and Dauphins, Aunt Sallies, Colonel Sherburns, and Wilkses—civilizers all. Certainly we are not to assume that Huck self-consciously knows the full meaning (even the full moral meaning) of what he says here. Yet we cannot conclude that this allusion is simply a matter of Mark Twain speaking out in his own person. Huck's view and Mark Twain's, in a culminating irony, here become one. Huck's prescience is, within the limits of the narrative, a matter of intuition, forced into expression by his hardheaded sense that he has almost always been one step "ahead of the rest." He can say his final "Yours Truly" and yet must be willing to go to hell for saying it.

III

I think we must conclude that Huck is not meant to survive. He is so powerfully a being of truth as against conscience, self as against society, that he exists not as an actuality but as a possibility. In him Mark Twain projects the American's sense that somewhere, at some point—even if only in the imagination—it would indeed be possible to regain access to the truth, if only we could cut through the shams of conscience and of the institutions that form and justify it. But in the present situation, Mark Twain despaired of that possibility and in Huck, his nature, and his history saw it only as impossible. Huck, then, is that ideal, perhaps never-to-be-attained type—in Wallace Stevens's phrase, an "impossible possible philosopher's man." Huck, then, stands as witness to his experience, totally unaware of the irony whereby it becomes at once an aspect and a function of our experience. In rendering the witnessing, Mark Twain makes us, if we but grasp the irony, the judge of that experience—Huck's and our own—and the world in which it is shaped. It is inappropriate to regret that Huck does not follow through on his own to free Jim. That is not Huck's proper role; for it would be the role of someone in whom conscience and truth were to a significant degree harmonious. Huck, for whom conscience always means role-playing, in whom the naked truth must finally be overpowering, stands, as I have said, not as possibly one of us but rather as our means of judging his world and Mark Twain's—and, along with it, ours.

We can take Mark Twain's preliminary "Notice" to *Huckleberry Finn* with the deadly serious levity with which it is meant: "Persons attempting to find a motive in the narrative will be prosecuted; persons attempting to find a moral in it will be banished; persons attempting to find a plot in it will be shot." "Motive" and "plot" are, however, not so much absent as negative. Huck's motive is to survive; and we know that the conditions of his life and of his society are such that survival is impossible. The plot of his *Adventures* lays out the pattern of the impossibility; Huck's is a history of whose meaning he cannot be conscious and still be his truest self. Above all, the story has no "moral." Rather it is an exercise in the use of such moral sensibility as remains with us. Knowing what Huck is, we can know what we have become and measure the cost and the worth.

F. Scott Fitzgerald wrote in 1935,

> Huckleberry Finn took the first journey *back*. He was the first to look *back* at the republic from the perspective of the west. His eyes were the first eyes that ever looked at us objectively that were not eyes from overseas. There were mountains at the frontier but he wanted more than mountains to look at with his restive eyes—he wanted to find out about men and how they lived together. And because he turned back we have him forever.

The condition of his turning back, however, is that we cannot demand that he be one of us. He stands as witness, bound to his own truth, so that we might go forth and be likewise.

DOUGLAS ROBINSON

Revising the American Dream:
A Connecticut Yankee

Twain's "inspiration" for *A Connecticut Yankee* is recorded in an oft-quoted journal entry from the mid-1880s, an ambiguous "dream" that may have been Twain's own ("I dreamed last night that..."—a random nocturnal image) but that also, Twain's elliptical syntax allows us to conjecture, may have been invented entirely for future use ("Have a character dream that..."—a mythic expression of the national hope). The journal entry, in fact, with its complex mixtures of times and attitudes, in important ways presents in embryo the novel Twain later wrote:

> Dream of being a knight errant in armor in the middle ages. Have the notions & habits of thought of the present day mixed with the necessities of that. No pockets in the armor. No way to manage certain requirements of nature. Can't scratch. Cold in the head—can't blow—can't get at handkerchief, can't use iron sleeve. Iron gets red hot in the sun—leaks in the rain, gets white with frost & freezes me solid in winter. Suffer from lice & fleas. Make disagreeable clatter when I enter church. Can't dress or undress myself. Always getting struck by lightning. Fall down, can't get up.

This is farce in the root sense of the word, as a man of the nineteenth century is most indecorously "stuffed" (from the Latin *farcire*) into a confining suit of armor. The dream encapsulates the novel precisely as an index of

---

From *American Apocalypses: The Image of the End of the World in American Literature*. © 1985 by The Johns Hopkins University Press. Originally entitled "Revising the American Dream."

Twain's driving concern with the problems of stuffing the nineteenth century into the sixth century, the present into the past, an after (*post*) into a before (*pre*)—which indeed, etymologically speaking, makes it a "preposterous" farce. Hank is stuffed into the past-as-prison, and he engineers his escape by first modifying (through his "civilization") and finally destroying (in the Battle of the Sand-Belt) the confining suit or era—only to find that the prison or shell thus destroyed was not merely a covering or vestiture but the very body that gave him life, and without it he is not just naked but dead.

I borrow this expanded sense of "preposterous farce" from Harold Bloom's discussion in *A Map of Misreading* of the trope/image/defense cluster that he cites as the central Romantic mode of victory over time: metaleptic introjection. In traditional rhetoric, metalepsis (or transumption) signifies the continuing of a trope in one word through a succession of meanings; but Bloom takes some rather interesting liberties with the trope, combining it with the imagistic cluster of early and late and with the Freudian defenses of projection and introjection to generate a complex theoretical tool. Bloom's metalepsis is double—doubly dialectical. In one dialectic, it portrays the "throwing forward" (projection) of past into future, a proleptic form of representation in which the "dreamer" (my word, not Bloom's) casts his or her own past self prophetically into the dim future. In the second dialectic, the dreamer farcically "stuffs" the before with the after (preposterous), the past with the future, self with other, in a "throwing inward" (introjection). Bloom notes in *A Map of Misreading* that the latter may become a vehicle for apocalypse—and while the former is the more obvious candidate (metaleptic projection clearly being the standard trope of apocalyptic expectation), in the context of *A Connecticut Yankee* it is easy to see the aptness of Bloom's notion of apocalyptic farce as well. Hank, trapped inside that suit of armor, obsessed with technological improvements and the elimination of anything that hinders him, points unmistakably from farce to apocalypse. Metaleptic introjection becomes apocalyptic farce precisely because the past cannot contain the future; nestled uneasily in the womb of the past, the future must burst out, even (or especially) at the expense of the womb itself, and even at the expense of the future's own existence. The spectacle of the future trapped in the past is incongruous, hence ludicrous; it is funny to watch its discomfort there, as well as its misadventures getting out. But it is also an explosive incongruity, a dangerous form of humor, as the ending of Twain's novel convincingly demonstrates.

What metaleptic apocalypse offers in terms of Lewis's and Carpenter's contention over the *direction* of the American myth is a dialectic in which regression and progression stand as alternative routes to the same goal: victory

over time. Metaleptically, both Lewis and Carpenter are right; and one of
the tensions at the heart of Twain's novel is that between a regressive and a
progressive path to bliss. Might technological progress be mankind's con-
veyance to a utopia? Or has it meant mankind's irrevocable fall from the
paradise of Twain's pre-Civil War youth, the agrarian garden of young America? The ambivalences surrounding this movement from garden to city in
Twain's attitudes toward his own life charge *A Connecticut Yankee* with a vital
tension, one between regression and progression. On the one hand, as Henry
Nash Smith reminds us, "Mark Twain, in common with virtually all his
contemporaries, held to a theory of history that placed these two civilizations
[King Arthur's Britain and nineteenth-century America] along a dimension
stretching from a backward abyss of barbarism toward a Utopian future of
happiness and justice for all mankind." On the other hand, somewhere back
before that "abyss of barbarism" lay the Garden of Eden, the primal garden
from which we all fell; and Twain's progressive faith was inextricably mixed
with a strong strain of nostalgia, a vestigial longing for a return to Eden, to
childhood, to the womb. Justin Kaplan reports that

> in other early notes for the book, the Yankee, like Mark Twain
> yearning for Hannibal as he remembered it to have been in his
> boyhood, yearns for an Arcadian past which "exists" only in his
> dream, a pre-Boss Camelot (purified, for the moment, of poverty
> and slavery) which is as drowsing and idyllic—"sleeping in a
> valley by a winding river"—as that other fictive town, the "St.
> Petersburg" of *Tom Sawyer* and *Huckleberry Finn*. And the Yankee,
> even as first conceived, has already lost the power and desire to
> escape from this dream. "He mourns his lost land—has come to
> England and revisited it, but it is all so changed and become old,
> so old—and it was so fresh and new, so virgin before."

The apocalyptic path to happiness, one might say, lies either backward,
to a lost childhood world of "freshness" and "newness," or forward to a
future utopia, a technologically advanced society that is as unlike the barbarism of the distant past as day is unlike night. Two paths—and one Dream.
The problem for Twain, then, became the working out of the American
Dream in a novel, with its demands of temporal consistency. Hank Morgan
can go back in time and return to his starting point in the present; what he
cannot do is go *both* forward and backward at once, back past Camelot all
the way to Eden, perhaps, and forward past the nineteenth century (not too
far, Twain hopes—perfection *must* be near) to the American millennium.

As I mentioned earlier, progression to an end and regression to an origin in a logological perspective constitute essentially the same transcendental movement, from a medial position in the flux of time to a paradisal stasis in eternity. For novelists (or, for that matter, theologians), who must concern themselves with narrative sequence, the problem is in fact rather more complicated, since the irreversibility of the temporal sequence of history involves the time-traveler in numerous paradoxes that underscore the radical differences between traveling back and traveling forward in time: paradoxes that science fiction, beginning with Twain's *Connecticut Yankee*, has explored at length and that will be taken up again later in this [essay]. First, however, it is useful to point out the significant parallels between progression and regression. Kenneth Burke notes in *The Rhetoric of Religion* that he is concerned with "principles," *principia* or beginnings, "first things." In a literal sense a concern with the apocalypse is, contrariwise, a concern with "terms," *termini* or endings. But the Latin *terminus*, like the Greek *eschaton*, is not simply an end—not simply the "last things." Just as the *eschaton* is a boundary at *any* edge of either time or space, a *terminus* may be either a *terminus a quo* (boundary from which, or beginning) or a *terminus ad quem* (boundary to which, or end). The apocalyptic "term" may thus well lie at either the beginning or the end of time; it divides time from the paradisal eternity beyond it, whether we conceive of that eternity as a primordial Eden or as a final New Jerusalem.

In English, of course, there is a curious semantic inversion by which term as boundary comes to mean precisely that which is bounded: we speak of a term of office or of pregnancy, or of a school term. But this "terminological" inversion is in fact significantly paralleled in the imagination of an apocalyptic transformation, in which the "term" of history stands to the "term" as boundary as type stands to antitype, anticipation to fulfillment. But this comparison introduces an important qualification. Type and antitype in the typological schemes of the New Testament are fixed in temporal sequence, type always pointing *forward* to an antitype in which Erich Auerbach calls "phenomenal prophecy"; but the term-antiterm relationship I am suggesting here would seem to subvert that sequence, positing an antiterminal fulfillment or culmination of the historical term at either the beginning or the end of time. Typologically, Adam is the "first man" (*protos anthropos*), Christ the "last Adam" (*eschatos Adam*, 1 Cor 15:45); terminologically, Christ as the messianic mediator is both *protos* and *eschatos*, first and last (Rev 22:13), which would imply a reciprocal relationship between the two temporal boundaries. In this sense, Adam or mortal man is the bounded and Christ is the boundary, Adam is the center and Christ is the circumference. Christ encloses or bounds the historical term by standing between time and eternity and embodying the transition.

But the image is more complicated still, for in the same place at the end of the Book of Revelation Jesus refers to himself also as the *arche* and the *telos*: that is, he is not merely the first and last *in* time, but also the atemporal origin or source of time (*before* the first) and its atemporal end (*after* the last). Jesus is both the mediatory boundary and the unbounded realm mediated by the boundary—the former in his redemptive role as *man* (first and last), the latter in his creative role as *God* (origin and end). This suggests that the apocalypse should be thought of precisely as a terminal inversion, in which the bounded term of history from Creation to Apocalypse is turned inside out, the boundaries placed within the bounded and what before was bounded transformed into the unbounded state of eternity. Christ as mediatory circumference becomes transformed from "inside," or bounded absence, to "outside," or unbounded presence. Time as a terminal enclosure or prison becomes, as the conclusion of Dante's *Paradiso* suggests, an infinite wheel with Christ at the hub.

This implies that, metaleptically, both the "late" mode of expectant (progressive) apocalyptic projection and the "early" mode of farcical (regressive) introjection are imagistically feasible; the apocalypse may be conceived as either the projective transformation of the self into other-as-future-self or the introjective transformation of self into other-as-original-self. The former is the orthodox route; the latter is perhaps reminiscent of Neoplatonism, as we imagine the generations rolling up one by one into Eve's womb, Eve into Adam's side, and Adam himself back into not dust, of course, but the Creative Spirit of God.

But consider Twain's problem. To attain the presential society, he must either send a character ahead in time to the telos of temporal amelioration, as Edward Bellamy had done in *Looking Backward* (1888), or he must somehow accelerate progress in order to attain the presential state *now*, by sending a character back in time to redirect the stream of history at its source. The difficulty with either approach, however, is that both make it impossible to live in the nineteenth century. Bellamy's Julian West dreams he is back in 1887 and finds the dream a nightmare; he escapes back into "reality" by reawakening in the year 2000, but for the author and reader it is a dream-reality, a deferred future whose hoped-for presence reduces the nineteenth-century present to absence. Twain's Hank, propelled by an imagination wracked with the paradoxes of what it is attempting to portray, awakes from the nightmare of the past into the waking reality of the nineteenth century, but finds that reality more nightmarish than the dream. Having dismissed reality as dream-illusion, he flees back into the illusion of the dream-past, and dies. The irreversibility of time renders the revelations of time-travel

horrific: if Hank succeeds in his reverse-millennial task, he necessarily oblit-
erates the nineteenth century, for the nineteenth century is now *in* the sixth
century, and what was once the nineteenth century is now an inconceivable
other. Therefore, he must fail; but to fail is to lose his presential vision, to
return to the nineteenth century divested of the very American ideology of
progress that makes the nineteenth century what it is. Either way, Twain's
own time is revealed as illusion, as alien. The American quest for presence
across time ultimately uncovers only absence.

What Twain's artistic foray into the paradoxes of time-travel teaches
him, in the end, is the impossibility of the American Dream—a lesson that
Edward Bellamy confronts but (in Julian's waking from dream) quickly sup-
presses and that Balizet and Wigglesworth never even confront. On the one
hand, the peculiar reality of time gives it an immalleability, a resistance to
change, which renders the fruits of progress inaccessible. Since time will not
permit the acceleration or compression of the sequence that progresses from
bad to good to better to best into the duration of an individual's lifetime, to
remain *in* the temporal flux is to surrender to the moment, to one moment
among an endless series of moments, which shifts the "perception" of progress
from the realm of empirical verification into that of the projection of desire.
On the other hand, the escape from time or victory over time imaged in
time-travel does not put one in control of time, but undermines its reality,
reduces it to an illusory absence. To travel back to the "abyss of barbarism"
in the sixth century, as Hank Morgan does, or ahead to the millennium in
the year 2000, as Bellamy's Julian West does, is to see the ameliorative
development but, by the same token, to be denied participation in it, indeed
to be excluded from its reality. To dream of amelioration from within time
is to discover perceptual absence; to perceive amelioration from outside of
time is to reveal its presence as dream.

But this succinct statement of the paradoxes at the heart of Twain's
novel needs unpacking, through a closer look at the movement of the narrative
itself. Twain realized that one of the principal obstacles to the fulfillment of
human desire was human beings' puny statures: their mortality and brief life
span, their frail bodies, too weak to carry out the will of an unrestrained
imagination, their ultimate passivity before fate. If, as in the Biblical apocalypses of Balizet and Wigglesworth, God is the apocalyptic agent, human
beings are forced to play a waiting game—a game in which potentially infinite
deferral guarantees no winners. Suppose instead, Twain postulates, that *man*
is the apocalyptic agent—no passive Briton but an American, a hero, a world-
historical figure who shapes his times rather than being shaped by them.
Suppose, that is to say, the American is a god—or a devil—it doesn't matter

which, so long as his power is sufficient to control his temporal and spatial environment. The American hero must therefore be either elevated to divine status so as to be able to create, like God, *ex nihilo*, or lowered to satanic status so as to be empowered to combat the tyrannies of worldly ignorance and superstition through iconoclastic revolt. Harold Bloom associates this elevation and lowering with *hyperbole*, the great Romantic trope of high and low, of the sublime and the grotesque; and it is clear that Twain is at some pains to hyperbolize Hank—in both directions—throughout the novel. Hank is never seen as a mere man in Camelot; he is always apparently either superhuman or subhuman, a god or a demonic sorcerer, and nothing loath to abet the Britons in their misconceptions. "I was no shadow of a king," he gloats in chapter 8; "I was the substance; the king himself was the shadow. My power was colossal; and it was not a mere name, as such things have generally been, it was the genuine article." "I was admired, also feared; but it was as an animal is admired and feared." "Here I was, a giant among pygmies, a man among children, a master intelligence among intellectual moles; by all rational measurement the one and only actually great man in the whole British world."

In fact, there is no little warrant for this hyperbolic elevation. Hank *is* superior to the Britons, at least in every way important to an American of the nineteenth century. And as Henry Nash Smith notes, his imagination is if not divine at least titanic. "Despite the Yankee's antics and the side-splitting predicaments he falls into," Smith writes, "his command of technology makes him at least potentially a hero of epic dimensions, a man with a world-historical mission. His plan of industrializing Arthur's Britain resembles Prometheus' defiance of the tyrannical gods for the sake of bringing to man the priceless gift of intellectual light and technological power." What is interesting in this self-conception, however, is the change Hank undergoes from his initial wonderment at his hyperbolic elevation to gradual acceptance of it as not hyperbolic at all, but *natural*. So as long as his memory of Hartford stands as Hank's norm of identity, he finds his elevation to near-divine stature by the Britons slightly amusing, to be exploited for business purposes but certainly not to be taken seriously. Increasingly, however, Hank comes to hyperbolize himself, losing that sense of difference between hyperbole and norm that binds him to humanity. By the time of his duel with Sir Sagramour, Hank has romanticized himself (and, significantly enough, the fraudulent Merlin as well) into the very god-demon his audience has long considered him:

all the nation knew that this was not to be a duel between mere men, so to speak, but a duel between two mighty magicians; a

> duel not of muscle but of mind, not of human skill but of su-
> erhuman art and craft; a final struggle for supremacy between the
> two master enchanters of the age. It was realized that the most
> prodigious achievements of the most renowned knights could not
> be worthy of comparison with a spectacle like this; they could be
> but child's play, contrasted with this mysterious and awful battle
> of the gods.

What irony remains here, what sense of the difference between hyperbole and
reality, is largely habitual; when Hank starts shooting the knights the reader
is increasingly convinced that he does indeed think of himself as a god.

What is interesting in this ostensible apotheosis, however, is that Hank
includes Merlin in it as well. In the temporal schema with which he started,
Hank's gigantic stature was directly tied to his nineteenth-century origin:
the hyperbolization had in effect been brought about by temporal amelioration, so that nineteenth-century beings stood alongside sixth-century beings
as would *homo sapiens* alongside an ape (or a worm, Hank would say). But
here Hank places a sixth-century man on his own level—a subtle indication
that there is something wrong with the ameliorative schema. Either Merlin
is anachronistically gigantic, achieving through magic the stature Hank was
given at birth by technological progress—which would undermine the notion
that nineteenth-century science is uniquely progressive—or human stature
has nothing to do with progress in time. . . . Time-travel, whether in the
mind or in the world, involves the traveler in scale distortions by which
people of an earlier age come to be seen either as giants from which present-
day pygmies degenerated, or as pygmies from which present-day giants
evolved; and to the extent that other humans serve the time-traveler as mir-
rors, reflections of the time-traveler's own humanity, that distortion skews
self-perception as well. The attempt to define himself as a god in contrast
to the puny Britons takes Hank through the discovery of Merlin as an equal,
to the reverse hyperbolization of himself in the disintegration of his personality at the end.

While Hank's faith in his own hyperbolical elevation lasts, however, he
stands tall as Twain's version of the Romantic American hero: the agent, not
the agency, of the apocalypse. In this sense the "syntax" of Twain's American
apocalypse might be characterized not as copulative, as it was in the Biblical
apocalypses of Balizet and Wigglesworth, but, rather, as factitive. Since the
apocalyptic "factor" is now not God but a human being, the utterance would
read not "The world shall be a paradise" but "I will make the world a
paradise." (Note that while the copulative syntax is embedded in this struc-

ture, the emphasis is now not so much on the transformation as on the transformer.) God is now human—or human beings are divine, setting themselves up as transformative gods who propose to enact an apocalypse upon a group of peers whom they mentally degrade to the status of creatures. If the Britons are worms, then Hank can—indeed *must*—play God to them. Since Hank lacks God's power to transform by a simple performative utterance, however, it is perhaps better to examine his factitive apocalypse not syntactically at all, but dramatically, as the outcome of a dramatic action that is coordinated by a composite playwright-director-actor: Hank himself.

Here Burke's dramatistic pentad is apposite, developed at length in *A Grammar of Motives* as the reduction of all motives to five motivational terms: act, agent, agency, scene, and purpose. The factitive apocalypse, clearly, would involve a ratio of two of these, scene and act; the apocalyptic drama might be stated simply as a scene-act-scene progression, specifically from scene$_1$ through the transformative act to scene$_2$. As I mentioned previously, however, this movement is complicated by Hank's reverse millennialism; where the "postmillennial" proponents of ameliorative evolution in Twain's day sought to restore on earth a paradise that was lost at the beginning of time, Hank seeks to restore in Camelot a paradise that was lost, figuratively speaking, at the end of time, in the nineteenth century. God created the world perfect, and at its fall looked forward to a future restoration; Hank falls from a Hartford that he chooses to recall nostalgically as perfect, to a corrupted, barbaric, virtually bestial state that he strives to convert into a restoration-as-anticipation of the future Eden. In the apocalyptic terms that he imposes on his experience, he alone recalls the loss of Eden and anticipates its recovery; he is an Adam who needs no Gabriel to tell him of apocalypse; he is, in fact, Christ himself, come to deliver the Britons from their bondage to tyranny and ignorance.

(Note that in the retrospective flights of Scott, Twain's nemesis, the retreat into the medieval past was conceived not as a fall at all, but as a regressive approximation of Eden. And Hank could well have imagined his trip back in time in similar terms, working to enculturate himself as fully as possible into the already existing British society, for example. But he doesn't, for the important reason that his presential locus is not the Origin but the nineteenth-century End. The movement of time takes Scott's characters ever further from their lost paradise, and so must be *resisted* through traditionalism, whereas for Hank, the movement of time brings the lost paradise ever closer, so that it must be accelerated through revolution. Traditionalist nostalgia is not only to no avail against the structure of time, it is counterproductive: the *nostos* or return of Hank's nostalgia is directed toward a future source,

not a past. On the other hand, Hank's reaction to the achievement of that
nostos at the end—his withdrawal into delirious dreams of Camelot—suggests
that there is more to his hyperbolization than simply a desire for restoration
to Hartford. Hank elevates himself to divine/satanic status in large part in
order to achieve a Romantic isolation from society; a flight into the mind
that . . . subsequent American writers resist and undercut.)

Hank's factitive act, his revolutionary transformation, is of course his
civilization, his *imitation* of Hartford that he implants in the midst of sixth-
century Britain. Here is the famous description from chapter 10:

> Four years rolled by—and then! Well, you would never imagine
> it in the world. . . . My works showed what a despot could do
> with the resources of a kingdom at his command. Unsuspected
> by this dark land, I had the civilization of the nineteenth century
> booming under its very nose! It was fenced away from the public
> view, but there it was, a gigantic and unassailable fact—and to
> be heard from, yet, if I lived and had luck. There it was, as sure
> a fact and as substantial a fact as any serene volcano, standing
> innocent with its smokeless summit in the blue sky and giving
> no sign of the rising hell in its bowels. . . . I stood with my hand
> on the cock, so to speak, ready to turn it on and flood the midnight
> world with light at any moment. But I was not going to do the
> thing in that sudden way. It was not my policy. The people could
> not have stood it; and, moreover, I should have had the Estab-
> lished Roman Catholic Church on my back in a minute.
>
> No, I had been going cautiously all the while. I had had con-
> fidential agents trickling through the country some time, whose
> office was to undermine knighthood by imperceptible degrees,
> and to gnaw a little at this and that and the other superstition,
> and so prepare things gradually for a better order of things. I was
> turning on my light one candlepower at a time, and meant to
> continue to do so.

Hank describes his civilization as a rich fullness of potentiality, hidden
away inside fences or inside a seemingly harmless mountain—troping it (in
Bloom's terms) both as a metonymy of emptiness/fullness and as a metaphor
of internality/externality. The problem Hank faces is exactly analogous to
the problem raised by Balizet and Wigglesworth of realizing imaginative
designs in history, only now Hank's design is no syntax, nothing so im-
palpable as language, but a *material* fiction, a "gigantic and unassailable fact."
With the positivist's blithe faith in the reality of things and mistrust of

deceiving words, Hank *builds* his paradise. Whereas Balizet and Wigglesworth relied by faith on the inherent resemblance of God's syntax to their own, hoping therefore that God would pronounce the performative utterance for them, Hank constructs his paradisal society materially and plots to transform the old society by supplanting it. Significantly, however, Hank's civilization is as much a figure as any shaped by Balizet and Wigglesworth: it is a metonymy of Hartford, and specifically, in Bloom's sense, a metaphorical metonymy, an apocalyptic metonymy conceived internally in Hank's factitive imagination. Hank's civilization is a rich potentiality, a source of much anticipation and an outlet for much creative effort, only in the fullness of internality; but internality as fullness depends upon *external fulfillment*, the successful bringing out of the civilization. Paradoxically, the civilization exists as an outside fullness only inside Hank's mind, in his memory of Hartford; outside his imagination, the civilization can exist in material form only hidden away inside an enclosure that *tropes* Hank's mind. The civilization as fullness seems restricted to internality; and as long as it remains inside, Camelot remains for Hank an external emptiness.

This restriction generates a tension in Hank's apocalyptic design that finally proves fatal. Left to itself, King Arthur's civilization would in time— over thirteen centuries—bring forth Hank's civilization in the fullness of externality. But then nothing would be changed, there would be no apocalyptic transformation, no primordial revelation of the nineteenth century. Hank itches for an apocalypse in the root sense of the word: he wants to "flood the midnight world with light." But he is also shrewd enough to predict the inevitable failure of a too-rapid unveiling: "The people could not have stood it; and, moreover, I should have had the Established Roman Catholic Church on my back in a minute." Hank's dilemma combines the problem of the historical realization of imaginative designs, the problem of human stature, and the problem of change over time—three of the most central concerns in the American experience. If human beings accept their limitations (as Balizet and Wigglesworth do to an orthodox extreme), they are reduced to a waiting game in which their only hope is that there is a significant parallel between their imagination and God's, who will therefore bring on the apocalypse that they desire. If, on the other hand, men and women hyperbolize themselves into gods and seek to effect real change by altering the structure of time (and its twin constitutive forces, the structures of material reality and of people's minds), they must confront the built-in resistances of that structure. However elevated by technological knowledge to a god's power over material nature, Hank lacks a god's power over human nature and so finds himself powerless in the end to effect a revolution;

however elevated by the accident of his time-travel to a god's foreknowledge of the future, he lacks a god's eternality (temporal unboundedness) and so finds himself powerless to oversee an evolution with patience. "If I lived and had luck," he says, revealing the anxiety of his impotence before both time (mortality) and fate (luck). Unless he moves quickly, he will never see the fruits of his labor; but if he does move quickly, the fruits of his labor will be destroyed.

And so, although in chapter 40 Hank paints a rosy picture of the "unveiling" of his civilization, the external fullness of his apocalyptic metonymy of Hartford, in the next chapter, "The Interdict," the Church steps in and *empties* that fullness:

> I approached England the next morning, with the wide highway of saltwater all to myself. There were ships in the harbor, at Dover, but they were naked as to sails, and there was no sign of life about them. It was Sunday; yet at Canterbury the streets were empty; strangest of all, there was not even a priest in sight, and no stroke of a bell fell upon my ears. . . . It was the INTER-DICT! . . .
>
> Of course, I meant to take the train for Camelot. Train! Why, the station was as vacant as a cavern. I moved on. The journey to Camelot was a repetition of what I had already seen. . . . I arrived far in the night. From being the best electric-lit town in the kingdom and the most like a recumbent sun of anything you ever saw, it was darker and solider than the rest of the darkness, and so you could see it a little better; it made me feel as if maybe it was symbolical—a sort of sign that the Church was going to *keep* the upper hand now, and snuff out all my beautiful civilization just like that. I found no life stirring in the somber streets.

When externality is thus revealed as emptiness, Hank finally realizes that it's all over; he is left with no recourse but to empty out what internality remains. He gives the order to vacate the Man-factories just as the Church had vacated the streets, and when the time is ripe, detonates his secret mines and blows them up: "In that explosion all our noble civilization-factories went up in the air and disappeared from the earth." Hank's dream of a brave new civilization in the heart of barbarism is thus reduced to the illusory fragments of dream dissipating in a bitter waking: "My dream of a republic to *be* a dream," he laments, "and so remain." Two dreams: the former a fullness of the imagination projected onto reality; the latter an emptiness of reality that engulfs the imagination. Imaginative dream destroyed reduces to illusory dream; Hank is already left, at this stage prior to the final battle, with nothing.

In another sense, however, nothing is what Hank had been going on all along. The eventual emptying out of his dream into illusion is prefigured even earlier in the novel by his penchant for the gaudy illusion of showmanship, a short tolerance for the unexciting that is inextricably tied to his American dreaming. "I never care to do a thing in a quiet way," he declares; "it's got to be theatrical or I don't take any interest in it." This is the side of Hank that Martha Banta aptly calls *Sawyerism*, "the curse placed upon those fascinated by the gaudy effects of crises." Hank Morgan is a grownup Tom Sawyer, with all the irrepressible immorality that made Tom's antics delightful, but with a new ethical attachment to his pranks, born of his "world-historical mission," that adds a degree of frightening seriousness to his tricks. Banta analyzes Twain's novel almost entirely under the rubric of this disease, suggesting finally that the book demonstrates the dangers of the apocalyptic imagination: "Mark Twain considers," she claims, "whether death offers the most effective dream-escape." "The only solution to stasis, Mark Twain implies, is for the imagination to get to work with catastrophe." This vision, which . . . would be annihilative apocalypse, Banta contrasts with tragedy, a more positive acceptance, despite pain, of time's built-in resistances: "Mark Twain recognized that farce (even more than melodrama) has a bang-up, fast-paced ending, while the tragedy is a world without the benefit of apocalypse—an existence in which suffering and the exactions of patience are endless. He came in time to prefer the profits of the farce, while Adams and the Jameses chose the tragic mode with its costs."

Certainly in terms of the main narrative of the novel, this is true. Hank's final explosive attack on knighthood is annihilative apocalypse as puerile escape; and the groundwork for that escape is laid throughout the novel, wherever Twain provides the imagery of apocalypse. All of the apocalyptic threats in the tale, as they are usefully discussed by David Ketterer in *New Worlds for Old* figure dream as gaudy illusion, a kind of sleight-of-mind that takes its effect partly through the ignorance of the spectators, partly through the human love of lurid spectacle. The eclipse, the destruction of Merlin's tower with fires from heaven, the firework display at the Valley of Holiness, the Battle of the Sand-Belt—all are undertaken largely for effect. Hank has more at stake in some of his apocalyptic effects than in others, but the *form* of each is explicitly designed to wow the rubes—and of course to gratify Hank's craving for glory. It is all theater; if someone is killed, so what? In a theater murders are perpetrated, and after the curtain falls the dead men stand up and wash off their make-up—while the audience cries, "Author,

author!" over thunderous applause. For Hank, Camelot is such a theater, a
stage on which to act out his apocalyptic drama, with the same real men and
women for both actors and audience.

The crucial difference between real theater and Hank's, of course, is
that theatergoers know they are watching a drama and enjoy the illusion of
reality. In Hank's theatricality, on the other hand, the illusion *is* reality, or
is palmed off on the Britons as such. Hank deceives by presenting dream
effects as real magic, absence as demonic presence, much as Huck Finn
convinces Jim that getting lost in the fog was a dream, and has him interpret
it. Jim and the Britons are the sort of literal-minded people that are easily
taken in by the dream peddler; but neither Huck nor Hank can leave it at
that. Both have to demonstrate their superiority by revealing the illusion
after it has been accepted as reality, revealing presence as absence: Huck by
pointing to the trash on the raft, Hank by revealing that "serene volcano,
standing innocent with its smokeless summit in the blue sky and giving no
sign of the rising hell in its bowels."

To crystallize this aspect of Hank's personality in Bloom's terms, one
could say that Hank's penchant for gaudy effects manifestly involves him in
an *ironic* dialectic of presence and absence, in which he seeks to combat
Merlin's presence by revealing it as absence, through a series of illusions that
he himself exposes as absence—but in so doing he inescapably leads the
Britons to treat his messianic civilization (the only real presence he has) as
absence also. One sees Hank's dilemma: in order to supplant Merlin's "British
Dream" of chivalry with his American Dream of industrial democracy, Hank
must convince the Britons that his dream is more real than Merlin's. But as
soon as one introduces the concepts of "dream" and "reality," of absence and
presence, it becomes almost impossible to prevent the collapse of all reality
into dream, all presence into absence. The reality of dreams is too much a
matter of faith for it to stand much scrutiny; to destroy one dream is to
destroy them all. It little avails Hank, therefore, to insist that Merlin's dream
is absence masquerading as presence, while his is a *future* presence that is
available right now. What future? the Britons rightly demand. Future presence *is* an absence.

Both Hank and Merlin are essentially dream peddlers, of course, and
their conflict throughout the novel is ultimately a contest for control of the
Britons' minds. Twain wants to establish a radical difference between science
and superstition, between technology and magic (truth and falsehood, presence and absence), by placing the two visions side by side in Hank and
Merlin and testing their relative efficacy; but his imagination keeps resisting
his ideological desires, revealing science and magic to be not different at all

but ultimately very similar dream tools, both illusionistic devices for the manipulation of the masses. (As Henry Nash Smith points out, Hank's magic in the destruction of Merlin's tower by "fire from heaven" is as unscientific as any of Merlin's, and Merlin's magic works on Hank in the end.) Like his creator, Hank would like to think of his contest with Merlin as revolving around the question of *truth*. He finally comes to realize (perhaps) that truth or falsehood is secondary, that the contest actually revolves around the question of *power*. Neither Hank's nor Merlin's vision of man and society—neither Hank's American Dream of capitalism nor Merlin's British Dream of chivalry—is *truer* than the other; both are illusions or fictions that, if successful, will grant their shapers access to ultimate channels of control.

For this sort of fiction to succeed, however—for its fictional absence to be shazammed into ontological presence—the magician/scientist requires absolute credibility, which is why we find Hank crowing throughout the novel that "Merlin's stock was flat again." But with Hank's overriding love for the kind of fiction that establishes a fraudulent credibility, for effects that seek to convince the ignorant that absence is presence, he cannot himself sustain credibility long. Thus it is that when the Church imposes the Interdict, although everyone in the kingdom still believes (or *fears*) that Hank is a powerful magician, they can no longer afford to believe in his vision of mankind; and the dialectics of fullness and emptiness, of inside and outside, and of presence and absence begin to converge:

"The Church is master now [Clarence says]. The Interdict included you with Mordred; it is not to be removed while you remain alive. The clans are gathering. The Church has gathered all the knights that are left alive, and as soon as you are discovered we shall have business on our hands."

"Stuff! With our deadly scientific war material; with our hosts of trained—"

"Save your breath—we haven't sixty faithful left!"

"What are you saying? Our schools, our colleges, our vast workshops, our—"

"When those knights come, those establishments will empty themselves and go over to the enemy. Did you think you had educated the superstition out of those people?"

"I certainly did think it."

"Well, then, you may unthink it. They stood every strain easily—until the Interdict. Since then, they merely put on a bold

outside—at heart they are quaking. Make up your mind to it—
when the armies come, the mask will fall."

Superstition (Merlin's tool) is an absence that is *in*, and Hank fails to educate
it *out*; the Church's threat of eternal damnation, the substance of the Interdict,
remains for the Britons a most powerful presence, God's judgmental presence, which banishes Hank's dream to the "bold outside," to a "mask" that
must eventually "fall." Just as Hank "stuffed" the suit of armor with his own
body, so he stuffs his "establishments" with hand-picked workers and their
minds with hand-picked ideas; but the *divine* threat wielded by the Church
remains sovereign, and all the "establishments will empty themselves" of
Hank's dream.

The Battle of the Sand-Belt is then really no more than the physical
enactment of Hank's failure, the emptying out of his dream into illusory
absence. His boast at the close of the duel with Sir Sagramour—"name the
day, and I would take fifty assistants and stand up *against the massed chivalry
of the whole world and destroy it*" (emphasis Twain's)—decodes into a frightening
dehumanization of Hank's one-time "agencies": chivalry to Hank is an "it,"
an abstraction, which he can destroy only by killing "them," every body
that harbors Merlin's chivalric dream. "English knights can be killed," he
later tells his "boys," "but they cannot be conquered. . . . We will kill them
all." Hank's intention is an implicit admission of defeat. Unable to rid the
Britons of the parasite of superstition, unable to supplant the chivalric dream
with his American dream of industrial democracy, he is forced to destroy
the host body. Having done so, Hank finds himself trapped, paradoxically, inside Merlin's cave, all alone, symbolically incorporated into Merlin's mind at last. Merlin then sneaks in to cast his most successful spell,
drugging Hank to sleep thirteen centuries and to wake, finally, back in his
own time.

But here the novel takes a puzzling turn. Why must Hank return? Why
must he survive his own apocalypse to confront the nineteenth century once
more? The apparent reason is to provide "M.T." with the palimpsest manuscript, of course; but M.T. could just as easily have discovered the manuscript
in the cave himself. Why does Hank revive—and, more puzzling still, why
does he die almost immediately upon M.T.'s completion of the story?

We must seek answers to these questions in yet another version of *dream*
developed in the novel, a version that provides the rationale for Hank's
science-fiction excursion back in time. The novel itself is in a sense a "dream
palimpsest," in which Mark Twain dreams Hank dreaming himself back in
Camelot; for when M.T. first meets Hank in Warwick Castle, he already

finds *himself* being transported back into Hank's dreamworld: "As he talked along, softly, pleasantly, flowingly, he seemed to drift imperceptibly out of this world and time, and into some remote era and old forgotten country; and so he gradually wove such a spell about me that I seemed to move among the specters and shadows and dust and mold of a gray antiquity, holding speech with a relic of it!" Hank moves both himself and his listener "out of this world and time" into an "old forgotten country" that, mythologically, might be the land of the dead, where "specters and shadows" dwell—or, psychologically, a dreamland, a land of mythic fantasy. Like Nathaniel Hawthorne in "Young Goodman Brown," Twain is careful not to tell us whether Hank actually did go back to King Arthur's time and return, or whether it was all a dream; Hank dreamed it, and it really happened.

This joint time-travel/dream-travel, undertaken simultaneously by teller and told, is further complicated when Hank begins his narration later that evening, in M.T.'s room. Hank describes the blow on the head that somehow mysteriously sent him back in time—"Then the world went out in darkness, and I didn't feel anything more and didn't know anything at all—at least for a while"—and shortly after, almost as if telling about the blow had the same effect as the blow itself, Hank begins to fall asleep. As Hank's mental world in the main narrative goes "out in darkness," so also, simultaneously, does that world in the narrative frame. The manuscript Hank hands M.T. just before dropping off is Hank's dream record of his stay in Camelot, written while holed up in Merlin's enchanted cave; and the act of reading it transposes the dream into M.T.'s imagination. Indeed, we might even assume that Hank is redreaming the entire episode while he sleeps, and that the act of dreaming and the act of reading are the same, Hank's manuscript in M.T.'s hands a synecdoche for his dreaming mind. For when M.T. finishes reading the manuscript, Hank comments on it *in his sleep*, adding the final touches that the manuscript lacks, and then dies, of no apparent cause. Healthy and chipper when he went to sleep in the opening frame, he dies mysteriously in the closing frame, almost as if the dreamworld of Camelot *were* his only reality, as he deliriously claims, and the dream over, he must die.

To read the novel in this fashion, of course, is to blur the distinction between world and mind; Hank's dream adventures in King Arthur's Court, the dream manuscript, and the dream ravings that end the novel come increasingly to look like mutually interchangeable tropes for Hank's *mind*— external parts that represent an internal whole. This terminology suggests a fifth and final borrowing from Bloom's "map of misreading": here the part/ whole dialectic of synecdoche is conjoined with the inside/outside dialectic of metaphor to form a composite trope for ethical growth. Where the conjunction of metaphor with metonymy in Hank's conception of his civilization permitted us to trace the emptiness and fullness of hidden (inside) and revealed (outside) experience in the *world*, the synecdoche-metaphor conjunction directs us to the problematic part/whole relations between world and mind: between outward action (including the act of narration) and inward mental action, between experience in the world and inner growth.

Does Hank grow, then? What inward action does the novel trace? Reading the novel in terms of synecdochic metaphor, I suggest, points us to the root of Hank's true failure: for he doesn't grow, doesn't learn, and that is finally a greater failure than the mismanaging of a revolution. Like a host of American heroes before and after him—Hollingsworth, Ahab, Gatsby, Sutpen—Hank betrays a significant kinship with the obsessional personality of Job: throughout the novel he really *sees* only his dreams, his imaginative recreation of reality, relegating alien reality to the status of illusion and elevating dream to the reality that must displace that illusion. Job demands that God conform to his moral standards, and he uses every form of coercion he knows to compel conformity. Hank demands that Arthur's Britain conform to his dream, and tries to annihilate it when it resists. Unlike Job, however, who does learn moderation in the end, Hank learns nothing; he remains obsessional to the last.

David Ketterer suggests that Merlin's cave, in which Hank is trapped at the end, is also Plato's cave; but if that is true, Hank is symbolically trapped in Merlin's cave throughout the novel. Despite his claims of Yankee practicality and common sense, Hank lives in a cavernous realm of shadowy illusions, of dreams, of gaudy effects and utopian schemes, and clings to those shadows even when representatives of reality—or rather of *alternative* illusions that would force him to acknowledge the relativism of his particular illusions—would thrust him out of the cave toward the light. In an important sense, in fact, "Plato's cave" is as much Hank's own as it is Merlin's, for the two illusionists are indeed congruent in the novel's symbolic scheme. Hank is trapped, finally, inside his own head (or inside Merlin's head); he is trapped inside the apocalyptic imagination, which would transform the world into the image of the individual's desire. The American hero's task, here as elsewhere, is to climb up out of Plato's cave not into the realm of transcendental form (that illusory realm is where he is trapped now), but into the real world of men and women, the *social* or communal world. The American solution to this problem, as Faulkner conceives it in *Absalom, Absalom!* and as Barth conceives it in *Giles Goat-Boy*, is my focus [elsewhere]; for now let me simply note that Twain had the makings of a solution in the storytelling situation of Hank and M.T., and rejected it. M.T. is an innocent abroad, a Yankee in Warwick Castle; Hank is, one would think, no innocent, but still a Yankee, an American in Europe whose experience spans two continents and thirteen centuries. Together they incorporate the relevant polarities—innocence/experience, America/Europe, present/past—into a potential image of community, the community of speaker and listener by which those polarities might be collectively and progressively understood. Instead, Hank falls asleep and dies; M.T. is left with a mind, an imaginative enclosure troped by the palimpsest MS. itself, a Platonic cave in which he is, like Hank before him, trapped. Twain reaches the threshold of a solution, but backs away, will not pass through; he remains too attached to Hank's American Dream, perhaps, to view its destruction with equanimity. The dream dies and reduces reality to dream. The extremes of Hank's experience cancel each other out, and nothing remains—except bare alien reality, of course, which Hank refuses to recognize as such:

> And such dreams! such strange and awful dreams, Sandy! Dreams that were as real as reality—delirium, of course, but *so* real! Why, I thought the king was dead, I thought you were in Gaul and couldn't get home, I thought there was a revolution; in the fantastic frenzy of these dreams, I thought that Clarence and I and a handful of my cadets fought and exterminated the whole chivalry of England! But even that was not the strangest. I seemed to be a creature out of a remote unborn age, centuries hence, and even *that* was as real as the rest! Yes, I seemed to have flown back out of that age into this of ours, and then forward to it again, and was set down, a stranger and forlorn in that strange England, with an abyss of thirteen centuries yawning between me and you! between me and my home and my friends! between me and all that is dear to me, all that could make life worth the living! It was awful—awfuler than you can ever imagine, Sandy. Ah, watch by me, Sandy—stay by me every moment—*don't* let me go out of my mind again; death is nothing, let it come, but not with those dreams, not with the torture of those hideous dreams—I cannot endure *that* again. . . . Sandy? . . . (ellipses Twain's)

His American Dream destroyed, Hank's apocalyptic imagination is now reversed: having achieved the *nostos* or return that informed his nostalgia while in Camelot, he flips the apocalyptic alignments and desires a return to a lost time that now lies not in the future but in the past, as in Scott. Before, the temporal movement had brought him ever closer to future restoration, inspiring in him a revolutionary spirit that, he knew, still could

never successfully bridge the gap between the sixth century and the restoration of an American paradise in the nineteenth. Fortuitously enabled by
Merlin to bridge the gap in a thirteen-hundred-year sleep, Hank now finds
himself, pathetically, being taken ever further from a *past* restoration by that
same temporal movement. Rather than retreating into a reactionary ideology
of conservation (for what good would that do?), he retreats into delirium,
dreaming that he only dreamed of the thirteen-century abyss that separates
him from his paradise. Whatever time Hank inhabits, in whatever terms he
thinks of his predicament, there remains that abyss between desire and its
fulfillment: that definitive feature of apocalyptic imaginings that Twain understands but cannot get past. As my later discussions of American apocalypses will show, the archetypal American solution to Hank's imaginative
dilemma is to plunge into the "abyss of thirteen centuries" that yawns between desire and fulfillment and to generate a productive energy from its
iconic habitation. Like Tiresias, first man then woman then man again, Hank
has passed through the extremes of his experience and thereby stands at the
threshold of a mediatory understanding that could transform his life as the
simple desire for restoration never could.

What the apocalyptic dream-farce of *A Connecticut Yankee* reveals, in the
end, is no historical crisis but character, Hank's *ethos*, the failure of an individual to learn. Hank's final delirium, which transforms dream reality into
an illusion more real than reality itself, brings us back through the novel's
dream inversions to the original frame, the *fiction* in which all dreams and
all realities—and all apocalypses, real or dreamed—are illusions that do not
pretend to deceive. Dream as hyperbolic metonymy passes through near-
total annihilation in the dream-as-irony that concludes the main narrative,
emerging in the book's P.S. as an internalized synecdoche that yet retains
much of the ironic awareness of absence. Hank dreams to create, to destroy,
and finally to escape the necessity of choice. Synecdochic dream remains,
in the end, Hank's most effective escape from death; but the escape is cheap,
for it is based on a self-deluding denial of absence.

As the reader has no doubt noticed, the five modified Bloomian tropes
generated by my reading of *A Connecticut Yankee* bear an uncanny resemblance
to the five apocalyptic hermeneutics I offered . . . [elsewhere]—a resemblance
that suggests a number of directions my argument might take. To note that
metalepsis complexly transforms the Biblical hermeneutic, hyperbole the
Romantic, metonymy the continuative, irony the annihilative, and synecdoche the ethical is to set a fairly obvious (if not entirely hazard-free) course
toward neat formal correspondences. Rather than follow that course, which
requires no great ingenuity for the reader to work out on his or her own, I

want to close this [essay] by taking a brief look at how Twain returned in his last, unfinished novel, *The Mysterious Stranger*—particularly in the novel's last chapter, the one constant in the shifting textual debate—to solve the dilemma to which *A Connecticut Yankee* had led him. Whereas *A Connecticut Yankee* had failed to make the move from irony's annihilative absence to synecdoche's ethical internalizations, *The Mysterious Stranger* at least sketches a rough chart for that move, succeeding where the other book failed by reconceiving the synecdochic perspective as grounds for hope, hope of an ultimate personal redemption. Hank dies as deluded as he had lived; August Feldner or Theodor Fischer finally learns, finally comes to understand, and what he understands is Twain's last thrust at an American solution to the apocalypse.

This is by no means the established reading of the chapter, however. Most critics tend to see in it unmitigated nihilism, a bitter attack on human life and human knowing that places it, as R.W.B. Lewis suggests in "Days of Wrath and Laughter," in the extreme fringes of annihilative apocalypse:

> Mark Twain ends his parable with a peculiarly inventive sort of metaphysical or even ontological catastrophe: not the reported end of the world in ice or fire, but the revelation that the world, the very universe, does not even exist and never has. "*Nothing* exists," Satan informs the narrator Theodor at the moment of his disappearance; "all is a dream. God—man—the world—the sun, the moon, the wilderness of stars—a dream, all a dream; they have no existence. *Nothing exists save empty space and you.*"
>
> Beyond that uncovering of absolute nothingness, the apocalyptic imagination can hardly venture.

Or, as John R. May summarizes this position: "The world is not literally destroyed by catastrophe; its reality, however, is dissolved by demonic fiat."

What Lewis and May discover in the chapter, of course, is the ironic revelation of presence as absence, which is a central trope in the annihilative apocalypse. But not all irony is apocalyptic, and Lewis and May have to stretch this passage to make it an annihilation. In the first place, the "revelation that the world . . . does not even exist and never has" is not at all a metaphysical catastrophe and not therefore (since ontology is a branch of metaphysics) an ontological catastrophe either. If it is a catastrophe at all, it is an ethical one: August/Theodor unlearns a false ontology and learns the true one, an internal transition that gives David Ketterer his cue for the "philosophical apocalypse." If the universe never existed, it cannot be "dissolved;" and 44's, or Satan's, words to the narrator can therefore be no *fiat*.

Read in this way, the chapter is solipsistic, perhaps even nihilistic—but certainly not apocalyptic, unless one considers ethical growth apocalyptic.

But notice further that 44/Satan nowhere uncovers "absolute nothingness"—what he uncovers is a world of "*empty space—and you*," which is a rather different matter. Empty space may not be the fullness of God, humanity, the world, sun, moon, and stars—but it does exist, in an empty metonymical way. The narrator exists too. Where then is that nothingness? "And you are not you," 44/Satan tells August/Theodor—"you have no body, no blood, no bones, you are but a *thought*." Still, better a thought than nothing at all. 44/Satan continues: "I myself have no existence, I am but a dream—your dream, creature of your imagination. In a moment you will have realized this, then you will banish me from your visions and I shall dissolve into the nothingness out of which you made me. . . . " (ellipsis Twain's). Creation *ex nihilo*: this existence as a mere "thought" is beginning to look increasingly godlike. And in 44/Satan's next paragraph he makes his finest statement of hope:

> I am perishing already—I am falling; I am passing away. In a
> little while you will be alone in shoreless space, to wander its
> limitless solitudes without friend or comrade forever—for you
> will remain a *Thought*, the only existent Thought, and by your
> nature inextinguishable, indestructible. But I your poor servant
> have revealed you to yourself and set you free. Dream other
> dreams, and better!"

The narrator has thus been revealed to *himself* as a lonesome god, set free from old dreams, "pure and puerile insanities, the silly creations of an imagination that is not conscious of its freaks," to *create anew*: to dream better dreams, better gods, better worlds, better individuals into shadowy existence. Twain images this revelation as loss, loss of the external world that seemed so substantial. But to despair of this loss is to remain squarely within the positivistic world view that Twain is attacking. The strong sense one gets of irony, of presence horrifically revealed as absence, suggests that Twain probably remained a positivist at heart even while undermining the very foundation of positivism; but the almost messianic tone of 44/Satan's last two sentences in the passage just cited reveals another Twain as well, a Twain finally not far from the Blake who insisted that all externality was a fallen projection. Forty-four/Satan sets August/Theodor free, by revealing him to himself—and this is, clearly, a step not back into the abyss of nihilism but forward into some new form of self-understanding. It is in this sense that I find the chapter a *hopeful* shift from irony, with its insistence upon absence, to the inward perspective of synecdoche. If irony prevails, all that remains is *external* absence, a terrifying alienation of matter from mind; and this would, perhaps, point to an apocalyptic annihilation. But if external absence is revealed as a synecdoche for the dreaming mind—or rather, for the mind-about-to-dream—then the question of presence and absence no longer matters. What matters is one's inner vision, which *constitutes* reality by reseeing it.

Re-creation by revelation, the synecdochic incorporation of externality in the internality of vision: these *are* Blakean notions, though it is clear that Twain had never read a word of Blake. But he didn't need to; he had two potent American sources for the apocalyptic visions toward which he strove, two seminal American apocalyptists to whom we turn in chapter 4:

> Every spirit builds itself a house; and beyond its house, a world; and beyond its world, a heaven. Know then, that the world exists for you. For you is the phenomenon perfect. . . . Build, therefore, your own world. As fast as you conform your life to the pure ideas in your mind, that will unfold its great proportions. A correspondent revolution in things will attend the influx of the spirit.

OINOS. —Then all motion, of whatever nature, creates?

AGATHOS. —It must: but a true philosophy has long taught that the source of all motion is thought—and the source of all thought is—

OINOS. —God.

AGATHOS. —I have spoken to you, Oinos, as to a child of the fair Earth which lately perished—of impulses upon the atmosphere of the Earth.

OINOS. —You did.

AGATHOS. —And while I thus spoke, did there not cross your mind some thought of the *physical power of words?* Is not every word an impulse on the air?

OINOS. —But why, Agathos, do you weep—and why—oh why do your wings droop as we hover above this fair star—which is the greenest and yet most terrible of all we have encountered in our flight? Its brilliant flowers look like a fairy dream—but its fierce volcanoes like the passions of a turbulent heart.

AGATHOS. —They *are!*—they *are!* This wild star—it is now three centuries since with clasped hands, and with streaming

eyes, at the feet of my beloved—I spoke it—with a few
passionate sentences—into birth. Its brilliant flowers *are*
the dearest of all unfulfilled dreams, and its raging volcanoes *are* the passions of the most turbulent and unhal-
lowed of hearts.

The first passage is Emerson, from the conclusion to *Nature*; the second
is Poe, from "The Power of Words." Both confront the physical power of
the imagination to create worlds, worlds of the imagination that are real and
are not real—worlds that at once apocalyptically supplant and iconically
express the world we know. What difference does it make that Emerson's
American dreamer is a poet, recreating by reseeing the world in time and
space, while Poe's is an angel, creating worlds of beauty and turbulence
beyond the space and time of "the fair Earth which lately perished"? It is a
question Poe himself would take up in his poem "Israfel," and it is closely
allied to Twain's significant shift from an angelic alter ego in "The Chronicle
of Young Satan" to a dream-self in "No. 44, The Mysterious Stranger." The
notion of the Other as double, of the alien as mirror image, raises focal
questions both of spatial relation (here and there, earth and heaven: material
self and spiritual or imaginative self) and of temporal relation (now and then,
present and future: self and to-be-imagined self), questions that, I suggest,
iconically define the central concerns of American apocalypses as being concerns of mediation. The works we [have examined] throughout this study
are most obsessively preoccupied with that transformative interface; that
boundary between now and then and between here and there, the point at
which the status of the self can be scrutinized in relation to the inscrutable
beyond.

CLEO McNELLY KEARNS

The Limits of Semiotics in Huckleberry Finn

*It is sometimes claimed that modern literary theory is an impossibly esoteric affair,
offensively elitist in its barbarous jargon. The truth is that such theory has always
been more acceptable to the ruled than the rulers. Oppressed peoples are natural
hermeneuticists, skilled by hard schooling in interpreting their oppressors' language.
They are spontaneous semioticians, forced for sheer survival to decipher the sign
systems of the enemy and adept at deploying their own opaque idioms against them.*
—TERRY EAGLETON, *New York Times Book Review*, December 9, 1984

*"Dah, now, Huck, what I tell you?—what I tell you up dah on Jackson islan'? I
tole you I got a hairy breas', en what's de sign un it; en I tole you I ben rich
wunst, en gwineter be rich again; en it's come true; en heah she is! Dah, now!
doan' talk to me—signs is signs, mine I tell you; en I knowed jis' 's well 'at I
'uz gwineter be rich again as I's a stannin' heah dis minute!"*
—JIM, *Huckleberry Finn*

*"Tom's most well, now, and got his bullet around his neck on a watch-guard for a
watch, and is always seeing what time it is, and so there ain't nothing more to
write about, and I am rotten glad of it, because if I'd a knowed what a trouble it
was to write a book I wouldn't a tackled it and ain't agoing to no more. But I
reckon I got to light out for the Territory ahead of the rest, because Aunt Sally
she's going to adopt me and sivilize me and I can't stand it. I been there before."*
—HUCK, *Huckleberry Finn*

Jim's outburst, "signs is *signs*, mine I tell you," in the final chapter of
Huckleberry Finn, proclaims his status as the novel's semiotician par excellence.

Indeed, his general performance in that role seems to confirm at least some of Terry Eagleton's claims for the "spontaneous" semiotic activities of the oppressed. Throughout the novel, Jim displays dazzling powers over signs, decoding in his own inimitable way texts as diverse as the natural indices of the body and the complex stories of the Bible. He finds signification everywhere, from the hair on his breast to the figments in dreams, and his ability to "read" these signs gives him a sense of control over his own fate which helps him survive the multiple indignities of life as a slave. Jim reads signs intensely, both to ward off the despair of his and Huck's situation and to challenge Huck's (slight but important) advantages of greater knowledge and greater mobility. As he does so, Jim becomes the novel's own model of what it means to read in semiotic terms, helping us to bring into focus through his "opaque idioms" the advantages and limitations of an acute attention to signs.

Those limitations, however, become more and more evident the more Jim's practice as a semiotician comes under scrutiny. In the first place, Jim is himself a sign, a sign produced by Huck's narrative. His "sign-reading" abilities are very much those assigned to the stereotypical stage darky, full of a superstition which is the more fascinating for its occasional flashes of insight or retrospective justification. Only the gaps, the fissures, the "breaks" in Huck's own presentation of Jim, the places where his sense of Jim's skill as a sign-reader breaks down or is transformed into something else, allow another dimension of Jim's character to appear and offer a genuine challenge to Huck's own reading of their situation. At these moments—the moment on the raft when Huck challenges Jim to interpret a fictive dream and the moment when his consciousness of a danger neither he nor Jim can control causes him to tear up his own piece of sign-making, the note turning Jim in—can Jim's presence in the novel indicate a real and liberating sense of power. This power is expressed not through the prognosticating and passive activity of sign-reading or semiotic decoding, but either through a genuine act of hermeneutic interpretation, one which affirms the moral and social responsibility of the interpreter and his prophetic role in making the meaning he purports to "see," or through a complete rejection of all sign-systems whatever for a liberating, if evasive, silence.

Jim's form of prophetic interpretation not only transcends semiotics but is framed by Huck's skeptical and evasive response, which makes a counterclaim for another kind of attitude to semiotics, a rather Joycean "silence, exile and cunning." Huck's tacit rejections of Jim's semiotic skills, and his own violations of all forms of coding, from the expectations of his mentors to the activity of writing itself, indicate a very different sense from Jim's of semiotic constraints. Jim seeks to transcend those constraints on behalf of a social and fraternal concept of liberation: Huck seeks to escape them on behalf of an individual and self-authorizing freedom. The tension between the two is at the heart of the novel and informs its interpretation both within and without the text.

Like those who dabble in divination, itself an instance and a telling paradigm of semiotic activity, Jim often operates, superficially at least, on the assumption that meaning is already coded in and that he gets his authority only as a "reader" of what is already there. This assumption usefully averts the crippling anger and despair generated by the powerlessness of his position, but it also reduces his function to that of mere prognosticator or diviner, a kind of tool of the texts he reads. While he does find relief in semiotic activity, Jim does so at the risk of submitting himself to the control of a system of identities—signs is signs, x is y—which are already fixed in advance. In assuming this position, Jim not only underestimates his own power and responsibility, but puts himself in constant danger of becoming nothing more than a comic butt. His audience, which includes Huck, Tom, and the reader, recognizes his prognostications to be naive, and they see all too clearly, in Jim if not in themselves, the motives of self-defense and self-aggrandizement that prompt such reductive semiosis. It is only in those moments when he (and we) abandon "spontaneous semiotics" and take on the full responsibilities of a wider and deeper kind of interpretation that any possibility of liberation from racial stereotype and oppression can be glimpsed in the discourse of the novel.

Furthermore, as this novel makes abundantly clear, the existence of many "natural" strategies of interpretation is not in itself a guarantee of liberation, and the variety of these strategies may involve more vital issues than a casual embrace of theory-at-large would allow. Jim, after all, is not alone on his raft, and his experiments in interpretation do not go unchallenged, either by his enemies or by his friends. Huck himself, for instance, offers another, very potent alternative to the "spontaneous semiotics" and "opaque idioms" of Jim's usual mode of interpretive activity. While Huck is, for the most part, lost in wonder at Jim's semiotic skill, and more than vocal in his admiration for it, he also constantly tests that skill and seeks to reveal its narrow base. Faced with Jim's apparent and insistent faith in the complete, direct, reciprocal, and transparent relationship between sign and meaning, Huck constantly deconstructs this semiotic activity by bringing into play a deeper skepticism and a far more radical sense of the unrepresentability of any signified by any material sign. Huck is, furthermore, vexed in a way Jim is not by the implications of determinism in semiotics. He recognizes that both he and Jim are far more implicated in the making of the codes they pretend merely to "read" than his partner would seem to admit, even though this recognition leaves him, too, in an uncomfortable position of entanglement and uncertainty. The two interpreters are, then, often engaged in a struggle for mastery between different and incommensurable ways of reading, one which, as each of them comes to recognize, makes any easy resolution by "natural," "spontaneous," or semi-conscious theories out of the question.

This struggle is motivated in part by some degree of competition for mastery over the narrative itself. There are times, for instance, when it is unclear, from a genre point of view, whether this novel is meant to mimic the narrative of an escaped slave or the deposition of a boy on trial for abetting that slave (See Harold Beaver, "Run, Nigger, Run: The *Adventures of Huckleberry Finn* as Fugitive Slave Narrative." *Journal of American Studies* 8 (1974): 339–61). Beneath this generic difficulty lies a tension between the two figures of Huck and Jim which makes us wonder whose story this really is, after all. Huck has control over the actual writing, it appears, but Jim often has a far superior grasp of the action and a deeper understanding of its significance for their fate. As long as Jim remains only a decoder of signs these deeper dimensions do not come into play. When, however, he is able to rise to Huck's challenge and to use his deeper powers of interpretation and prophecy to transcend the role of mere semiotician, he becomes Huck's great antagonist—becomes, indeed, *so* strong that he very nearly usurps Huck's role in the story altogether.

Jim's exuberant assertion that "signs is *signs*" indicates, then, one attitude toward signification: an affirmative and hopeful attitude insisting on the fullness and richness of the sign, with its promise of future meaning and future wealth. This attitude is in part Huck's construct, however, and is undercut by moments when his own sign-making activity breaks down, revealing a deep skepticism both about the adequacy of signs and about the codes on which they depend. These two attitudes are juxtaposed throughout the novel, contributing both to its comic effects and to its near brushes with tragedy, as issues at stake in questions of interpretation become more and more vital to each character's life and fate.

These two attitudes toward semiotics are worked out in terms of a running analogy between monetary relations, prediction, and textual interpretation. Money is useful here because it shows both the great power of signifying systems, able as they are to convert one kind of value into the terms of another, and their inherent limitations, the danger of collapse as those values prove incommensurable after all. All signs, like all currencies, can be inflated with values they cannot sustain or used reductively to indicate conversions that cannot be performed. Indeed, the central problem on which this novel rests is precisely a problem of such reductions: the reduction in this case of a human being to a unit of monetary worth, a slave. Prediction, too, can be inflated or reduced, especially in the form of divination, which denies human freedom and reduces those who indulge in it to the level of pawns in a rigged game. Analogous, as well, are the most debased forms of textual interpretation represented here: the overly literal readings of religious fundamentalism and the overly spirited ones of romantic fiction, each of which falsifies the value of the signs with which it deals either by inflation or by reduction. To these are opposed the true use of money, the genuine function of prophecy, and the sane, contextually rooted interpretation of literary and religious texts. These are distinguished from the false use of signs by their assumption of freedom of the will and their dedication to that fully realized political and ethical liberation which is the novel's ever-receding goal.

We can trace this interweaving of money, prediction and textual interpretation throughout the novel. It is no accident, for instance, given their counterposed attitudes toward signs, that the story begins with Huck trying to give up a fortune and ends with Jim looking forward to one. In chapter 2 the analogy is even more fully worked out. Here Huck and Tom steal three candles from under a sleeping watchman's nose, leaving a five-cent piece for pay. The watchman turns out to be Jim, and Tom compounds the mischief by taking Jim's hat off while he sleeps and hanging it on a tree over his head. When Jim wakes up, the boys are gone, and he begins to make quite a reputation for himself by claiming that "witches" have charmed him and ridden him down to New Orleans and back and even around the world, hanging his hat on a limb to show "who done it." In this inventive semiotic scheme, the five-cent piece becomes the gift of the devil, having curative powers as well as powers of command over the witches. Money is closely related to magic, and Jim is their would-be master. The whole business makes him quite a celebrity—the founder, indeed, of his own little community of interpretation—and he is, Huck tells us with a note of childish jealousy, "most ruined" for a "servant" on its account.

At first look this is a simple piece of local color and class and race stereotyping. We see Jim as a caricature, a stage darky, a superstitious, comic, and pretentious character, just about to get "above" himself—and very much the butt, rather than the equal, of Tom's boyish pranks. The events of the story do, however, in some ways confirm, figuratively speaking, Jim's sense of himself and of his adventures. He does indeed get "taken for a ride" by a certain kind of white-boy witchery, a ride which takes him very nearly to New Orleans and enlarges his scope as if he had indeed gone "around the world." His recovery from that ride and his mastery over it are also very much dependent on the possession of that "five-center piece." Money is a talisman of command over the manipulations to which Jim will be subject as the tale goes on. Even at their most apparently simplistic, Jim's semiotic interpretations have an unconscious or subconscious truth, a truth which is part of their charm. At this point he does not surpass that charm, but remains enmeshed in the code he purports to read. This reading is consoling and enabling, helping Jim and us to believe that his fate is not entirely sealed, that he can understand, anticipate, and circumvent trouble, and that good fortune, however far in the future, is destined to be his. It does not, however, allow Jim to engage consciously in creating the meanings to which he points, and its illusions eventually prove more disconcerting than enabling.

The complex connection between money and signs becomes even clearer in Jim's next appearance. In chapter 4 Huck has just discovered that his father is back in town and looking for him—no doubt for access to his little fortune, won in the earlier tale *The Adventures of Tom Sawyer*. Here Huck provides the first of many tacit and complex reversals in the strength and weakness to be gained by the activity of semiotics. The incident opens with Huck seeking Jim's advice. It seems that Jim is in possession of a hair-ball which predicts the future, but which requires, Jim claims, a little wherewithal in order to prompt its powers. This claim leads to a strong suspicion that Jim himself has an all-too-materialist analysis of the nature of sign-reading, but Huck is by no means an easy mark for this game. He tries to avoid being taken for all he has by remaining discreet about the full dollar in his pocket and proffering a visibly spurious counterfeit quarter instead. Accepting the premise of the hair-ball's powers, he *explains* that the quarter is counterfeit, but suggests that maybe the hair-ball won't know the difference! This piece of innocent but self-defeating guile (who does Huck think he's kidding, the hair-ball or Jim?) is, however, completely outdone, both morally and in terms of the comedy, by the talisman's owner, who promptly scoops the scene by advancing a plan for *improving* the counterfeit so that it will pass in the local market.

In undertaking this task, Jim makes himself Huck's confederate rather than his antagonist in this game of true and false significations, and indicates, by the same token, his complete ease with apparently contradictory signifying codes. While the rationalist reader is busy working out who believes what here, Jim moves with ease from the code of soothsaying, where he clearly believes his words to be true, to the code of money, where truth-value is irrelevant, as long as the sign is superficially credible. Combining these codes, he proceeds, in cooperation with the hair-ball, to deliver a prophecy which is partly a perfectly accurate guess as to the nature of Huck's father's actions, partly an expression of the rather Manichaean dualism associated with divination, and partly the healing and consoling message of an older person to a younger one. (According to the hair-ball, Huck's father has two angels hovering around him, one white and one black, and their alternation of ascendancy dictates his instable actions; Huck himself will have both trouble in his life and "consid'able joy," and is destined to be either hung or drowned. The prophecy at this point is somewhat muddled, but we may note that hangings and drownings do lie ahead in this tale as its violence and danger increase.) In this scene, then, a spurious coin becomes, by a semiotic operation, "as good as real," and likewise a spurious bit of fortune-telling becomes "as good as true" as the false coinage of superstition is redeemed by Jim's practical wisdom. Here Jim has begun to demonstrate powers of conversion, conversion of false coinage into true, of monetary relations into relations of collaboration and friendship, and even, to some extent, of superstitious divination into prophetic wisdom. The coin, however, is still counterfeit at base, and the limits of the power of semiotics to convert one sign into another at will are beginning to become apparent.

As the novel progresses, Jim is more and more construed by Huck as the master semiotician. "Jim knowed all kinds of signs," Huck says, "indeed, he knowed most everything." In chapter 8, Huck even presses Jim for some insight into the semiotic theory on which he works. His first concern is why Jim constantly draws attention to *bad* signs, rather than *good* ones. Jim's answer is incontrovertible and pragmatic: the only reason to interpret signs is to prompt corrective action, and in the case of good coming, it is better to let well enough alone. There are, besides, "mighty few" good signs, and the most useful ones are those that predict something far off—like wealth. "You see," Jim explains, "maybe you's got to be po' a long time fust, en so you might git discourage' en kill yo'self 'f you didn't know by de sign dat you gwyne to be rich bymeby." Signs are useful for their pragmatic impact on the present, as forms of encouragement or despair.

Jim uses as a case in point here the prophecy of his own riches as indicated by the hair on his breast, and Twain takes the occasion for another comic excursus on the complex relation of signs and money. This time the signs are linguistic and even literary, rather than magical, and they provide a lesson in the limitations, as opposed to the strengths, of Jim's semiotic powers. Jim, it appears, once had fourteen dollars, but he took to speculation and lost it all. Jim's form of speculation was a series of bad investments which were bad in part because they rested upon deep confusions of figurative and literal meaning. He invested, he tells Huck, first in "stock." The "stock," however, turns out to have been "livestock"—in the form of one cow, which died. He then put the money in a bank scam, itself a literal misreading of the nature of the banking enterprise by a fellow-slave, and invested the putative return in a wood-flat which was stolen, while the "bank" went bust. Finally, prompted by a dream, he offered ten cents to a fellow named Balaam, who had taken literally a preacher's injunction that money given to the poor would come back tenfold. Needless to say, there was no immediate return. The apotheosis of this continual, comic melange of figurative and literal meanings comes when Jim remarks, ironically, that in spite of all these failures, he must already be rich because he owns himself, and he is, after all, worth eight hundred dollars on the open market. "I wisht I had de money," he concludes. The underlying lesson of these misadventures is the frequent untranslatability of one kind of sign into another, of money into real goods, of words into their literal counterparts, or of cash value into flesh and blood. Too reductive a semiotic equation, "signs is signs," x is y, will eventually break down, both in theory and in practice: a lesson Jim has yet to learn.

Twain liked to read aloud this excursus on signs and money together with a later passage in the novel, also revealing of Jim's semiotic strategy— the very funny exchange between Huck and Jim as each tries his interpretive powers on a classic text, one of the Biblical stories of Solomon. Solomon comes up in chapter 14, in the context of Huck's reading to Jim from books all about "kings, and dukes, and earls and such." The conversation calls into play the conflict between at least three different codes of signification: Biblical fundamentalism, romantic adventurism, and proverbial wisdom. Jim, like a zany student, poses a marvelously off-the-wall but cogent question, one which links money with a different kind of social and economic power. "How much do a king git?" he asks. Huck, caught off guard, provides a makeshift answer, in the course of which the notion of a harem comes up. Jim adroitly elicits a definition of this hitherto unknown term, and then masters it by a neat analogy. (This analogy can only be described as "metaphysical": a harem must be like a boiler room, the latter equally noisy, but more productive, and you can shut it off. The conceit of the harem-boiler room will later reach nightmare proportions in Richard Wright's *Native Son*.) Jim then turns his attention to his own ingenious interpretation of the passage from 1 Kings 3:16–18 which describes how Solomon found the true mother of a child by threatening to cut it in half. This project, Jim argues, was criminal folly;

why didn't Solomon first "shin aroun' mongs' de neighbours" and *find out* to whom the child belonged before indulging in this cruel form of experimental vivisection? Charged by Huck with completely missing the point—the child wasn't *really* going to be cut in half—Jim rises to heights of dialectical casuistry that leave us gasping: "De 'spute warn't 'bout a half a chile, de 'spute was 'bout a whole chile; en de man dat think he kin settle a 'spute about a whole chile wid a half a chile, doan' know enough to come in out'n de rain."

This dazzling rejoinder is a classic semiotic response, a manipulation of signs as it were in air, with little responsibility toward that complex relation between literal and figurative meanings they entail. Necessity is here the mother of invention, for Jim, as Huck presents him, is clearly compensating for lack of knowledge by the overwhelming exercise of his interpretive ingenuity. At the same time, he demonstrates unconsciously that all semiotic activity is far more context-bound than it appears. An equation within a code in one situation is no equation at all in another. Jim's method of resolving the dispute over the child comes as deeply out of the tribal and proverbial context of a close-knit slave community as Huck's does out of the fundamentalist Biblical culture to which he has been half-exposed. The two codes are incommensurable, and the significations of one do not convert easily into those of the other. Confronted with this lack of fit, Huck, his whole being actively and consciously bound up with the contradictions between these codes, experiences an understandable despair, and he inaugurates that strategy of withdrawal he will later pursue to the end. "I see it warn't no use wasting words," he concludes, and, taking refuge in a raw and unmediated privileging of one code over the other, "you can't learn a nigger to argue." He is himself the "divided child" over which they have been arguing, and he cannot heal that division with signs, but only with his own particular version of silence, exile, and cunning.

There are, however, problems with Jim's semiotic play here and with the stock role Huck makes him occupy. Indeed, in asserting him as the novel's great semiotician, Huck is exposing Jim to ridicule as the perfect type of the superstitious darky. In light of this stereotype, the ability to read "signs" appears less as a skill than as an illusion, a pretension produced by events and motives that a more liberal, more sophisticated, and perhaps more cynical audience can understand better than either character. After all, we know, because we have followed Huck and Jim through the story, the rational causes of the events they experience, and we can imagine, all too easily, the psychological needs and defenses which give rise to these grand and reductive semiotic equations. Huck's glorification of sign-reading in Jim, then, takes place to the disadvantage of his own reliability as narrator, as well as playing to a stereotype that can only confirm the audience's superiority, rather than involve that audience in the dangers, responsibilities, and inadequacies of submission to a genuine, but flawed, process of interpretation.

As the novel progresses, Jim steps out of his two-dimensional stereotype and begins to assert this genuine hermeneutic power. He does so by breaking through Huck's expectations of him to inaugurate a very different kind of interpretive activity from sign-reading or prognostication. (How this effect is created through the constructs of Huck's discourse is, of course, a mystery of Twain's craft; *that* such an effect is created seems beyond dispute.) A particularly sharp demonstration of the difference between semiotic divination and prophetic interpretation comes at the novel's turning point, in chapter 15, in which Huck's relation to Jim reaches a moral crisis. During the events of this chapter, the friends are separated by fog, as Huck's canoe breaks from the raft and is swept to the other side of an approaching island. Later, Huck manages to return to the raft and finds Jim asleep, with one oar broken and a litter of dirt all around him to testify to his efforts to find the boy again. When Jim wakes up, Huck, possessed for the moment of the spirit of adventurist elaboration that animates Tom Sawyer, tries to tell him that this separation and struggle have been only a dream. Jim is hard to convince, but once duped, he sets himself to interpret this so-called "dream." He does so with his usual brilliance. The dream is a *warning*, a warning of danger ahead, and of the necessity for waking up and paying attention to signs, so the two can get out of the fog and into the "big clear river" again. Jim is not, in figurative terms, entirely wrong here. Huck's lie and the fictional experience it refers to *are* a kind of warning, a warning of the fog of false consciousness which can divide the two and make them lose their ethical moorings.

Both lie and fiction, moreover, seem to call out for decipherment, the need for which Jim himself insists upon. The events of the so-called dream are, Jim claims, important calls to action, and if the two of them didn't "try hard to make out to understand them" the dream events would take them *into* bad luck instead of keeping them out of it. Jim concludes with a major semiotic equation, itself one of his not infrequent excursions into literary troping. He identifies, Huck tells us, the "big clear river" figuratively with "the free States." Jim reads signs here as a writer of fictions might read them, with a kind of literary sensibility that is revealing but also artificial. Furthermore, his reduction of signs to pragmatic indications involves all kinds of logical contradictions he does not explore.

Huck, however, at once tries to puncture this literary mode of signification and to reveal its lack of ground. He is apparently operating under the not-unfamiliar critical assumption that simply by pointing to a text's base in a fiction he can deflate its semiotic claims. "Oh well, that's all interpreted well enough, as far as it goes, Jim," he says, "but" (pointing to the leaves and rubbish and the smashed oar, incontrovertible proofs of the fictionality of the dream, not to mention of his own cruel and self-aggrandizing lie) "what does *these* things stand for?" Jim gazes at the evidence of the facts, a harder set of signs than he has hitherto confronted, and a set which makes the question of the human intentionality behind them explicit. He is at first stunned, and simply looks back and forth. At this moment of defeat, far from giving up, however, Jim, in a remarkable *coup de théâtre*, abandons the mode of semiotics proper for the greater mode of interpretive insight and prophetic power. With superb dignity, he shifts the ground of argument from the dubious discourse of divination to the compelling one of moral truth, a truth which includes the human subject as an essential element. Turning to Huck, he asserts an interpretation stronger than any he has made, one which draws its strength not from reductive identities, or from some elaborately literary turn of speech, but from the force of his own perception of the *willed* nature of the situation. Looking from the things on the raft to Huck he says:

> "What do dey stan' for? I's gwyne to tell you. When I got all wore out wid work, en wid de callin' for you, en went to sleep, my heart wuz mos' broke bekase you wuz los', en I didn' k'yer no mo' what become er me en de raf'. En when I wake up en fine you back agin', all safe en soun', de tears come en I could a got down on my knees en kiss' yo' foot I's so thankful. En all you wuz thinkin' 'bout wuz how you could make a fool uv ole Jim wid a lie. Dat truck dah is *trash*; en trash is what people is dat puts dirt on de head er dey fren's en makes 'em ashamed."

This speech has a ring of authenticity which lifts Jim permanently out of the category of stereotype and makes him one of the strongest characters in American literature. The word *trash* here is one indication of that strength, for it is about the most telling term Jim could have chosen to bring Huck to his senses. It has a literal and a figurative application, and for once they cohere. Huck is "trash" in the literal sense, a part of the flotsam and jetsam the current has swept back to the raft. He is also "trash" in figurative terms; he is under-animated, so to speak, by any human difference or power of self-determination which would distinguish his attitudes from the detritus of those of the worst of his class, race, and time. There lingers behind this word a hint of the only term of abuse that outweighs *nigger* in contempt, *white trash.* This term of abuse represents social degradation without the alibi of racial discrimination, and it has great pejorative force. Huck escapes this appellation only by a hair's breadth, perhaps, indeed only by virtue of Jim's own restraint, which will not allow him to stoop to a particularized application of the universal human law of brotherhood.

In making this interpretation of the bits and pieces on the raft, Jim deliberately exaggerates the language of signification. "What do dey stan' for?" he repeats after Huck, with scornful emphasis, "I's gwyne to tell you," and he does, with great underlining of the copula, the primary linguistic indicator of reductive equation: "Dat truck dah is *trash*; en trash is what people is dat puts dirt on de head er dey fren's." The repeated, sarcastic "is" serves to draw attention less to Jim's office as a semiotician than to the fact that there are limits to that office. Here, the need for a specialist in signs becomes itself an indication of shame, of the lack of a fully developed and awakened consciousness. "We hold these truths to be *self-evident*" begins the founding document of Huck and Jim's conflicted nation. For some things— liberty, equality, and fraternity, for instance—Huck does not need a reader of hair-balls or an interpreter of dreams, but a prophetic reminder of the free will in which signification must be grounded and the goal of liberation which it must seek.

Huck is forced, as it were, by Jim's strength here to acknowledge his greater power and moral force, though he narrates this acknowledgment with the faintest trace of defiance, as if aware of an internal and external voice of pride which regards such an acknowledgment as a shame rather than a virtue. In general, Huck is careful to evade or avoid such moments of conscious fraternity, abjuring all forms of consensual relationship whether of broth- erhood, sisterhood, adoption, or even the subtle but implicit contract between writer, reader, and character. Huck associates these consensual relationships very much with the realm of women and slaves, which he wishes to leave behind for a direct, unmediated experience of male freedom. Huck is always looking for, losing, and reasserting interpretive priority—over himself, his own life, and the facts of his narrative as well. Like his blood father, he rejects domestication, and in his strategies of evasion he keeps alive—like Joyce's Stephen, like Rimbaud—the possibility that he will become the real master of his own debatable Territory. On that Territory, so unlike the fluid, changing River, he will, in some receding future tense, be able to make his mark and write the story of his own dominance, a dominance not only over Jim, over Tom, Aunt Polly, and the Widow, but even, at times, over the author and audience of his tale, whose expectations only complete silence will allow him to evade.

Throughout the novel, Huck constantly acts out the contradictions of this relationship to the very sign-systems which allow him to speak. At one point or another, he breaks every code of signs he can encounter or imagine, from speech to writing, from the letter he himself has composed turning Jim in to the signifying systems that make possible the novel he writes. At the same time, he revels in all of these modes, exploiting them to the full for a number of cross-purposes, ranging from the preservation and maintenance of his own distinct and superior identity to the defense of his relationship with Jim. To write and to speak are, for Huck, ways of asserting in the face of Jim's often superior power of interpretation a countervailing mastery over signs. They are also ways of rescuing, in the face of a society which would annihilate both Huck and Jim, the individuality that gives them life and the fraternal bond that holds them together. Huck can no more escape these activities than he can fly, for his entire narrative is constructed by them: on the one hand, by a certain "literariness" (which we may read sometimes as static on the line created by Twain himself, sometimes as the precociousness of a boy just becoming aware of an audience for his charms) and on the other hand, by the lively presence of one of the most purely *spoken* voices in all literature.

Speech and writing are, as Huck comes to learn, inextricably tied to and entangled in codes of signification which leave no place for his own experience and which threaten his exclusively boyish and anarchic little world. Rather than bend and reform these codes, as Jim seems to do, by sheer force of will and interpretive strength, Huck chooses to step outside them altogether and to break with the matrix of civilized behaviors they inevitably entail. Writing, as Huck has occasion to know, and as he tells us in the opening paragraphs of his tale, is not innocent. It is, on the contrary, fraught with lies or "stretchers." Huck accepts this as part of the game, but he worries about it nonetheless. Furthermore, Huck's own writing is, as we have seen, rather deeply motivated by a struggle with Jim over narrative priority and interpretive power, a struggle which causes him to lose confidence, now and then, in their common ground. Finally, Huck has had what social workers love to call a "bad history" with many forms of writing. He has been early exposed to that highly reified and dangerous reading of the Bible produced by fundamentalist literalism, and his later experience of tales of romance as interpreted irresponsibly by Tom has proved a dangerous substitute. In every case, writing has left Huck no space for his own commitments and experiences, but rather with a sense of codes and systems which are threatening, but which he cannot quite dismiss from his mind. Speech proves equally deceptive, for, among other things, in this realm Jim is supreme, and he consistently gets the upper hand—and by beating Huck at his own game.

Huck's rejection of writing and speech marks another limit of semiotics, a limit marked not by its transcendence into strong interpretation, but by its fall into silence. We have already seen how, when confronted with Jim's dazzling powers of dialectic over the Solomon story, Huck decides that it is useless to waste words arguing with "a nigger." Just as he withdraws from speech when confronted with Jim's superior power, so Huck withdraws from writing when confronted with the superior power of "sivilization." In a direct attack on signs, he simply tears up his own letter turning Jim in. Huck's wrestling-match with his conscience in this case is typically confined, as is much semiotic activity, to a set of yes-or-no acceptances of a particularly literalistic and reductive code. He cannot, it seems, learn to bend, break, or transcend this code so as to make it adequate to his ethical and political needs. (It is Jim's function in the novel precisely to raise and keep alive the hope of this revisionary interpretive activity.) Huck's decision to tear up his letter represents both a genuine step forward in maturity and comprehension and a gesture of despair and blind will, one not unlike his refusal to go on arguing with Jim. These withdrawals reach their climax when Huck decides to "light out for the Territory" and stop writing altogether—the only point at which his decisions and thoughts become genuinely unanswerable, either within the novel or without.

Of course, this attack on signification conceals a deep uncertainty in Huck about his own powers of persuasion and, as many would argue, a regressive and self-defeating desire to escape from consensual reality as well. Huck's decision, however, calls into question not only "sivilization" but "civilization" (a distinction that, like the *a* in Derrida's *differance*, can *only* be represented in writing). Among other things, it throws into relief the assumptions and reading strategies of that largely liberal, white, and Northeastern audience for which this book would seem to be written. This audience, with its confident expectation that the moral code is self-evident, that the characters will receive their just deserts and that the tensions between Jim, Huck, and society can be dissolved in conventions of genre, receives from Huck's decision to "light out for the Territory" a genuine moral shock. This shock marks an absolute limit of the power of semiotics to resolve all forms of difference, and it keeps alive the possibility of Huck's own individual freedom to operate outside the codes and bonds of a previously established system.

We cannot forget, however, in the sensation of this shock, the continued power of Jim's role in the narrative. The final pages of *Huckleberry Finn*, pages in which Jim makes his famous assertion that "signs is *signs*," are pages of very rapid denouement, which describe the continued turns of a wheel of fate that Huck's abrupt departure does not entirely stop. Here, in quick succession, Jim learns not only that he is free and has, under the terms of Miss Watson's will, been free for some time, but also that his freedom is to be underwritten by Tom Sawyer to the tune of forty dollars. (We are tempted to interpret, retrospectively, the moment of Miss Watson's death as precisely the moment Jim utters the word *trash* on the raft.) Confronted with this offer, it is true, Jim does not respond with anything like what a weaker or more stereotypical character might have said in a more sentimental tale. He utters no Beecher-Stoweish "Praise de Lor'," no "bless yo' soul, Marse Tom," no "shucks, ole Jim ain't worth so much turr'ble fuss as all *dat*." Nevertheless, his "signs is *signs*," and his prediction of future happiness and wealth, although they may indicate a kind of poetic justice, ring hollow with the hollowness of a repeated stereotype, a hollowness Huck's silence—for he does not say a word here—tends to underline.

Jim makes a partial recovery from this stereotypical role when he is able to interpret another set of signs in an apparently more genuinely liberating way. Just here, at the climax of the story, Huck tells us that he remembers his absent father, authorizer of all kinds of signs, as deeply terrifying a figure to Huck's mind now as when he lay in wait unexpectedly in his son's room at the very beginning of the tale. Jim, however, seems able to reinterpret Huck's experience so as to defuse this threat. First, he reminds Huck of a body they had found on the river whose face Huck "didn't want to see." "Doan' you 'member de house dat was float'n down de river, en dey wuz a man in dah, kivered up, en I went in en unkivered him and didn' let you come in?" he asks. Then he reveals its "true" meaning: "Well, den, you k'n git yo' money when you wants it; kase dat wuz him." Here, as Tina Zworg has pointed out, Jim's interpretive skill enters Huck's narration on a conscious level and enters the reader's as well, giving us the power either to go back and recover a deeper sense of it on our own from "between the lines" of Huck's story or to continue to block its implications by "lighting out for the territory." Jim reveals that he has defied what is for Huck and for all weak interpreters a great taboo; he has "unkivered" the dead, and in doing so he has demystified once and for all an obscure and threatening entity so as to master it, to render it harmless, beyond any further capacity to frighten or disturb. Like the famous "Mistah Kurtz—he dead," in Conrad's *Heart of Darkness*, but in celebration rather than dismay, Jim's "dat wuz him" predicts a great hope: the death of an old, violent, patriarchal order and the promise of a new, fraternal one—but only if we will consent to forget Huck's construction of this story and his continued skepticism and fear and to reinterpret it in Jim's own light.

Huck's response to this news, however, is by no means as ecstatic as Jim's careful, therapeutic, and self-assured questioning might lead us to expect. Rather, as he has on similar occasions, Huck chooses silence as a response, passing instead to a curt and somewhat caustic wrap-up of what has happened to Tom since these revelations took place. Huck's silence, his change of subject and his decision to "light out for the Territory" express not only a touch of boyish annoyance at Jim's and Tom's claims to have known more about his life than he does, but a skepticism towards all forms of interpretation, from semiotic decoding to genuine prophecy. It is Huck, after all, who, even if only mimicking Jim's restraint, has withheld from *his* audience the crucial information of the father's death until the last moment, and it is in part a way of setting Jim up for deflation (for surely things cannot work out quite as well as they here seem to) that Huck has allowed him to break the news in the tale. Now, dropping Jim completely and leaving Tom dangling his watch-fob in a haze of rather contemptible self-congratulation, Huck takes the occasion to express, as succinctly as possible, his jaundiced attitude toward the whole business of narration and interpretation. Not only is there "nothing more to say," he tells us, but he is "rotten glad of it," because if he had known what a trouble it was going to be to write a book, he wouldn't have done it in the first place, and he certainly isn't going to undertake it again. Instead he will "light out for the Territory" and forgo any situation, even the situation of writing, where he has "been before."

Huck's skeptical and evasive response to Jim, to Tom, and even to his own good fortune here, suggests a countervailing hope to Jim's—the hope of a willed and even willful priority, a total and utterly individual future command over audience, character, and even the author of his own tale. The novel is indeed constructed by the difference between these two definitions of liberation—liberation as brotherhood and equality and liberation as self-authorizing paternity and priority. Both of these kinds of liberation move the novel beyond the limits of semiotics to prophecy on the one hand and silence on the other. To choose between these alternatives is to lose sight of Twain's point: their complete contradiction of and their absolute necessity to one another.

Chronology

1835	November 30, Samuel Clemens is born in Florida, Missouri, to John Marshall Clemens and Jane Lampton.
1839	Family moves to Hannibal, Missouri.
1847	John Marshall Clemens dies; Samuel leaves school and begins career as a printer.
1853–54	Clemens travels as a journeyman printer to St. Louis, New York, Philadelphia, and Iowa.
1856	Plans trip to South America. Stops in Cincinnati and writes *The Adventures of Thomas Snodgrass*.
1857	Apprenticed to a river pilot.
1861	Volunteers for a Confederate Civil War brigade; leaves after a few weeks. Heads for Carson City.
1862	Works as a miner and reporter. Adopts the pen name Mark Twain.
1864	Travels to California; meets Bret Harte.
1866	Sent to Sandwich Islands as a feature writer.
1867	Publication of *The Celebrated Jumping Frog of Calaveras County and Other Sketches*.
1869	Publishes *The Innocents Abroad*.
1869–71	Writes for the *Buffalo Express*.
1870	Marries Olivia Langdon.

1871   Moves to Hartford where he lives and writes for the next sixteen years. In Hartford he also embarks on several business ventures and accumulates debts.

1872   Publishes *Roughing It*.

1873   *The Gilded Age.*

1876   *The Adventures of Tom Sawyer.*

1880   *A Tramp Abroad.*

1884   *Adventures of Huckleberry Finn.*

1889   *A Connecticut Yankee in King Arthur's Court.*

1892   *The American Claimant.* Disastrous investment in typesetting scheme.

1894   *Pudd'nhead Wilson.* Twain departs on a worldwide lecture tour to pay off debts.

1896   *Joan of Arc.*

1898   Finishes paying off debts.

1900   Writes "The Man That Corrupted Hadleyburg."

1904   Twain's wife dies.

1906   Begins working on autobiography. Publishes *What Is Man?* privately and anonymously.

1907   Receives honorary D.Litt. from Oxford University.

1909   Daughter Jean, the last of his four children, dies.

1910   April 21, Twain dies, leaving many unpublished papers, among them the incomplete drafts of "The Mysterious Stranger."

Contributors

HAROLD BLOOM, Sterling Professor of the Humanities at Yale University, is the author of *The Anxiety of Influence, Poetry and Repression,* and many other volumes of literary criticism. His forthcoming study, *Freud: Transference and Authority,* attempts a full-scale reading of all of Freud's major writings. A MacArthur Prize Fellow, he is general editor of five series of literary criticism published by Chelsea House.

BERNARD DE VOTO won the Pulitzer Prize for nonfiction in 1948 with the publication of *Across the Wide Missouri.* His *Mark Twain's America* remains a central study of Mark Twain.

F. R. LEAVIS was a major British literary critic. His works include *The Common Pursuit, The Critic as Anti-Philosopher, Culture and Environment,* and *Re-evaluation and Development in English Poetry,* and his classic study, *The Great Tradition.*

J. HILLIS MILLER is Frederick W. Hilles Professor of English and Comparative Literature at Yale University. His books include *The Disappearance of God, Poets of Reality,* and *The Linguistic Moment: From Wordsworth to Stevens.*

ROBERT PENN WARREN won the Pulitzer Prize for fiction in 1947 with *All the King's Men* and Pulitzer Prizes for poetry in 1958 and 1978. His most recent book is *Poems: 1935–85.*

JUDITH FETTERLEY is Professor of American Literature at S.U.N.Y., Albany. Her writings include *The Resisting Reader: A Feminist Approach to American Literature.*

CYNTHIA GRIFFIN WOLFF is Director of the University Honors Program at the University of Massachusetts, Amherst. Her criticism includes *Samuel Richardson and the Eighteenth-Century Puritan Character.*

225

BRUCE MICHELSON teaches at the University of Illinois, Urbana.

ALFRED KAZIN is Distinguished Professor of English at the City University of New York. His many books include *The Inmost Leaf*, *New York Jew*, *On Native Grounds: An Interpretation of Modern American Prose Literature*, and *A Walker in the City*.

JAMES M. COX is Professor of English at Dartmouth College. His best known work is *Mark Twain: The Fate of Humor*. He is a prolific essayist and is the editor of *Robert Frost: A Collection of Critical Essays*.

ROY HARVEY PEARCE is Professor of American and English Literature at the University of California, San Diego. His principal works include *The Continuity of American Poetry* and *Historicism: Once More*.

DOUGLAS ROBINSON is Associate Professor of English Philology at the University of Tampere in Finland and is the author of *John Barth's* Giles Goat-Boy: *A Study*.

CLEO McNELLY KEARNS is Associate Professor of English at Rutgers University, and the author of the forthcoming *"What Krishna Meant": Indic Philosophy and Religion in the Work of T. S. Eliot*.

Bibliography

Anderson, Frederick, ed. *Mark Twain: The Critical Heritage*. London: Routledge and Kegan Paul, 1971.

Asselineau, Roger. *The Literary Reputation of Mark Twain: A Critical Essay and Bibliography*. Paris: Marcel Didier, 1954.

Auden, W. H. "Huck and Oliver." *The Listener* 50 (1953): 520–41.

Bellamy, Gladys. *Mark Twain as a Literary Artist*. Norman: University of Oklahoma Press, 1950.

Bier, Jesse. *The Rise and Fall of American Humor*. New York: Holt, Rinehart and Winston, 1968.

Blair, Walter. *Mark Twain and Huck Finn*. Berkeley: University of California Press, 1960.

———. "Mark Twain and the Mind's Ear." In *The American Self: Myth, Ideology, and Popular Culture*, edited by Sam Girgus. Albuquerque: University of New Mexico Press, 1981.

Bliss, Percy. *The American Mind*. Boston: Houghton Mifflin Co., 1912.

Branch, Edgar. *The Literary Apprenticeship of Mark Twain*. Urbana: University of Illinois Press, 1950.

———. "The Two Providences: Thematic Form in *Huckleberry Finn*." *College English* 9 (1950): 188–95.

Budd, Louis J. "Deconstructing Mark Twain's White Suit." *Publications of the Arkansas Philological Association* 9 (1983): 1–16.

———. *Mark Twain: Social Philosopher*. Bloomington: Indiana University Press, 1974.

———. *Our Mark Twain: The Making of His Public Personality*. Philadelphia: University of Pennsylvania Press, 1983.

Cox, James M. *Mark Twain: The Fate of Humor*. Princeton: Princeton University Press, 1966.

———. "Remarks on the Sad Initiation of Huckleberry Finn." *Sewanee Review* 62 (1965): 389–405.

De Voto, Bernard. *Mark Twain's America*. Boston: Little, Brown, 1932.

Eliot, T. S. Introduction to *The Adventures of Huckleberry Finn*. London: Cresset Press, 1950.

Fatout, Paul. *Mark Twain in Virginia City*. Bloomington: Indiana University Press, 1960.

──────. *Mark Twain on the Lecture Circuit*. Bloomington: Indiana University Press, 1960.

Feidelson, Charles, Jr. *Symbolism and American Literature*. Chicago: University of Chicago Press, 1953.

Ferguson, DeLancey. "Huck Finn Aborning." *The Colophon* 3 (1938): 171–80.

Fetterley, Judith. "The Sanctioned Rebel." *Studies in the Novel* 3 (1971): 294–304.

Fiedler, Leslie. *Love and Death in the American Novel*. Revised edition. New York: Stein and Day, 1975.

Gerber, John. "The Relationship Between Point of View and Style in the Works of Mark Twain." In *Style in Prose Fiction*. New York: Columbia University Press, 1959.

──────, ed. *Studies in* Huckleberry Finn. Columbus, Ohio: Charles E. Merrill Publishing Company, 1971.

Gribben, Alan. *Mark Twain's Library: A Reconstruction*. Boston: G. K. Hall, 1980.

Hill, Hamlin. *Mark Twain: God's Fool*. New York: Harper and Row, 1973.

Hoffman, Michael J. "Huck's Ironic Circle." *The Georgia Review* 23 (1969): 307–22.

Howe, Irving. "Anarchy and Authority in American Literature." *Denver Quarterly* 2 (1968): 5–30.

Howells, William Dean. *Literature and Life*. New York: Harper and Brothers, 1902.

──────. *My Mark Twain: Reminiscences and Criticism*. New York: Harper and Brothers, 1912.

Kahn, Sholom. *Mark Twain's Mysterious Stranger*. Columbia: University of Missouri Press, 1979.

Kaplan, Justin. *Mr. Clemens and Mark Twain*. New York: Simon and Schuster, 1966.

Lauber, John. *The Making of Mark Twain*. New York: American Heritage, 1985.

Leary, Lewis. *Southern Excursions: Essays on Mark Twain and Others*. Baton Rouge: Louisiana State University Press, 1970.

Long, E. Hudson. *Mark Twain Handbook*. New York: Hendricks House, 1957.

Lorch, Fred. *The Trouble Begins at Eight: Mark Twain's Lecture Tours*. Ames: Iowa State University Press, 1968.

Lynn, Kenneth. *The Comic Tradition in America: An Anthology*. London: Victor Gollancz, 1968.

──────. "Huck and Jim." *Yale Review* (1958): 429–40.

──────. *Mark Twain and Southwestern Humor*. Boston: Little, Brown, 1959.

Marx, Leo. *The Machine in the Garden: Technology and the Pastoral Ideal in America*. New York: Oxford University Press, 1964.

Neider, Charles, ed. Introduction to *The Complete Essays of Mark Twain*. Garden City, N.Y.: Doubleday, 1963.

Paine, Albert Bigelow. *Mark Twain: A Biography*. 3 vols. New York: Harper and Brothers, 1912.

Parsons, Coleman. "Down the Mighty River with Mark Twain." *Mississippi Quarterly* 22 (1968–69): 1–18.

Pettit, Arthur G. *Mark Twain and the South*. Lexington: University of Kentucky Press, 1974.

Reimer, Earl. "Mark Twain and the Bible: An Inductive Study." Thesis, Michigan State University, 1970.

Salvaggio, Ruth. "Twain's Later Phase Reconsidered: Duality and the Mind." *American Literature TriQuarterly* 12 (1979): 322–29.

Sattlemeyer, Robert, and J. Donald Crowley, eds. *One Hundred Years of* Huckleberry Finn: *The Boy, His Book, and American Culture.* Columbia: University of Missouri Press, 1985.

Simpson, Claude M., ed. *Twentieth Century Interpretations of* Adventures of Huckleberry Finn: *A Collection of Critical Essays.* Englewood Cliffs, N.J.: Prentice-Hall, 1968.

Sloane, David. *Mark Twain as a Literary Comedian.* Baton Rouge: Louisiana State University Press, 1979.

Smith, Henry Nash. *Mark Twain's Fable of Progress: Political and Economic Ideas in* A Connecticut Yankee. New Brunswick, N.J.: Rutgers University Press, 1964.

———. *Mark Twain: The Development of a Writer.* Cambridge: Harvard University Press, 1962.

———, ed. *Mark Twain: A Collection of Critical Essays.* Englewood Cliffs, N.J.: Prentice-Hall, 1963.

Stone, Albert E. *The Innocent Eye: Childhood in Mark Twain's Imagination.* New Haven: Yale University Press, 1961.

Tenney, Thomas A. *Mark Twain: A Reference Guide.* Boston: G. K. Hall, 1977.

Trilling, Lionel. *The Liberal Imagination: Essays on Literature and Society.* Garden City, N.Y.: Viking Press, 1966.

Tuckey, John. *Mark Twain and Little Satan: The Writing of* The Mysterious Stranger. West Lafayette, Ind.: Purdue University Press, 1963.

Varista, Raymond. "Divine Foolishness: A Critical Evaluation of Mark Twain's *The Mysterious Stranger.*" *Revista* 5 (1975–76): 741–49.

Acknowledgments

"Mark Twain and the Great Valley" (originally entitled "Introduction") by Bernard De Voto from *The Portable Mark Twain*, © 1946, renewed 1974, by The Viking Press, Inc. Reprinted by permission of Viking Penguin, Inc.

"Mark Twain's Neglected Classic" (originally entitled "Mark Twain's Neglected Classic: The Moral Astringency of *Pudd'nhead Wilson*") by F. R. Leavis, from *Commentary* (February 1956), © 1956 by F. R. Leavis. Reprinted by permission of Chatto & Windus. This essay originally appeared as an introduction to the Zodiac Press edition of *Mark Twain* (Chatto & Windus, 1955) and was later reprinted in *Anna Karenina and Other Essays* by F. R. Leavis.

"First-Person Narration in *David Copperfield* and *Huckleberry Finn*" (originally entitled "Three Problems of Fictional Form: First-Person Narration in *David Copperfield* and *Huckleberry Finn*") by J. Hillis Miller from *Experience in the Novel* edited by Roy Harvey Pearce, © 1968 by Columbia University Press. Reprinted by permission.

"Mark Twain" by Robert Penn Warren from *Southern Review* 8, no. 3 (July 1972), © 1972 by Robert Penn Warren. Reprinted by permission of the author.

"The Anxiety of Entertainment" (originally entitled "Mark Twain and the Anxiety of Entertainment") by Judith Fetterley from *The Georgia Review* 33, no. 2 (Summer 1979), © 1979 by the University of Georgia. Reprinted by permission of *The Georgia Review* and Judith Fetterley.

"*The Adventures of Tom Sawyer*: A Nightmare Vision of American Boyhood" by Cynthia Griffin Wolff from *The Massachusetts Review* 21, no. 4 (Winter 1980), © 1980 by The Massachusetts Review, Inc. Reprinted by permission.

"Deus Ludens: The Shaping of Mark Twain's *Mysterious Stranger*" by Bruce Michelson from *Novel: A Forum on Fiction* 14, no. 1 (Fall 1980), © 1980 by Novel Corp. Reprinted by permission.

"Creatures of Circumstance: Mark Twain" by Alfred Kazin from *An American Procession* by Alfred Kazin, © 1984 by Alfred Kazin. Reprinted by permission of Alfred A. Knopf, Inc. and the author.

"*Life on the Mississippi* Revisited" by James M. Cox from *The Mythologizing of Mark*

Twain edited by Sara de Saussure Davis and Philip Beidler, © 1984 by The University of Alabama Press. Reprinted by permission.

" 'Yours Truly, Huck Finn,' " by Roy Harvey Pearce from *One Hundred Years of Huckleberry Finn: The Boy, His Book, and American Culture* edited by Robert Sattlemeyer and J. Donald Crowley, © 1985 by the Curators of the University of Missouri. Reprinted by permission of the University of Missouri Press.

"Revising the American Dream: *A Connecticut Yankee*" (originally entitled "Revising the American Dream") by Douglas Robinson from *American Apocalypses: The Image of the End of the World in American Literature* by Douglas Robinson, © 1985 by The Johns Hopkins University Press, Baltimore/London. Reprinted by permission.

"The Limits of Semiotics in *Huckleberry Finn*" by Cleo McNelly Kearns, © 1986 by Cleo McNelly Kearns. Published for the first time in this volume. Printed by permission.

Index